"If we have learned anything in the past year, it was the urgent need for allies in all facets of life. I've had the honor of working and partnering with Melinda over the years and she has modeled what it means to be an active ally. This book brings together what she has learned into powerful action-oriented frameworks. As a disabled woman of color, I'm grateful this book exists so that I can be a better ally for communities that look like—and don't look like—mine. I highly recommend this book as a must-read for business leaders and anyone committed to building a more inclusive and empathetic world."

—TIFFANY YU, CEO & Founder, Diversability

"*How to Be an Ally* invites you to pull up a chair, examine your approach to life, and actively build a better world for everyone."

—NATALIA VILLALOBOS, Google's "Feminist in Residence"

"Wanting to be an ally doesn't mean that you're an ally. If you want to understand what allyship can feel like and look like at work, *How to Be an Ally* is a concise guide that shows you how to move from awareness to action."

—DAISY AUGER-DOMÍNGUEZ, Chief People Officer, VICE Media Group

"*How to Be an Ally* is the book we've all been waiting for. It's simple, practical, and impactful. So many of us struggle with our own privilege. But privilege isn't a bad thing when it's used as a tool to help those who have been discriminated against. *How to Be an Ally* demystifies diversity, equity, and inclusion and provides everyday steps we can all take to change our communities and workplaces for the better.

"The exercises and also wealth of information make this book a go-to guide for every aspiring Ally and a one stop shop for advocates who need to explain their work to others. When we talk about educating oneself or changing a company or playing your part, this is the book we all need on our bookshelves."

—MANISHA AMIN, CEO, Centre for Inclusive Design

"What does it mean to be an ally? Melinda captures her years of research and personal connections to convey an empathetic and vulnerable walk from intent to allyship, which she aptly describes as 'being a good human.' A must-read for everyone."

"We can all be better allies to those of our coworkers who lack the benefits of our privilege and have, as a result, all too frequently been marginalized, indeed disrespected. For those white guys amongst us who, like me, want to grow our understanding of the issues and make a commitment to better appreciate and support *all* of our colleagues, Melinda's book is an accessible must-read! She provides thought-provoking historical context and, crucially, offers up many tangible ways to combine understanding and empathy in concrete actions that will make for a better workplace—as well as simply making us better people."

"As a DEI practitioner myself, I always look to Melinda to further my own learning about how the DEI conversation is developing in the tech industry because in many ways, she is steering it! *How to Be an Ally* is full of tangible action steps—big and small—that all leaders can take to advance equity in the workplace in new and innovative forms. Melinda challenges how we've approached DEI in the past, and turns her critical eye toward building a more inclusive future that lasts."

"Melinda Briana Epler is one of the most inclusive and thoughtful leaders I have ever encountered. In her timely debut book, Epler, director, producer, and tech equity CEO & Founder, writes from the perspective of a white woman who has detailed her own journey from apathy to advocacy for justice and equity for others. Anyone reading this illuminating and instructional book will find themselves on their own journey from apathy to full-on advocacy by its end. Epler shows vulnerability, bravery, empathy, and great courage as she outlines the lessons she's learned along her own personal journey in what I hope will aid readers from stumbling along the allyship path. I'm excited to share this book with my entire organization as a part of our foundational learning on equity, inclusion, and diversity."

—**RACHEL WILLIAMS,** Head of Equity, Inclusion & Diversity, X - The Moonshot Factory

"The term 'thought-leader' is tossed out casually, however that is exactly what Melinda Briana Epler epitomizes. She is a leader who through her work, gently but forcefully, guides all of us to reexamine long-standing beliefs on meritocracy and then to take incremental, meaningful, and daily actions to build truly inclusive workplaces. Hers is a counsel I seek, and I'm always put on a more considered path for applying Melinda's guidance."

—**J. KELLY HOEY,** investor and author, *Build Your Dream Network*

"Melinda's dedication to creating safer, more inclusive organizations has had a profound impact on the tech industry. Having partnered with her for several years now, I've had the opportunity to watch her work in action and bear witness to the evolution of several corporate cultures. I'm grateful she's taken the time to share her learnings so that individuals and companies across industries can begin their own journeys in action."

—**KATELIN HOLLOWAY,** Founding Partner, Seven Seven Six

HOW TO BE AN ALLY

HOW TO BE AN ALLY

ACTIONS YOU CAN TAKE FOR A STRONGER, HAPPIER WORKPLACE

MELINDA BRIANA EPLER

New York   Chicago   San Francisco   Athens   London   Madrid
Mexico City   Milan   New Delhi   Singapore   Sydney   Toronto

1 2 3 4 5 6 7 8 9   LCR   26 25 24 23 22 21

ISBN   978-1-264-25793-5
MHID   1-264-25793-7

e-ISBN   978-1-264-25794-2
e-MHID   1-264-25794-5

Library of Congress Cataloging-in-Publication Data

Names: Epler, Melinda Briana, author.
Title: How to be an ally : actions you can take for a stronger, happier workplace / by Melinda Briana Epler.
Description: New York : McGraw Hill, [2021] | Includes bibliographical references and index.
Identifiers: LCCN 2021007771 (print) | LCCN 2021007772 (ebook) | ISBN 9781264257935 (hardback) | ISBN 9781264257942 (ebook)
Subjects: LCSH: Diversity in the workplace. | Discrimination in employment. | Personnel management.
Classification: LCC HF5549.5.M5 E65 2021 (print) | LCC HF5549.5.M5 (ebook) | DDC 658.3008—dc23
LC record available at https://lccn.loc.gov/2021007771
LC ebook record available at https://lccn.loc.gov/2021007772

McGraw Hill books are available at special quantity discounts to use as premiums and sales promotions or for use in corporate training programs. To contact a representative, please visit the Contact Us pages at www.mhprofessional.com.

For my grandfather Joe Epler, who shared a century of wisdom with me; my grandmother Helen Rumble, who shared her compassion with me; and my husband, Wayne Sutton, who is my greatest ally.

CONTENTS

PREFACE

No one is born a great ally, knowing everything people are going through, how you can best support them—and also how not to hurt them. Allyship is a journey, and each of our journeys looks a bit different.

I certainly was not born an ally. I've been working on it for many years. As a White[1] girl, I feel lucky that I grew up in Oakland and South Seattle, both areas that were very racially, ethnically, and economically diverse. My friends were from many cultures, and about equally mixed boys and girls (I didn't have any nonbinary[2] friends that I knew of at the time). I learned from my friends who celebrated Chinese New Year and went to Chinese churches, Samoan Americans who celebrated and shared their cultural traditions with pride, Japanese Americans whose families had lost their homes when they were interned in World War II and worked to heal and re-earn their wealth, recent Laotian refugees trying hard to fit in and build a new life, friends who grew up poor and Black[3] or wealthy and Black, very privileged White sons of lawyers and politicians, and daughters of parents with disabilities[4] just barely getting by. My family was White middle class, living on a majority White, upper-middle-class street in a very economically, racially, and ethnically mixed part of town.

My schools were majority-minority, where my high school reading list included the White male "canon"—William Shakespeare, Leo Tolstoy, George Orwell, Charles Dickens, and Nathanial Hawthorne—but also authors like John Okada (*No-No Boy*), Anne Frank (*Diary of Anne Frank*), Malcolm X and Alex Haley, et al. (*Autobiography of Malcolm X*), Ntozake Shange (*For Colored Girls Who Have Considered Suicide/When the Rainbow Is Enuf*), Michelle Cliff (*No Telephone to Heaven*), Alan Paton (*Cry, the Beloved Country*), and James Welch (*Fools Crow*). My teachers quite literally filled in the gaps of standard curriculum with cultures and perspectives left out of our history books. I supplemented this further with lots of books by Latinx[5] and Indigenous[6] authors, and in college I continued to read, expanding deeply to Middle Eastern, Latin American, and Indigenous authors.

My family traveled to Mexico in middle school, where I met girls my age selling handmade baskets to tourists instead of going to school, and that was when I first began to understand the disparities and inequities in our world today. In high school, I led my school in an exchange program with the USSR during the Cold War—my family welcomed Soviets to stay in our home, and I stayed in a family's home in Uzbekistan (then part of USSR) to help bridge peace. Homelessness, economic disparity, gun violence, and the threat of nuclear war consumed my thoughts, as did prom, physics, varsity soccer, and—yes—band practice.

I grew up deeply believing that our breadth and depth of uniqueness matters. I learned how important it is to find commonalities among our differences. Reading, having diverse friends, and traveling: together they created in me an internal value that difference was important and wonderful. And I grew up knowing that we had work to do as a world, to bridge peace and understanding, and to right very deep-seated wrongs.

But it wasn't until my first quarter in college that I realized that racism still exists, that we do not live in a post-racial society:

> During my first few weeks of college, I'm walking through the quad in the center of the University of Washington campus and happen upon a group of Black students talking about the injustices they face daily and working through what they are going to do about it. I listen for some time. At first, I go through denial: "They are just stirring things up," I think. Then I hear more about their experiences, and it sinks in. My denial turns to anger, frustration, sadness, and guilt.
>
> I was very wrong. How could I have been so wrong?
>
> How do we live in a world that pretends racism and discrimination are in the past, when the reality is that my colleagues and friends experience it every day? In classrooms, walking down the street or into a store, getting a job—basic things I take for granted are daily barriers for them.

Despite having seen the entire *Roots* series four or five times in school (from a film projector) and reading Black authors from around the world, I had in my head that it was history. While the racial and ethnic injustices

I learned about might still exist in other countries like South Africa, I thought—and I was taught—that they were well in the past for the United States. Today I am still ashamed I didn't recognize it sooner.

I spent the next nine years in college sampling different courses and degrees, learning new perspectives and tools, trying to figure out how I was going to change the world and make it better. I'm still paying off that college debt (!) but I'm grateful for all that I learned. I studied cultural anthropology and Native American history, Black social psychology and literature, Middle Eastern history and literature, Latin American film and literature, LGBTQIA+[7] studies, and environmental injustice. And—equally important—how change happens over time in societies when someone or a group of people stand up and work together for collective good. Then I moved to art school in New York, followed by film school in Los Angeles, to learn how storytelling can create movements and change the way people think and feel.

To pay my way through school, I worked with kids who were Somalian and Ethiopian refugees, kids of parents recovering from addiction, kids without housing. I worked on research projects that studied facial expressions and empathy. And of course, I worked some typical student jobs, including waitressing (which brings a whole other set of patience and empathy skills) and cashiering (which due to repetitive injuries gave me a temporary disability in both arms for about a year and left me with lifelong chronic pain). I watched films from around the world. I also spent my school breaks backpacking and camping throughout Latin America and the United States and saw firsthand the injustices Indigenous people face, the richness of cultures, and resilience of people across our continents.

It wasn't until many years later that I realized that sexism exists around me too, when I studied art and learned just how many women artists have been literally written out of history by men. At the time, Black and Latinx artists were often placed in a box called "outsider art"—a coded term for not being properly educated in art and not interacting with the art "canon." The moment I realized history is usually written by elite White men was a big one for me—this unfortunately continues to play out in today's go-to sources for facts on the internet, like Wikipedia and Google. History is written through a biased lens that—whether intentional or not—erases diverse leaders and experiences, cultural knowledge, and unique, diverse truths.

It was several more years before I recognized my own experience with sexism in the workplace; it had to knock me down before I did. Looking back, I experienced pretty severe sexism and harassment in several of my early jobs, but I didn't recognize it. If you are just now awakening to racism, sexism, ableism, and other forms of oppression—you are not alone. We don't see what we don't see—what we don't want to see, what the world doesn't want us to see. Until our awareness opens, and then we might begin to see it *everywhere*.

It was several years later before I recognized the challenges faced by women with intersectional identities (Latinas, Black women, Indigenous women, trans women of color, women born in places where gendered violence and severe discrimination are socially normalized and accepted), people with disabilities, veterans, anyone in the LGBTQIA+ community, religious minorities, people who have been incarcerated, and people with many other underrepresented and historically marginalized identities. And I'm still learning.

Allyship unfolds throughout our lives as we receive new information, meet new people, and put ourselves in new and often uncomfortable situations so we can learn. Your journey of allyship will no doubt be different from my own. And yet when each of us embarks upon our own journey of allyship, collectively we have the power to make the world a better place for us all.

The world's systems, processes, and popular culture are out of balance, tipped in favor of some of us in the world—at the expense of the rest. This does not mean that we don't all work hard to get where we are; it means that some people have to work much harder to succeed due to many barriers put before them.

Allyship is understanding this imbalance in opportunity and working to correct it. It's taking action on your values of fairness, justice, and giving back. As allies we learn, unlearn, and relearn. We work to do no harm ourselves, we advocate for people, and when we're ready, we lead the change.

We will explore some of the many ways to take action as an ally in the coming pages. Your allyship doesn't have to be big or take a lot of time, you get to decide what type of ally you'd like to be. An ally takes a little risk, gets a little uncomfortable . . . then takes another risk, and another. Over time we become better allies and, as a result, *better humans*.

The first time my partner, Wayne Sutton, and I put together an allies panel at our Tech Inclusion Conference in 2015, it was new and awkward—the folks on that panel were brave.[8] It was early in my own discovery about the concept of allyship. Since then, we've invited many people on stage around the world to talk about allyship, I've spoken on many stages and at many executive tables teaching allyship globally, and we've worked with several hundred global companies and organizations, and thousands of individuals, to drive diversity, equity, inclusion, and allyship.

In the following chapters I'll share with you what I've learned as I've worked to become an ally, as well as some of my own struggles as someone who needs allies as well. I've had the honor of interviewing and hosting a number of people on stages around the world about allyship, and I interviewed a number of people for my podcast and this book who will share their experiences here as well. This book also draws on a global study we did at Change Catalyst, learning what people want most from allies, why allies do what they do, what the biggest challenges are for allies, and how allyship can impact the workplace.

Allyship may be a new idea to you, or you may have been an advocate or activist for years. I wrote this book for all of us. Many new allies were born with the rise in awareness about racism after George Floyd was murdered in 2020, and the violence against Asians and the Asian American and Pacific Islander (AAPI)[9] communities during the COVID-19 pandemic. If you're one of those folks, welcome! This book is for you to learn some of the context and skills to create much needed change by being an ally. If you have been focused on allyship or advocacy for women or for LGBTQIA+ folks, but haven't really done much around being an ally for people with disabilities, Muslims, Indigenous, or Latinx folks—this book is for you. No one is a perfect ally for all groups; I've added context around allyship for people with many different identities. If you're an executive, employee resource or affinity group leader, or focused on learning and development, human resources, diversity, equity, and inclusion, this book is for you. Perhaps you are thinking about how to put a program together to build empathy and allyship—I've added some frameworks and discussion-generating questions you can use to facilitate deeper conversations and actions.

Take your time with this book, read at the pace that works for you, allow yourself to explore the kind of ally you'd like to be, and take the steps to become that person.

ACKNOWLEDGMENTS

Thank you to all those who have pushed me to be a better ally. William Albright for advocating for himself having an American Sign Language (ASL) interpreter and Zeeshan Khan, who is Blind, for advocating for a visual guide at our first Tech Inclusion Conference so they could fully participate. Without these two, I may not have gone down the path of understanding and allyship for people with disabilities. Along with friends and collaborators Aubrey Green and Alex Tabony, they inspired us to codevelop an Ability In Tech Summit in 2016. And because of them we continue to advocate for people with disabilities to be included in diversity, equity, and inclusion work. Together we have created an impact rippling far beyond us, as now disability inclusion is regularly discussed in the tech industry.

Thank you to the Black students organizing on the University of Washington campus many years ago—for allowing a privileged White woman to listen in. And to all the people who have pushed me to be a better ally and who have advocated for me and with me over the years. There have been hundreds and I appreciate each of you.

Thank you to Doe Mayer, one of my film teachers at the University of Southern California, who encouraged me to learn the value of storytelling told through the lens of behavior change, to create more lasting social change. This fundamentally shifted my work to build upon behavioral science and change management strategies that effect systemic and sustainable change. Over the years I've learned that change occurs when you combine passion, storytelling, and science with collaborative, empathetic leadership.

Thank you to all my fellow diversity and inclusion advocates and activists, who work day in and day out every day to create change. Including those who have been there supporting our work from the beginning: Rachel Williams, Natalia Villalobos, Mary Grove, LaFawn Davis, Michael

Thomas, Ritu Bhasin, Jennifer Brown, Vanessa Roanhorse, Aubrey Blanche, Tarsha McCormick, James Grate, Tiffany Price, Chris Genteel, Maica Gil, Tina Lee, Karla Monterroso, Mandela Schumacher-Hodge Dixon, Susan Geear, Jill Wesley, J. Kelly Hoey, Lusen Mendel, Phil Dillard, Claire Lee, Priya Rajan, Lisa Mae Brunson, Sonja Gittens Ottley, Jessica Loché-Eggert, Michael Seiler, Jennifer Tacheff, Lionel Lee, David Ortiz, Jennifer Anastasoff, Felecia Hatcher, Sharon Vosmek, Cindy Alvarez, Natalia Oberti Noguera, Y-Vonne Hutchinson, Fallon Wilson, Katelin Holloway, Lisa Gelobter, Bronwen Clune, Lesa Mitchell, and Hollie Haggans. Many folks provided input as I wrote this book, special thanks to Ritu Bhasin, Manisha Amin, and Lisa Abeyta. I'm also grateful to the journalists who write about diversity, equity, and inclusion and help hold our industries accountable. And the many advocates and activists who had paved the way to where we are today, and who keep working even when they're exhausted. This work is hard, simultaneously invigorating and utterly draining, and difficult to do well. I see you and appreciate you.

Thanks to my team who has worked with me on the research and learning through several years: Wayne Sutton, Salem Kimble, Renzo Santos, Ariyah April, Antonia Ford, Shivaani Lnu, Sally Moywaywa, Juliette Bouquerel Roy, Emilie Maas, Merve Bulgurcu, Justin Cobb, GG Mahmoud, and Olivia Wirsching . And the many incredible team members who have worked with us over the years, our clients, partners, and the hundreds of speakers at our events I've learned from.

And a very special thank-you to my husband, Wayne Sutton, who among many other things supported me in speaking my truth at TED and writing this book. We've learned so much from our work together, as well as through countless long breakfast and dinner conversations, and motorcycle rides. What an incredible privilege the two of us have to be in an interracial relationship where we see and debrief the daily biases and barriers each of us uniquely faces, and learn from each other. Wayne is my greatest ally.

INTRODUCTION

How I Hit the Glass Ceiling and Bounced Back

I n 2013, I hit the glass ceiling hard, and still to this day I have shards from it embedded deep beneath my skin.

The glass ceiling exists for many people rising to the top of their fields and companies, where we hit the limit of what opportunities are open to us because of our identity (gender, race, ethnicity, disability, sexual orientation, and/or other historically marginalized identities). It's glass, so we might not see it right away, and the people around us usually can't see it either.

All my life I've worked to make the world a better place. I began my career as a documentary filmmaker. After several years, my work evolved to creating movements of change by combining storytelling with behavioral science. I partnered with nongovernmental organizations (NGOs), governments, and Fortune 500 companies to build social change using social marketing, branding, behavior change strategies, and storytelling. I also advised social entrepreneurs, became a popular sustainability blogger, and volunteered and served on the boards of multiple nonprofits and advocacy organizations.

While leading several global branding, marketing, and social impact campaigns with my clients, I was offered a job in-house as an executive at an international engineering firm in San Francisco. Like many companies, this organization was working to stay strong in an industry dominated by ever-enlarging global conglomerates. This company wanted to be the go-to firm for women in engineering and wanted me to help them get there. That sounded fantastic.

They told me my branding, storytelling, and marketing experience was exactly what they needed to shake up their brand positioning, storytelling, and marketing strategy. My experience in organizational and cultural change was exactly what they needed to build a healthier and more scalable culture, put human resources operations in place, and manage process and culture integration in a few upcoming mergers and acquisitions. And my social impact and behavioral science expertise was perfect for leading a new business service for our healthcare clients to help them improve sustainability metrics through behavior change initiatives.

The CEO had courted me for about a year before I finally said yes. Three times he asked me to work for him. I said no each time, because my business as a brand consultant was growing quickly and I liked working with multiple clients to make a positive impact in the world. Finally, I decided to take a leap. So I closed down my successful business and moved across the country to start changing the world in a new way.

I was Chief Experience Officer, leading marketing and culture, and also responsible for building a new service line for clients on sustainability behavior change in the healthcare industry. I worked with some of the nation's largest healthcare systems, using technology and culture change to radically reduce their waste, energy, and water use and improve their social impact. It was my dream job in many ways. I was creating real change in the world and making a significant positive impact on the company's sales, marketing, and engagement.

But that job became the worst professional experience of my life. While I was doing meaningful work in the field, I was miserable as soon as I got back to the office. I was the only woman on the executive team. And while I was used to being the "only" in my life, I was not ready for the deep assault on my expertise, the lack of respect, and being undermined and belittled throughout my time there. While there were bigger issues, most of what happened involved behavioral patterns and personal slights that slowly chipped away at my ability to do my work well. Here's an example:

> *I'd spent the first few weeks in my role hitting the ground running on client delivery and listening, learning, and developing a plan to meet the marketing and culture goals I'd been hired to achieve. My first major presentation at the company was to share the strategy I developed with my 19 colleagues on the leadership team.*
>
> *After being introduced by the CEO, I looked around the room at my fellow executives, eager to share and discuss my plan. And I watched . . . as they immediately picked up their phones and looked down at their computers. They're not paying attention. As*

I start to speak, I'm thinking they will begin to pay attention out of
respect and hopefully interest. But they don't. Instead they quickly
jump in and interrupt me before they've even heard what I have
to say. People talk over me, again and again. Some of my ideas
are flat out dismissed, and then a few minutes later brought up by
someone else and championed.

It was deflating, and as it turned out, it was not an isolated experience. I soon began to realize that only a few leaders in the company truly believed in the CEO's vision of becoming the go-to firm for women. Many of my colleagues didn't care to be led by a woman and—they told me directly—they felt that to actively hire *more* women would be "lowering the bar." In my case, not only was I a woman executive, but I was also an outsider not directly from their industry. It was clear I didn't belong.

Data shows, and my CEO believed, that diversity was exactly what they needed to stay strong in the market: someone to bring new perspectives from many different industries, with a different set of innovative skills, and who would challenge leaders to make their work better. As a consultant I became good at quickly learning culture, language, and processes of new industries. I had already consulted with them for about a year so I knew their business, and I brought with me a lot of ideas and successes from other industries. But to many leaders at this firm, my being an outsider was another reason not to pay attention to my ideas. They absolutely were not going to give me an opportunity to succeed. From the start, they had made up their minds that as a woman and an outsider, I would fail.

Once on board, I learned the company did not have good experiences with the couple women executives they had hired in the past. Somehow, each of them turned out to be "not the right fit." Yet I was an idealist. I believed the CEO when he told me about flaws these women had and that by contrast, I was the perfect person for their company. I know the CEO believed this too. Sadly, we both had a lot to learn about the company's culture.

Several years earlier, I'd worked in the film industry where sexual harassment was an everyday experience for me. I thought it would be better in corporate America, yet in some ways, it was worse. While I experienced sexual harassment, a lot of what I experienced was more subtle, and I didn't understand it at first. I believe most of it was unintentional—my colleagues' behaviors were rooted in the norms established by the company culture and in their individual biases, which were formed over their lifetimes and perhaps handed down over generations.

The little negative behaviors and patterns I experienced daily from my colleagues slowly chipped away at my confidence, undermined my leadership, and reduced my capacity to innovate. Former White House Chief Technology Officer Megan Smith calls what I experienced "death by a thousand paper cuts." In this case, I think I was feeling shards of the glass ceiling along with these paper cuts!

> It's there, it's insidious, and so many people, women of all races, men of color, experience what I call death by a thousand paper cuts.
>
> —MEGAN SMITH[1]

When people experience acts of exclusion, there is a physiological as well as emotional consequence. Reflecting back to that room where I gave my first presentation: despite my years of experience and expertise, I was negatively judged before I'd said anything. Sure, I was a bit nervous for my first big presentation in front of this group, but I was prepared. I had done this many times before, my plan was a good one, and like a good corporate executive and coalition-builder, I had talked with many of my colleagues individually to get their input beforehand.

Yet I was knocked off my feet from a lack of people listening, the constant interruptions, and my ideas being taken as other people's ideas. I lost energy and confidence because my expertise was being questioned. Then my fear and stress response kicked in, and I experienced what's called the amygdala hijack.[2] My brain was stuck in fight, freeze, or flight mode. In social situations my brain often chooses flight—so my brain was focused on how to fly out of that room. I was no longer fully functioning as the innovative, confident, and challenging thinker that I am. I began to sound flustered and soon found I was saying a lot of ums and ahs in an attempt to keep people from talking over me. By the end, it had unraveled into a mediocre presentation at best.

When your voice and expertise are silenced, it's nearly impossible to be an effective leader. If the people in that room had challenged my ideas, then we could have had a robust debate. But they never heard my ideas. Or perhaps worse, they heard my ideas in passing and suddenly claimed them as their own.

I was the only woman in that room, except for the CEO's assistant. And I could have used an ally. An amygdala hijack can be interrupted at any time by someone who helps change the dynamics in the room. An ally could have recognized what was happening and helped stop the interruptions, could have asked people to put down their phones, and could have subtly pointed attention back to my ideas and strategy.

The disrespectful behaviors I experienced in that meeting room continued every single day I stayed at that company. Behaviors and patterns like this, when they happen over and over and over again, *wear you down*. Pretty quickly, my energy was tapped, my confidence was shot, and I was miserable.

Exclusion can break you. It can change how you show up, it can lower your self-confidence, change your work identity, make you less productive (because you're working against many barriers, and because it's exhausting), make you numb and distant, and lead you to build protective armor around yourself—which can cause all sorts of other issues. We will explore this more in the following chapters.

About a year into the job, I hit rock bottom and felt like a complete failure for the first time in my life. At a real low point, I read an article about toxic workplace culture and microaggressions. *Microaggressions* in the workplace are everyday slights, insults, and negative verbal and non-verbal messages—sometimes intentional, sometimes not—that impede someone's ability to do their work well, show up, and thrive as their best self.

That sounded familiar! I slowly began to realize that I wasn't failing, the culture around me was failing me. And data showed me, I was not the only one. Similar behaviors in the workplace affect people of all underrepresented identities.[3] This has a real impact on our colleagues, our companies, and our collective capacity to innovate.

I began to see microaggressions everywhere, every day, particularly from a handful of my colleagues I interacted with daily. First, I observed them in wonder and shock, and then with anger and frustration. I tried to point them out, and *that* was a disaster. I tried asking people to close their laptops and put down their cell phones in meetings. Awful idea—they became angry and shut down completely.

I tried sharing the data I analyzed in our company: we were losing women to turnover at alarming rates. Like several companies in the industry, we had a revolving door. On one side we were working on recruiting diverse talent, on the other side we were not retaining them. Women were leaving and going to our competitors. Astoundingly, company leaders told me they didn't care.

All this was devastating, and it took me some time to work out of a pit of despair and discouragement. What helped were long talks with my husband every night, finding ways to make a difference for people with underrepresented identities who worked for me, learning about how other companies improved their cultures, and reading stories of people who had experienced similar situations.

One day one of the principals in the company asked me to lunch and told me, awkwardly: "Um, I have been wanting to say something for a while and wasn't sure how to say it . . . I think people are treating you differently because you're a woman."

I was floored. I had no idea he was paying attention. He hadn't been in any meetings where I'd brought this up, and yet he noticed on his own. He told me he'd seen his wife struggle with the awful treatment she received from her colleagues in her career as an attorney, and he saw me experiencing similar things. Wow. Just that acknowledgment—that someone who I don't know well was seeing what I was seeing—that was enough to make me feel not quite so alone. It helped.

I found myself motivated to create societal change so that other people don't experience what I did, so that people of all backgrounds can be happier and truly thrive and lead in their workplace. My wheels were turning. In the meantime, I used my power of storytelling and behavior change to begin improving our company culture. I did this work while skirting the real issues. I did not talk about women, LGBTQIA+, Black, Latinx, and people with other underrepresented identities—no one wanted to hear it. Instead, I focused my work on emotional intelligence, employee engagement, and wellness. I call this covert culture change—use it if you have to! The culture started to change a little bit, particularly on teams led by principals like the one who took me to lunch. Some of the leaders began to get it. Our engagement numbers improved significantly, especially for women, and our turnover decreased.

When All You Can Do Is Create Change Covertly

Covert culture change is best when leadership and/or the culture overall is not ready to address diversity, equity, and inclusion directly. You can still move the needle in several ways to achieve the ultimate objectives of diversity, equity, and inclusion—without using those words at all. It can be taxing to work in a culture like this, but if you love your work and want to change the company culture, it's still possible.

Wellness programs can improve engagement levels and overall health and well-being. Mindfulness and emotional intelligence programs can improve empathy skills. If done at the leadership level, these can create more empathetic leadership overall, and sometimes even open up leadership teams to be more receptive to conversations about inclusion in the future. Leadership development programs can help people with underrepresented identities grow their careers and move into leadership roles, and generally improve engagement and belonging metrics. Employee resource groups (ERGs) or affinity groups can provide a safe space for people with underrepresented identities to meet and be more themselves. Over time, ERGs can gain power and influence in numbers and help demand change in the organization.

If your company's values have elements of inclusion within them, sometimes it's possible to focus on improving the culture so that it better aligns with those values. Company values often revolve around "respect," "learning," "curiosity," "collaboration," "openness," "doing the right thing," "relationships," "trust," "authenticity," "being yourself," and so on. If you have one of these values or something similar, you can work on training, programs, and/or processes that help team members aspire to these values. Respecting each other's viewpoints and expertise, creating a learning culture with a growth mindset, approaching each other with curiosity, improving collaboration, being more open to each other's input and expertise, and so on—if your company culture deeply revolves around these values, it will help foster inclusion.

You can also improve diversity, equity, and inclusion by updating processes to be more competitive in your industry (and perhaps better align with your values as well): for example, changing hiring practices to be more inclusive, adopting inclusive design methods, and tweaking processes in performance reviews and promotion to be more inclusive and equitable. Changing meeting processes can also make a difference in developing belonging. We'll explore several systemic changes you can make in "Step 6: Lead the Change" and "Step 7: Transform Your Organization, Industry, and Society."

Harassment and bullying are illegal in many countries, and most companies are worried about the risks here, so it's often easier to press for these to be addressed. These can be addressed with anti-harassment and antibullying policies and processes. Make sure it's a norm to report incidences, ensure people across the company know where to report, protect people who report, and of course take appropriate action when people do report.

It takes years for company cultures to deeply change, however, and I didn't want to stay where I wasn't welcome. I also wanted to have a bigger impact on the world, something I've been preparing for my whole life. So I transferred the change-making work to other people in the company who could continue what we started. And I left my job as an executive, to change the tech industry as a whole.

I started my own company with Wayne Sutton, my cofounder and now husband. At Change Catalyst, we build inclusive innovation globally through consulting, training, speaking, coaching, online courses and toolkits, and events. To date, we've worked with nearly 500 companies, innovation hubs, startups, and venture capital firms in cities around the world. I work a lot with leaders: developing their own skills in empathy, inclusion, and allyship, and helping them build companies that are diverse, equitable, and inclusive.

People share stories about the impact of our work every day—messages that fuel me to continue doing this hard work of change! We began our work in the tech industry and have since expanded our work to several other industries. Change at the industry level takes people and organizations working across the industry ecosystem to create change. In tech that means education, investment and entrepreneurship, workplaces, policy, advocacy organizations, and media—all of us must work together to create a fundamental shift in the industry. While it has not been easy, we are making progress as an industry.[4]

In 2018, I gave a TED talk on what I've learned over the years about allyship. I chose that topic because I was seeing so many people wanting to create change but not knowing how. I wanted to provide a framework of understanding and some tangible, actionable steps people can take to be better allies for each other. To my surprise and excitement, that talk has resonated with millions of people.[5] Since then, I continue to receive many requests for more information: how can someone like you, like me, step in and help someone else thrive? How can we be better leaders, better managers, better colleagues, better neighbors? How can any one of us interrupt the microaggressions, stereotypes, biases, and systemic inequities that keep people in our lives from thriving?

I wrote this book to answer these questions for all of us. This book is an evolution of that TED talk—it includes my experience from years of practicing allyship and training leaders and teams to be better allies. Carol Shields says that you should "write the book you want to read, the one you cannot find." I needed this book to help me be a better ally. In the following pages you'll learn about how we got here as a society, what the benefits are of being an ally, and how you can take small, medium, and larger steps to be an ally.

This book is about how we can all be better allies for each other—with an emphasis on allyship for people from groups that face discrimination and unfair barriers to opportunity, with identities that are generally underrepresented in the workplace. The pages of these book are written by myself, a White, cisgender, bi (and straight presenting[6]) woman who grew up in a middle-class family in the United States. I am an introvert who has anxiety and depression, asthma and other immune system disorders, and debilitating migraines. I'm still recognizing and exploring all these pieces that form my own identity. The more I explore my own identity, the better an ally I can become.

I have spent my life learning from people who have identities different from mine—especially people with disabilities and people who are Indigenous, Black, Latinx, Arab, Asian, and LGBTQIA+—so that I could expand my own worldview and become a better ally and advocate. Over the past few years, I've learned from thousands of people about what allyship means for them, my team and I have conducted an international allyship study, and I've intimately interviewed about 50 people for my podcast as research for this book. I also conducted a literature review of more than 300 articles and books, and colleagues have read these pages and provided me with invaluable feedback.

While I have dedicated my life to this work, my knowledge is not perfect—I'm not a perfect human and I'm not a perfect ally. *Nobody* is a perfect ally! Allyship is a continuous journey for each of us. Language and understanding are constantly evolving. And while I have worked to include geographically diverse language and examples, I am still learning how allyship plays out in different countries around the world, and there are many gaps in my understanding. Please use this book as a framework from which you continue to grow your own knowledge and form your own worldview, continuously learning from people with diverse identities and experiences.

Some of the terms and vocabulary used in this book are not in common use yet and may not be completely familiar to all readers. A companion glossary can be found at https://changecatalyst.co/glossary.

HOW TO BE AN ALLY

1
WHAT ALLYSHIP IS AND WHY IT MATTERS

The number one thing I have learned over years of doing this work with hundreds of companies is this: *There's no magic wand that creates diversity, equity, and inclusion. Change happens one person at a time, one act at a time, one word at a time.*

It's human nature to want quick solutions. Often companies new to diversity, equity, and inclusion believe one training will fix their problems, but that isn't how change works. There is no training that on its own magically fixes lack of diversity, inequity, and exclusion.

In the world today, we have a tendency to believe that technology can fix most problems in our workplaces. But there is no technology that magically fixes this either. There are some technology solutions working on pieces of the diversity and inclusion puzzle; there is some training that can help people learn specific solutions to creating more equitable systems, processes, language, and structures. However, the real change happens when each of us becomes part of the solution.

That's where allyship comes in: you and me, leading with empathy, changing how we do what we do, how we make people feel, working together to recognize and correct deep imbalances in opportunity that began centuries ago and continue today. As we reach a critical mass of allies, we create stronger and happier workplaces, companies, and industries together.

Data shows that people on diverse and inclusive teams are happier at work, we're more innovative and productive, and our companies are more profitable.[1] It's the right thing to do, it's the just thing to do—*plus* it's good for business and it makes us all happier. When we are there for each other and support one another, we thrive together.

Who Is an Ally?

Everyone, from every background. Yes, *all of us*.

As a White, cisgender[2] woman who lives in the United States—there are some ways I've been very privileged and other ways I have not. I work every day to use my privilege to be an ally for other people.[3] Plus, I still need allies too.

All of us have more to learn, and we need each other. We need you. For those of us who have identities that are often underrepresented, this is an extra burden to bear on top of all the barriers we face. But I firmly believe we will not fundamentally shift society without each of us working together—being there for each other and especially for those who have less privilege than we do. No matter who you are, there is always someone who has less privilege than you who needs an ally. So take care of yourself, take time out if and when you need it, and then show up for someone when they could really use your support. I see you and I appreciate you.

What Is Allyship?

Allyship is empathy in action. It's really seeing the person next to us—and the person missing who maybe should be next to us—and *first* understanding what they're going through, *then* helping them succeed and thrive with us. We use our power and influence to create positive change for our colleagues, friends, and neighbors. We recognize when someone isn't in the room who should be and work to get them in that room. And not just in the room but at the table, rebuilding that table together if it wasn't made for them, and leading the conversations at that table.

Allyship is learning by reading, observing, listening, and hearing other people's lived experiences. Allyship is stepping up and stepping in as an advocate—even sometimes stepping back—so that our colleagues can thrive. Allyship is also leading the change, taking action to correct unfairness and injustice. We remove barriers so everyone can rise and make sure no one is unfairly held down.

There are many terms that go hand in hand with allyship. Some say we need to go beyond allyship to being comrades, collaborators, coconspirators, accomplices, and advocates. To me, these are all forms of allyship and each is important. The work of allyship is not passive, it is *active*. Allies are not bystanders; allies do the work.

An alliance is an agreement to cooperate, a merging of efforts, helping each other when in need, mutually working toward a common goal. Between countries, this is often sharing weapons and supplies, fighting side by side in war—think Allied Powers in World War II. By working together, these allies won the war. Between people, often this is sharing our power and influence, working together to correct systemic barriers. Allies advocate for and with each other, we collaborate and conspire with people who have been historically marginalized to rebuild systems that are more equitable. We may start with small actions as allies, yet over a lifetime we grow into deeper actions.

What Does an Ally Do?

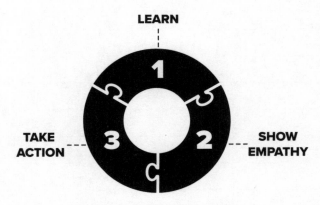

FIGURE 1.1 **How to Be an Ally**

As depicted in Figure 1.1, good allies learn, show empathy, and take action: we learn to better understand each other, to become aware of unintentional harm we might be causing, to make corrections to our own beliefs and actions, and to grow as inclusive leaders. We also learn when we make mistakes (which we all do!). Good allies are always learning.

EXERCISE

Take a moment to think about an underrepresented group you don't know enough about. Make a commitment right now to spend a few minutes this week reading an article or book, attending an event, or following new people on social media so you can begin to learn more about their experiences.

I commit this week to learning about: _____

_____

. . . by doing: _____

_____

Once you've completed this task, take a moment to write down a few things you learned.

I learned: _____

_____

_____

_____

_____

_____

_____

Continue to regularly spend time learning, and reflect and correct any misconceptions you may have along the way.

We show empathy for each other and recognize and value our unique experiences. We notice when people have been negatively impacted by marginalization or inequity, whether caused by ourselves, someone else, or an unfair system. Good allies are empathetic leaders, approaching people, ideas, and solutions with empathy.

We take action in ways that benefit people around us—especially people who have been oppressed and marginalized, and have faced inequity. This can be in little ways at first, then stepping into opportunities for bigger action.

This book is organized into seven steps for you to take action as an ally:

1. **Learn, unlearn, and relearn.** Learn about and recognize historical harm and its intergenerational impact, unlearn biases from history and cultural marginalization, and relearn from new perspectives.
2. **Do no harm—understand and correct our biases.** Work to change your behaviors and actions so that you don't unintentionally harm people with biases.
3. **Recognize and overcome microaggressions.** Develop your awareness and empathy skills to identify and eliminate microaggressions.
4. **Advocate for people.** Step up and advocate for people in small, everyday ways that can make a big difference.
5. **Stand up for what's right.** Intervene to stop microaggressions and support people who have been harmed.
6. **Lead the change.** When you're ready, take action to lead the change in your work, on your teams, and in your workplace.
7. **Transform your organization, industry, and society.** Address biases and inequities in your company and in the broader world.

Allyship is *not* charity; allyship is being a good human. Allyship helps correct and repair centuries of people not being treated equally, create equal access and opportunity, build better companies, and establish healthier, happier workplaces and communities.

Being a good ally takes some work: each of us challenging what we have learned our whole lives about ourselves and each other, reframing success and opportunity, getting uncomfortable, and going a bit out of our way to take actions that fundamentally change lives. Sometimes we make mistakes, it's part of allyship too—so we apologize for our mistakes, we grow as humans, and we keep learning, showing empathy, and taking action.

What Does Allyship Look Like?

Allyship can take on many forms. What's most important is what allyship feels like and how it creates a positive impact.

Octavia Spencer and Jessica Chastain

In 2017, two friends and colleagues Octavia Spencer and Jessica Chastain were having a deep discussion about pay equity for women. Both are actresses and producers. Jessica had been a vocal proponent of gender pay equity for some time, but in this conversation Octavia shared her experience as a Black woman and talked about the pay inequity between White women and women of color. Jessica listened and learned.

"I assumed—which is the dangerous thing—I assumed a woman like Octavia Spencer would be compensated fairly for the work she's done, and for the awards she's received for the work she's done," Jessica said. "And when she told me what her salary had been, that's what really shocked me."[4]

Then she took action. Jessica was developing and producing a new film, and asked Octavia to join her on it. Octavia responded, "I am gonna have to get paid." To which Jessica replied, "We're gonna get you paid on this film. You and I are gonna be tied together. We're gonna be 'favored nations,' and we're gonna make the same thing." She then wrote their equal pay into the pitch for the film. The two friends pitched the film together and sparked a bidding war with different studios vying for the production. In the end, both ended up with a salary five times higher than what they initially asked for.

"I love that woman because she's walking the walk and she's actually talking the talk," Octavia said. "The thing is, people say lots of things. And when it came down to it, she was right there, shoulder to shoulder—as a producer, as an actress. It's changed my whole perspective."[5]

In response to Octavia telling their story publicly, Jessica responded on Twitter, "She had been underpaid for so long. When I discovered that, I realized that I could tie her deal to mine to bring up her quote. Men should start doing this with their female costars."[6]

This story rippled through the Hollywood community as an example of how White women can be meaningful allies to women of color. "Jessica said to Octavia, 'I got you'. . . It's nice to go out and march, we can do that. It's nice to wear black at the Golden Globes, it's nice to do that. But what are we doing behind closed doors? And I gotta give our sister Jessica Chastain her props. She stood up for Octavia and put it down. And that's how we all need to do it for each other," said Jada Pinkett Smith.[7]

Other actors have also started to step up and help each other achieve pay equity. In 2020, weeks after Chadwick Boseman passed away from colon cancer, Sienna Miller, who costarred with Chadwick in the 2019 film *21 Bridges*, shared in an interview that he had given a portion of his own salary to ensure she was paid what she deserved.[8] Benedict Cumberbatch, Michael B. Jordan, Oprah Winfrey, Mark Wahlberg, Bradley Cooper, Chris Rock, and Shonda Rhimes have all stepped up for their colleagues in similar ways.[9]

[
Is there an opportunity in your life to help someone receive equal compensation or recognition?
]

Tommie Smith, John Carlos, and Peter Norman

At the 1968 Olympics, Tommie Smith and John Carlos, two Black athletes representing the United States, stood on the winners' platform—and in what was seen as a radical act, they raised their gloved fists high above their heads during the US national anthem. This historic moment is captured in Figure 1.2. The two said Tommie had raised his right hand to represent Black Power, where John raised his left hand to represent Black unity. They stood shoeless, wearing black socks to represent Black poverty. Tommie wore a black scarf to represent Black pride, John wore a necklace of beads that "were for those individuals that were lynched, or killed and that no one said a prayer for, that were hung and tarred. It was for those thrown off the side of the boats in the Middle Passage."[10]

Afterward Tommie stated, "If I win, I am American, not a black American. But if I did something bad, then they would say 'a Negro.' We are black and we are proud of being black. Black America will understand

FIGURE 1.2   Peter Norman, Tommie Smith, and John Carlos During the Ceremony of the 200-Meter Race at the 1968 Olympics in Mexico.
[Photo credit: Angelo Cozzi, Mondadori Publishers]

what we did tonight."[11] After receiving some criticism for their actions, Tommie replied: "They say we demeaned the flag. Hey, no way man. That's my flag . . . that's the American flag and I'm an American. But I couldn't salute it in the accepted manner, because it didn't represent me fully; only to the extent of asking me to be great on the running track, then obliging me to come home and be just another nigger."[12]

The third man on the platform was Peter Norman, an athlete from Australia. Peter wore the same patch that Tommie and John wore, from the Olympic Project for Human Rights. He wore it to show solidarity with Tommie and John, and to support the movement shining a light on human rights and racism at the Olympics.

All three athletes took a stand that day and paid a personal price. Tommie and John were condemned by the International Olympic Committee, withdrawn from all further races, and faced harsh public criticism. They and their families received death threats upon returning home. Peter also faced public criticism at home and was banned from future Olympics, despite repeatedly qualifying.

A few other allies stood up for Tommie and John at the time. Wyomia Tyus, a Black woman, publicly dedicated her gold medal win in the 4 × 100 meter relay to John and Tommie. The all-White Olympic crew team from Harvard issued a statement: "We—as individuals—have been concerned about the place of the black man in American society in their struggle for equal rights. As members of the US Olympic team, each of us has come to feel a moral commitment to support our black teammates in their efforts to dramatize the injustices and inequities which permeate our society."[13]

That moment on the Olympic platform in 1968 is seen as an important moment in the history of US civil rights. The actions of those three men live on far beyond that moment, inspiring generations to come. When Peter passed away in 2006, Tommie and John were pallbearers at his funeral. "Not every young white individual would have the gumption, the nerve, the backbone, to stand there," John said at the funeral. "We knew that what we were going to do was far greater than any athletic feat. He said, 'I'll stand with you.'" Tommie said, "Peter Norman's legacy is a rock. Stand on that rock."[14]

[
*What platform can you use to stand
with someone as an ally?*
]

Colin Kaepernick and Megan Rapinoe

In August 2016, 48 years after Tommie Smith and John Carlos raised their fists on the Olympic platform, San Francisco 49er quarterback Colin Kaepernick chose to sit on the bench during the US national anthem. In an interview following the football game, Colin said, "I am not going to stand up to show pride in a flag for a country that oppresses Black people and people of color. To me, this is bigger than football and it would be selfish on my part to look the other way."[15] Later he explained further, "There's a lot of things that need to change. One specifically? Police brutality. There's people being murdered unjustly and [their murderers] not being held accountable. . . . That's not right by anyone's standards."[16]

After public criticism of his actions from service veterans among others, Colin met with former National Football League (NFL) player and US veteran Nate Boyer to learn how to show more respect for veterans in his protest. The next week instead of sitting during the anthem, Colin took a knee along with his teammate Eric Reid. Nate stood beside them as an ally. In his statement following the game, Colin also pledged to donate $1 million to charities focused on racial inequality and police brutality.

That same day, Seattle Seahawks cornerback Jeremy Lane sat during the national anthem. As Colin continued to take a knee at game after game, other Black players across the NFL began to join the protest, including taking a knee, locking arms, or raising their fists.

> I think we can move on from losing alone to the belief in winning together.
>
> **—MEGAN RAPINOE**[17]

Two days after Colin kneeled for the first time, US Women's National Soccer Team star Megan Rapinoe took a knee during the national anthem at her match: "It was a little nod to Kaepernick and everything that he's standing for right now. I think it's actually pretty disgusting the way he was treated and the way that a lot of the media has covered it and made it about something that it absolutely isn't. . . . Being a gay American, I know what it means to look at the flag and not have it protect all of your liberties," Megan said. "It was something small that I could do and something that I plan to keep doing in the future and hopefully spark some meaningful conversation around it."[18] Megan is an advocate for LGBTQIA+ rights and has been active in the movement—and lawsuit—for equal pay for women's soccer players.

In response to Megan kneeling, the next week the stadium played the anthem before the players left the locker room—before she had an opportunity to kneel. The US Soccer Federation condemned her kneeling and passed a policy requiring players to stand during the national anthem. The next month, players and staff of the men's German soccer club Hertha Berlin took a knee in solidarity.

As a player who was getting older, who just returned from a serious knee injury, Megan's continued protest put her career in jeopardy: "If I want people to stand up for *my* rights, then I have to do that, and people should do that," she said. She faced significant backlash, including being left off the national team roster for five months. "I really thought maybe they were putting ol' Pinoe out to pasture. I thought maybe it was over."[19] But eventually she returned to the national team after working to prove herself. "I just knew that if I was to come back from it all, I had to be so undeniable."[20]

Megan's words about her protest echo those of Colin, as well as Tommie, John, and Peter before him. "I can understand if you think that I'm disrespecting the flag by kneeling, but it is because of my utmost respect for the flag and the promise it represents that I have chosen to demonstrate in this way," she wrote. "When I take a knee, I am facing the flag with my full body, staring straight into the heart of our country's ultimate symbol of freedom—because I believe it is my responsibility, just as it is yours, to ensure that freedom is afforded to everyone in this country."[21]

Four years later, French soccer player Marcus Thuram took a knee after the murder of George Floyd. Shortly after, English football clubs Liverpool, Aston Villa, and Sheffield United did the same. In response, FIFA—the global soccer governing body—publicly stated that such protests are "worthy of applause not punishment." After these protests and the FIFA statement, the US Soccer Federation board repealed their ban, and its new president personally apologized to Megan. The protests continued.

Megan continued to use her voice and platform to advocate for Colin and the fight against racial injustice in global sports and in the United States overall.[22]

"It's always worth it to [protest], whether people like it or not,'" Megan said. "Use your voice in whatever way that you can. I truly believe we have a responsibility to make the world better in whatever way we can do best."[23]

> This stand wasn't for me. This is because I'm seeing things happen to people that don't have a voice, people that don't have a platform to talk and have their voices heard, and effect change. So, I'm in the position where I can do that and I'm going to do that for people that can't.
>
> **—COLIN KAEPERNICK**[24]

While Megan received public criticism and condemnation for her actions initially, she was able to continue her career, eventually the ban was lifted, and she received a public apology. Colin did not have the same fate. Despite his "above-average" record as a young quarterback, no team signed him for the 2017 season.[25]

Colin's actions in 2016 and beyond—with the support of allies like Megan who knelt with him—have continued to shine a light on racial injustice in the United States.

> *How might you show solidarity for someone on your team, during a time where it would really be meaningful for them?*

Michael Siebel and Alexis Ohanian

Ten days after George Floyd was murdered in May 2020, Alexis Ohanian Sr., cofounder of Reddit, posted on Twitter that he was officially stepping down from the board.[26] He asked in his resignation that he be replaced with a board member who is Black.

"I co-founded Reddit 15 years ago to help people find community and a sense of belonging," Alexis said. "It is long overdue to do the right thing. I'm doing this for me, for my family, and for my country. I'm saying this as a father who needs to be able to answer his black daughter when she asks: 'What did you do?'"[27]

Reddit is one of the most visited websites in the world, with an incredible impact—and a history of harassment, bullying, racism, sexism, ableism, anti-Muslim, anti-Semitism, anti-LGBTQIA+ sentiment, and more on its platform. While they have done a lot of work in recent years to make the site safer, it could surely benefit from a more diverse board helping drive further safety, belonging, and innovation.

Diversity on boards is challenging to improve unless the board has term limits, someone retires, or someone steps down—so lack of representation on boards can take a generation or several to correct. Alexis taking this action allowed for an immediate change to Reddit's board diversity. "I believe resignation can actually be an act of leadership from people in power right now. To everyone fighting to fix our broken nation: do not stop," he said. And he further pledged, "I will use future gains on my Reddit stock to serve the black community, chiefly to curb racial hate, and I'm starting with a pledge of $1M to Colin Kaepernick's Know Your Rights Camp."[28]

Alexis's board seat was succeeded by Michael Seibel, Group Partner and Managing Director of Y Combinator and cofounder and CEO of Justin.tv (which later became Twitch).

"I want to thank Steve, Alexis, and the entire Reddit board for this opportunity. I've known Steve and Alexis since 2007 and have been a Reddit user ever since," Michael said in a statement. "Over this period of time I've watched Reddit become part of the core fabric of the internet and I'm excited to help provide advice and guidance as Reddit continues to grow and tackle the challenges of bringing community and belonging to a broader audience."[29]

[*Is there an opportunity in your life to step back to give someone else an opportunity to shine?*]

Activists and Allies in the Long Push for the Americans with Disabilities Act

In 2020, the United States celebrated the 30th anniversary of the Americans with Disabilities Act (ADA)—a landmark civil rights act that legislated basic rights for people with disabilities. While there is a lot more work to be done—and that work is slow like most human rights work—the ADA was an incredibly important foundation for people with disabilities.

As with many legislative acts of this scale, many activists spent years, even lifetimes, laying the foundations for this legislation to happen. And as with many large-scale human rights movements, those activists needed allies to use their power and influence to ensure its success. Discrimination and oppression often prevent people from becoming leaders that have the power to create systemic change—so allyship is often necessary for systemic change to occur.

In 1986, the National Council on Disability (then the National Council on the Handicapped) issued a report *Toward Independence*, which recommended congressional legislation that would provide equal opportunity for people with disabilities. The council was chaired by Sandra

FIGURE 1.3   **President George H. W. Bush Signs the Americans with Disabilities Act of 1990 into Law. Pictured (left to right): Evan Kemp, Reverend Harold Wilke, President Bush, Sandra Swift Parrino, Justin Dart Jr.**

[Photo credit: Joyce C. Naltchayan, George Bush Presidential Library and Museum/NARA]

Swift Parrino, an ally and a mother of two sons with disabilities. Sandra and her team worked with Justin Dart Jr., a disability activist (and an ally in his own right for women and minorities) to draft this report for Congress, suggesting Congress ratify "The Americans with Disabilities Act of 1986."[30]

Two years later, the first version of the Americans with Disabilities Act was introduced to Congress by Representative Anthony Coelho (D-CA) in the House and Senator Lowell P. Weicker Jr. (R-CT) in the Senate. Lowell was an advocate of public policy for people with disabilities throughout his 28-year tenure as an ally and parent of a child with a disability.

That same year, the Congressional Task Force on the Rights and Empowerment of Americans with Disabilities was created by Representative Major Robert Odell Owens, a civil rights activist. "The strategy was to link it to civil rights," said Major Owens. "It was the best route to get folks to understand segregation fast. Civil rights and women's rights had a clear history. Making the transition to rights for people with disabilities became easier because we had the history of the other two."[31]

"The disability community's success in passing the ADA would not have been possible without the opportunity, encouragement or support that Major Owens gave us. His contributions to advancing disability rights cannot be overstated," said Yoshiko Dart, a disability activist and ally who worked on the task force. The task force was chaired by Justin and cochaired by Elizabeth Boggs, who had been a disability activist for many years as an ally. It also included 38 volunteers—people with disabilities, activists, and allies. Together they worked to make the case for legislation.

In 1989, Senator Tom Harkin (D-IA) worked with Senator Edward Kennedy (D-MA) to improve the bill. Senator Harkin and Representative Coelho then reintroduced the bill to Congress. After much deliberation, compromise, and public demonstrations like the ADAPT Capital Crawl,[32] the Americans with Disabilities Act of 1990 was passed and signed into law, as shown in Figure 1.3.

Sandra Swift Parrino, Elizabeth Boggs, Major Robert Odell Owens, Lowell P. Weicker Jr, Yoshiko Dart, and later Tom Harkin all worked as allies to help ensure the ADA's success.

[
Is there an opportunity for you to help change unfair policies and/or to advocate for greater inclusion for people with disabilities?
]

I share these stories as examples of what allyship looks like. In each of these cases and in all allyship, we must center the work around the people we are working to be allies for. These moments in history are about the movements and the leaders of these movements—the allies are there supporting and working with them to create much-needed change.

These are just a few very public stories of the many ways people can show up as allies, of course. Many of the allies in these stories have also needed allies in their lives. I have personally benefited from many small acts of allyship throughout my life and career: a professor I asked for a recommendation, who went beyond and hand-delivered his recommendation in person to get me an interview. A friend who helped me push through my fears of public speaking, supporting me as I worked to become a successful speaker. Another friend who taught me negotiation skills so I could better advocate for a good compensation package. Even a stranger, who offered me a place to stay when I was a broke student looking for housing in New York.

Figures 1.4 and 1.5 show just a few of the many stories people have shared with us about how allies have helped them in their careers.

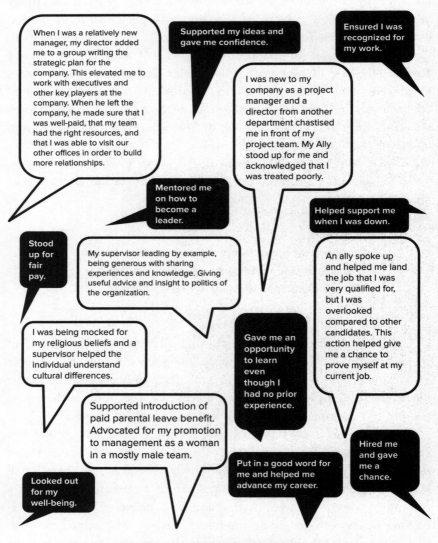

FIGURE 1.4   How Allies Help People

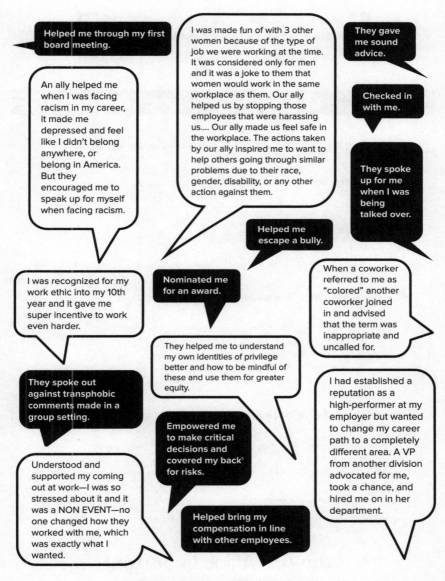

FIGURE 1.5 **How Allies Help People**

[*How have allies helped you in your life?*]

EXERCISE

Think about a time when an ally made a difference in your life.

What did they do? _____

_____

_____

_____

How did it help you in your career? _____

_____

_____

_____

How might you give back to someone else in a similar way?

_____

_____

_____

Why Are Allies Important in the Workplace?

Our companies have a responsibility to create inclusive cultures, build diverse teams, and correct systemic inequities in hiring, promotion, pay, and leadership. Yet we all make a mistake when we see diversity and inclusion as a side project for someone else to solve, rather than the work all of us need to do together. *We* are our companies—our workplace cultures and systems won't change without all of us taking action to change them.

To improve company cultures and systems, we must take an active role in learning how our own actions affect other peoples' abilities and opportunities to succeed and thrive, and correcting the systems and processes we use every day that may also cause harm. When you're being belittled, disrespected, bullied, or discriminated against, it's really difficult to create change. We can accomplish more when we work together to build a workplace where we all thrive.

This book isn't just about White, male allyship—though that is part of it, and I appreciate all of you who are reading and taking action. This book is for all of us. Like Megan Rapinoe—a White lesbian fighting for gender pay equity and LGBTQIA+ rights—kneeling in solidarity with Colin Kaepernick to shine a light on racial injustice. Like Representative Major Robert Odell Owens—a Black senator and civil rights advocate—working for the rights of people with disabilities by forming a committee that would put together a strong case for the Americans with Disabilities Act. And Sandra Swift Parrino, Elizabeth Boggs, and Yoshiko Dart, three women who were not disabled, dedicating their careers to advocating for and with people with disabilities. Being there for each other makes a difference.

History has shown time after time that we are more powerful together than we are on our own. Together we can build healthier, happier, more innovative and productive teams. Together we can correct imbalances in success and opportunity and make our workplaces inclusive.

Why Become an Ally?

As you dive into allyship, I encourage you to reflect on your own motivation for being an ally. Reminding yourself of this from time to time can keep you motivated when you're challenged, and can also clarify where you want to focus your allyship. Figure 1.6 shows the most common reasons people become allies from our research. Perhaps one or more of these reasons will resonate with you.

For me, several are important drivers, but my primary motivations are fairness and justice and making the world better for future generations. Spend a moment thinking about your primary motivation.

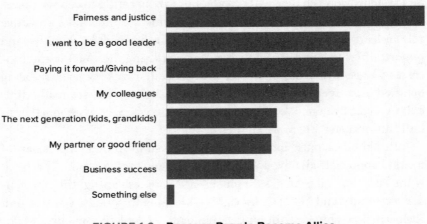

FIGURE 1.6   **Reasons People Become Allies**

EXERCISE

What motivates *you* to be an ally? Write this down and refer back to it later. You may want to think about what prompted you to pick up this book and read it. Whom do you want to be there for in your life? What kind of a leader do you want to become? What world do you want to help create?

My reason for being an ally is: _____

_____

_____

_____

When allyship gets difficult, or you've taken a break and want to come back to being a good ally, let this motivate you. And don't worry if you haven't quite honed in on the perfect answer. This can be a first draft that evolves as you learn.

Behavior change takes time, and each person needs different input to keep themselves going on the path of change. In the following pages, you'll find data, research, historical context, stories, quotes, and tangible, actionable steps you can take. Take what you need for your journey so you can lead the change you wish to see.

I've learned a lot in my journey to be a good ally over the years. And yet as I interviewed and analyzed the data from thousands of people's ideas about allyship and advocacy, I still found surprises that challenged my assumptions. Be open to new ways of seeing, thinking, listening, and doing. What we learn can challenge some deeply held beliefs we have had for years.

2

THE ROLE OF ALLYSHIP IN WORKPLACE DIVERSITY, EQUITY, AND INCLUSION

> If the Whites are hurting, Blacks are hurting, too. When Black people hurt here, White people do, too.
>
> —CLARISSA BROWN, a friend of Jonathan Price[1]

One night in 2020, before we went to sleep, my husband sighed a big sigh and put down his phone. I knew without him having to say a word: another Black man had been killed. It was Jonathan Price, 31, who worked for the government and was well-known and respected for giving back to the community. He was at a gas station and stepped in to help stop a domestic violence situation. When the police officer arrived later, Jonathan tried to shake his hand and explain the situation. The officer didn't listen; instead he tased and shot Jonathan four times, killing him.

My husband, family, friends, and colleagues experience regular examples of how their Black lives are not valued. And then they go to work, and experience biases and microaggressions that tell them their expertise is not valued. When police shoot innocent, unarmed Black men—and to be clear, they should not be shooting any unarmed person, innocent or not—it is often due to racism and/or fear that stems from biases. These same biases are happening in our workplaces.

In the workplace, biases affect how we scrutinize résumés and work experiences differently, and the subtle ways we pass people up for promotions, assume people aren't ready for a special project, and minimize and invalidate people's expertise. This affects people's careers, livelihoods, dreams, and ability to thrive based on their hard work, expertise, and merit.

From Our History to Our Workplaces

There is a direct line from historical oppression, systemic inequities, and cultural marginalization to our workplaces. Because our workplace and education systems were generally made by and for a dominant majority population—often decades before many of us had equal rights to an education and to earn a living—those systems are often inequitable, whether intentional or not. As a result, inequities and marginalization are often endemic in education systems, hiring processes, compensation and promotion, product development, marketing and advertising, and workplace cultures. They were never redesigned for *everyone*.

Intergenerational wealth and opportunity gaps, which we'll explore in "Step 1: Learn, Unlearn, Relearn," can also impact our prospects for education as well as what networks we may have—both are keys to getting in the door of most high-paying jobs today.

In a landmark decision by the US Supreme Court in the summer of 2020, people who are LGBTQIA+ finally became legally protected from workplace discrimination.[2] Until then, in more than half of the states it was legal to fire someone for being gay, lesbian, bisexual, or transgender. In an act of allyship and social justice prior to the decision, more than 200 major corporations filed a brief to the Supreme Court in support of LGBT employees. There is still much more work to do, however. Anti-trans legislation continues to be introduced at alarming rates across the United

States. Ninety percent of transgender people have faced harassment, mistreatment, or discrimination in the workplace—and can face additional barriers when traveling for work, like facing scrutiny at airport security, lack of safe restrooms, and conferences and meetings that can be unsafe.[3]

> A lot of states in the United States and across the world now have laws around bathrooms for trans folk. So there's now states where I can't pee in. And that's kind of troubling. Because I like to pee. You know . . . It's useful not to hold it in all day.
>
> —MARION DALY[4]

Globally, people with disabilities are severely under- or unemployed, with rates of employment as low as 10 percent in some countries.[5] In the United States, just 31 percent of working-age adults with disabilities are employed—compared to 75 percent of those without disabilities. Women and Black people with disabilities are even less likely to be employed.[6] There is also a severe pay inequity, where people with disabilities earn 37 percent less than their peers in comparable roles.[7] Myths and biases about people with disabilities are common in the workplace, with employers often wrongly believing people with disabilities are not productive, are unable to perform job tasks, need costly accommodation or to be "cared for," or that there is a lack of qualified talent with disabilities (a similar perception for overall talent from underrepresented backgrounds).[8]

One-third of veterans in the United States are underemployed, and 70 percent are more likely to take a step back in seniority when they return to work.[9] This is often due to perceptions of a "gap" in their résumé when they served, something returning parents and other caregivers also face.

While Black people are 13 percent of the US population and earn 10 percent of college degrees, they are 8 percent of corporate professionals. Moving up the ladder in an organization, Black people comprise 7 percent of managers, 3 percent of executives and senior managers, and less than 1 percent of CEOs.[10] Black employees are the most likely of any racial or ethnic group to experience racial prejudice and discrimination in the workplace, and they tend to spend more energy being authentic at work. They are also less likely than their White colleagues to have access to senior leadership and growth opportunities. Black women are also less likely than White women to receive support through allyship.[11]

COVID-19 exposed and exacerbated gender disparities, where several human rights organizations believe the pandemic set back women's rights by years, if not decades.[12] Women experienced significant additional work at home parenting children (a "double shift" duty many parents share, but women take on this work at a disproportionate level) and an increase in domestic violence (referred to as the Shadow Pandemic). Women, Black, and Latinx workers in the United States were more likely to be furloughed or laid off, and globally women were more likely to leave the workforce or reduce their hours to care for children and other family members. Women were also 70 percent of health and social workers globally, which meant they were more likely to be on the front lines, risking their lives every day.[13]

In the United States, women are 51 percent of the population and 47 percent of corporate professionals, yet only 38 percent of managers and 21 percent of C-suite executives.[14] A lot of my work is in the tech industry, where women, people with underrepresented racial and ethnic identities, first-generation students, and people from low-income backgrounds leave STEM (science, technology, engineering, and math) fields at higher rates than their counterparts—due to bullying, public humiliation, pay and promotion inequity, general unfairness, and lack of respect.[15] Just 30 percent of women who earn bachelor's degrees in engineering remain in their field, most moving on—and moving up—in other industries.[16] Women of color, who earn less than 10 percent of bachelor degrees in computer science, navigate both gender and racial microaggressions, as well as experiencing invisibility and lack of support.[17]

Diversity, Equity, and Inclusion in the Workplace

Over the past few decades, many companies have started to actively work to address diversity, equity, and inclusion. Initially, motivations—and success—varied. Some business leaders undoubtedly felt a personal moral obligation to address historical inequities. Others likely were driven by a desire to conform to shifting societal attitudes and to meet the expectations of employees, customers, and other stakeholders. And once some progress was made in creating more diverse and inclusive organizations, vitally important data emerged: diversity and inclusion is good for business.

Hiring a Diverse Team Is Not About "Lowering the Bar." It's About *Raising the Bar.*

The expression "lowering the bar" generally is used by people from a majority group or culture when talking about increasing the number of hires from a group that is underrepresented—usually women, people with underrepresented racial and ethnic identities, and sometimes people with disabilities. The incorrect sentiment behind this statement is that to find qualified people from an underrepresented group, you'd have to reduce the qualifications and expectations for that role. Further, that this person would become a burden to the person hiring and to the team, because they would be less qualified.

This idea may come about due to a person's fear, bias, unwillingness to try to find people with underrepresented identities for the role, a lack of understanding around what makes a quality employee, as well as not knowing or caring about the science that shows diverse teams are more productive, profitable, and innovative. Data actually shows quite clearly that diverse teams raise the bar.[18]

Often people assume that if qualified people with underrepresented identities don't apply for a position, they don't exist. Yet that's almost never the case. *Ask why* rather than *assume why.* Like any target market, you have to go where your customers are to find them, and you have to market to them. You have to know what they want and develop a product—in this case, job description, benefits, and culture—that draws them in.

Additionally, you have to develop a data-driven talent selection process that is designed to create the best, most innovative teams to solve the complex problems of your company. Most hiring processes are biased toward the majority, based on assumptions of what makes a good employee versus what actually does. For example, most tech companies and many Fortune 500 companies filter out candidates by education, prioritizing candidates from top Ivy League schools for consideration. Yet research shows education does not matter when it comes to how well someone ultimately performs in their role.[19]

Make diversity a core "value add" for the role, and design your hiring process to ensure you are seeking and hiring candidates with a wide diversity of experiences. Explore ways you might be inadvertently excluding good candidates due to incorrect assumptions or biases—and correct them. And go beyond hiring to ensure your culture is one where people from underrepresented identities feel safe, supported, valued, and that they truly belong. This will help you build a strong, talented team that develops innovative solutions for your diverse clients, customers, and stakeholders.

A large and growing body of data shows there is a real business case for diversity and inclusion. Diverse and inclusive teams and organizations are more productive, profitable, and innovative. That old rubric that hiring more diverse people "lowers the bar" has been proven to be completely false. The opposite is true—diversity raises the bar and improves everyone's performance. Organizations and business leaders have even more incentive to increase diversity and inclusion: it's good for the bottom line.[20]

Of course, understanding the case for diversity and making it work in an organization are two different things. As my story in the Introduction attests, hiring some people from underrepresented groups and asking them to work in a culture that is overtly or tacitly hostile to diversity is a recipe for failure. New hires will feel marginalized, disempowered, and unhappy. Many will leave.

As our research deepens, it's becoming clear that happiness and well-being are a key component of what produces positive business outcomes. People need to feel safe, valued, and respected in a diverse, equitable, and inclusive environment.[21] And allies—you and I—have such a key role in this: we can impact the culture and make a difference for our colleagues with one action at a time.

What People Want from Allies in the Workplace

Where allyship is prioritized and encouraged in the workplace, people's well-being at work improves significantly. When someone has at least one in their workplace, their likelihood of feeling psychologically safe increases by 35 percent. They are 81 percent more likely to feel they belong, 79 percent more likely to be satisfied with their workplace culture, and 94 percent more likely to be satisfied with their job.[22] We'll discuss the roles safety and belonging have in developing inclusion later in this chapter.

FIGURE 2.1   Word Cloud Showing Adjectives People Use to Describe Good Allies

Since 2014, my company, Change Catalyst, has worked with hundreds of leaders to build inclusive leadership, allyship, diversity, equity, and inclusion in their companies. We've trained and coached many thousands of people around empathy, allyship, and inclusive leadership. We have also conducted global research to learn more about allyship sentiments and how allyship can improve workplace diversity, equity, and inclusion. Some of what we found has been surprising.

While allyship can feel complex, Figure 2.1 shows that above all people describe good allies to be trustworthy, helpful, honest, supportive, loyal, caring, kind, and good listeners. We all have the power to embody these qualities. People report that having allies in their workplace help them feel more engaged, increase their happiness and sense of belonging, and improve their productivity. For people with some marginalized identities, especially those more likely to face discrimination, allies are also important to increase feelings of psychological safety in the workplace.

Looking at what people want from allies, we found 17 different themes in our research over the years, which are depicted in Figure 2.2. When asked to prioritize, however, overwhelmingly people want their allies to "trust me," "give me confidence or courage," and "mentor me." Allyship can be pretty simple—we already have many of these skills and attributes, we may just have to learn to activate them differently to become good allies.

HOW WOULD YOU MOST LIKE AN ALLY TO HELP YOU IN YOUR CAREER?

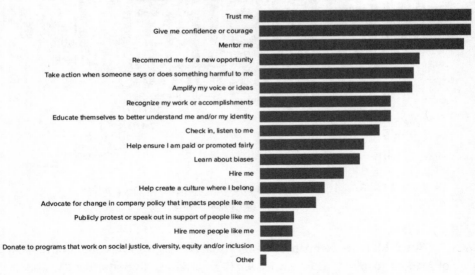

FIGURE 2.2 **What People Want from Their Allies**

Women most frequently want allies to give them confidence or courage, where men prioritize trust, and people who are nonbinary prioritize mentorship. When someone has experienced discrimination in their career, their allyship priorities shift: they want allies to help build their confidence and take action when someone says or does something to harm them.

Black people in the United States report the highest rates of any race to experience discrimination in their careers (73 percent) compared to their White colleagues (46 percent). They are more likely to prioritize that allies learn about their biases and to take action when someone says or does something to harm them. And allyship does improve their feelings of safety: Black people in the United States are 67 percent more likely to feel safe in the workplace when they have at least one—and that number grows the more allies they have.

Globally many groups report high rates of discrimination in the workplace, including people with disabilities (74 percent), veterans (73 percent), people from the MENA region (68 percent), Indigenous people (67 percent), and people who are LGBTQIA+ (65 percent).[23] Sixty-nine percent of people who are nonbinary report experiencing discrimination in their workplace, where just 46 percent feel they have a safe work environment, and 38 percent feel that they belong in their workplace culture. Rates of psychological safety and belonging are also very low for people with disabilities and people who are Indigenous, Latinx, Black, and from the Middle East North Africa (MENA) region.

Indigenous people and people who are LGBTQIA+ generally want allies, above all, to take action when someone says or does something harmful to them. Veterans look for allies to be mentors, whereas Latinx people most want allies to give them courage. Immigrants generally want their allies to mentor them and overwhelmingly want their organizations to do more around allyship, while first-generation citizens are more likely to prioritize that allies trust them. Asians also prioritize trust, while people from the MENA region want allies to amplify their voice or ideas. People with disabilities want allies to trust them, take action when someone says or does something harmful to them, and better understand their identity.

These are broad ideas for how individuals like allies to show up for them. No groups have monolithic experiences, and people often have intersectional identities. The best way to know what someone wants or needs is to ask.

The Foundations of Diversity, Equity, and Inclusion

The following pages include some foundational terminology about diversity, equity, and inclusion (DEI).[24] As an ally, this is important to understand these foundations so you can participate in conversations at work and improve your depth of allyship. Everyone who works on DEI has their own working definitions; the following are what we developed over the years at Change Catalyst through our work with clients, communities, and hundreds of leaders in DEI around the world.

Diversity

Diversity is bringing humans with different backgrounds to the table. That means you're hiring diverse people, you're inviting people with diverse identities to meetings and events, and there is diversity in your classrooms and boardrooms. When you look around the room—and more important, when you look at the *data*—you see that there is a broad range of people from different genders, races, ethnicities, disabilities, religions, ages, sexual orientations, and other aspects of someone's identity and background.[25] These other aspects could include culture, class, caste, political views, geographical origin (countries, regions, urban/rural/suburban), languages spoken, thinking styles, education, personality traits (e.g., introverts and extroverts), parental status, veterans, people who have been incarcerated, and more.

Companies working to increase diversity usually begin by improving their hiring processes through recruiting in new places and/or hosting events, where they can find candidates with underrepresented identities. They might work on improving their recruiting experience to remove biases and exclusionary practices, and make candidates with underrepresented identities feel more welcome. Companies who are working on diversity in a deeper way focus on hiring as well as retention, leadership, product development, customer acquisition, supply chain, board and investor diversity, and more. They set public goals for achieving greater diversity and executives hold themselves accountable for achieving those goals.

I often hear people say a person is "diverse." Someone might be biracial or mixed race, or from an underrepresented group, but no one person is diverse. Instead, you might say they have an underrepresented identity or are from a historically marginalized group. Or better, identify them by their specific identity (e.g., Vietnamese-Canadian woman with a disability). Whenever possible, identify people with their preferred identity language.

By the same nature, a group of people with the same identity is not necessarily diverse. For instance, a group of women is not diverse unless it includes a broad range of women from different races, ethnicities, disabilities, sexual orientations, ages, religions, and so on. A group of Black people is not racially diverse—though it may incorporate diversity in terms of ethnicity, disability, sexual orientation, age, and/or religion. The expression "diversity of thought" is often used to show that a group of White men is diverse because they have different thinking styles. This may be true, but to have true diversity on your team, you need to work to bring together diverse identities, experiences, and skill sets.

Intersectionality

> Intersectionality is a lens through which you can see where power comes and collides, where it interlocks and intersects. It's not simply that there's a race problem here, a gender problem here, and a class or LBGTQ problem there. Many times that framework erases what happens to people who are subject to all of these things.
>
> **—KIMBERLÉ CRENSHAW**[26]

When companies first begin working on diversity, frequently they will focus their work on one or two identities—this is often women, but is increasingly becoming racial and ethnic minorities (generally the focus is on Black and Latinx identities in the United States). However, when you only focus on one or a few groups, you often negate someone's intersectional identities and don't make space for them to thrive and feel that they belong. A person can be a woman who is queer, Afrolatina, and disabled, for example. Her intersectional identities make her unique, adding important diversity to your team, and also, she may experience compounding inequity and microaggressions throughout her life that are important to recognize and correct.

My experience facing microaggressions in the workplace as a White woman were significant. A Black woman in the same position might face those same microaggressions, as well as microaggressions targeted toward her identity as a Black woman. A Black woman who is Muslim and an immigrant may face additional microaggressions, biases, and systemic barriers to opportunity. Because people have intersectional identities, be sure to use *and* not *or* when you're talking about different groups—for example, "women *and* minorities." To say "or" would be to diminish a part of someone's identity.

Inclusion

Inclusion is inviting diverse humans to speak and encouraging and supporting them to lead. It's not enough for someone to be at the table, you actually need to invite and make space for them to speak, and deeply listen and value their ideas and experience when they do speak. For someone to feel truly included, they also must have the opportunity to lead—and to see people like them leading. Sometimes inclusion means collaboratively redesigning the table altogether.

Companies that focus on inclusion along with diversity programs benefit more from their diversity compared with organizations focusing on diversity as a stand-alone practice.[27] The work of inclusion begins by making sure someone feels welcome to walk in the door, then that they feel safe to be there, engaged and activated while they are there, committed to being there and contributing to the culture, and that they truly belong in that place. At Change Catalyst, we call these the Stages of Inclusion, which are shown in Figure 2.3. People slide up and down this scale depending on their experiences at a given time.

STAGES OF INCLUSION

FIGURE 2.3 Inclusion: From Welcome to Belonging

1. **Welcome.** I feel welcome to walk in the door. The company website, messaging, vision, and values resonate with me. People seem to care about my presence. I have a good experience in the hiring process, and the onboarding process speaks to my needs.
2. **Safe.** I feel safe to be who I am and share my ideas and experiences. I don't have to cover parts of my identity. I'm not harassed or bullied. I don't face regular microaggressions. And if I do face any of these, I know where to report them and am confident appropriate action will be taken for me to feel safe again.
3. **Engaged.** I am engaged with my team, actively contributing to my team's success. I am rewarded for my accomplishments and motivated to improve my work and increase the company's overall success. I understand the process for promotion. My manager cares about my growth and gives me regular feedback to help me grow. My ideas are valued and I contribute to innovation.
4. **Committed.** I am committed to being at this company for a while, and my company is committed to me. Leadership cares about me and my growth. I have opportunities to become a leader myself. I am fairly compensated and promoted. I contribute to my colleagues' successes and our company culture overall through mentorship, sponsorship, and/or other ways.
5. **Belong.** I belong here. I am valued for my unique experiences and contributions. I am proud of my accomplishments at this organization. I am connected to my colleagues and to the leadership of the company. I am supported in my own growth and can become who I want to be here.[28]

Many companies and individuals stop their strategy at bringing diverse people in the door (Stage 1). But this can create a revolving door if someone does not feel safe, engaged, committed, or that they belong. Little things we each do in our daily interactions can make a difference in how someone feels along this path of inclusion.

Some of the ways companies focus on inclusion are:

▸ Improving internal processes to be more inclusive of people with all identities

- ▸ Making physical spaces more inclusive for people of different religions and ethnicities, people who are transgender, lactating mothers, and caregivers
- ▸ Offering benefits packages that are inclusive of caregivers, trans folks, and people with disabilities
- ▸ Offering paid time off for people to celebrate their own religious and cultural holidays, and recognition for those holidays
- ▸ Supporting and funding ERGs or affinity groups for people with underrepresented identities to gather, learn, advocate, and be themselves
- ▸ Developing professional development programs to build diverse leadership
- ▸ Providing training and coaching around allyship, empathy, biases and microaggressions, inclusive leadership, and inclusive design
- ▸ Internalizing and operationalizing company values that incorporate inclusion

Creating an inclusive culture takes time, especially if the culture wasn't built inclusively from the beginning. Most companies are a work in progress, still implementing the needed structural and cultural change to become truly inclusive. This work requires adequate budget, staffing, change management expertise, and a leadership team that champions this work and holds themselves accountable for its success.

But it's worth it. In our research, we have seen a remarkable correlation between an employee's feeling of safety, belonging, and job satisfaction and how much their company prioritizes DEI. In companies where DEI is a key priority, 76 percent of people report feeling very safe in their workplace, 64 percent report a deep feeling of belonging, and 93 percent report they are satisfied with their job. By contrast, in companies that don't prioritize DEI, just 8 percent of employees report feeling very safe, 14 percent feel a deep sense of belonging, and 62 percent feel satisfied with their job.[29] This work matters.

Equity

Equity is correcting justice and fairness while addressing historical privilege and oppression. People and companies that address equity are acknowledging that throughout history to the present, some people have had more privilege while others have been oppressed and treated unfairly through our institutions and culture. We will explore this inequity in "Step 1: Learn, Unlearn, Relearn."

Workplaces focused on equity often start by looking at pay equity, usually finding a disparity based on gender and race. Given what we know of the compensation equity for people with disabilities, you might expand this work. Addressing promotion and leadership equity is equally important because people with underrepresented identities are less likely to be promoted or given a raise due to biases and unfair processes. Some companies address education equity by providing apprenticeship and internship programs as well, and partnering with schools like historically Black colleges and universities (HBCUs) and Hispanic-serving institutions (HSIs) in the United States. Knowing that law enforcement and criminal justice systems are severely inequitable, a few companies actively hire people who are incarcerated or formerly incarcerated. Sometimes companies will partner with organizations working to improve equity in their industry or across society as well.

Underrepresentation and Overrepresentation

Representation refers to diversity parity: whether the demographics of your workplace population is representative of the demographics in your region or customer base. If groups are not represented equitably, they are *under*represented.

In 2014, some of the major tech companies released their diversity numbers publicly for the first time and showed a very bleak picture: White and Asian men were very significantly *over*represented in the industry. For the companies that released their numbers publicly, it was a wakeup call to action: the press, their staff, the Obama administration, and sometimes even company investors demanded action.

Overall, where the US population was 51 percent women in 2014, tech companies were showing an average of just 32 percent women in their workforce—the majority in admin roles rather than higher paying technical roles. In terms of race and ethnicity, Latinx people were 16 percent of the population, yet just 10 percent of employees in tech companies, and Black people were 12 percent of the population, yet just 7 percent of employees in tech companies. By far the largest population of Black employees was at Amazon, which had a higher representation of Black people at their distribution centers. Many tech companies reported just 1 to 2 percent Black employees.[30]

At the time, and still today, many companies blame the candidate "pipeline" for this underrepresentation. However, the numbers don't match up. During the same period tech companies reported on average 2 to 3 percent combined Black and Latinx technical staff, about 20 percent of computer science degrees were earned by Black and Latinx students.[31]

My colleague Brenda Darden-Wilkerson reminded me recently that like "diverse," "underrepresented" should not be used in place of someone's identity. For example, Black women in the United States are often underrepresented in the workplace. But when identifying a specific Black woman, she may have an underrepresented identity but she is not an underrepresented *person*. She is a Black woman whose identity is underrepresented.[32]

"Underrepresentation" is a way of stating that we have work to do to improve our organization's diversity so that it represents the diversity of our communities. Practitioners in DEI have also used *historically marginalized*, *minorities*, *undervalued*, *underestimated*, *untapped*, and many other terms to call attention to the disparity. None are perfect terms, each categorizes people by their *lack* of something: *un*, *under*, or somehow *other*. I don't love any of them, so I'm hoping someone comes up with a better term we can agree to use in the future!

Let's Talk About Power and Privilege

If you have never had a Supreme Court decide if you have
the same rights as others, you have privilege.

—UNKNOWN

When I first started working on diversity and inclusion, I didn't want to hear the word *privilege*. I didn't like it. I worked hard, I've faced significant challenges, I have dedicated my life to improving the world, and I've made a lot of personal sacrifices to do this change-making work over the years. I didn't want to hear that I was somehow doing something wrong by having privilege.

But privilege isn't about doing something wrong, privilege is usually something you are born with.

I explored this in myself and realized even with the many challenges I have faced, I do have privilege other people don't have. I was born with White skin, which sadly gives me privilege in a lot of spaces—people treat me differently. Examining my privilege further: it includes thinking that racism was something in the past, as I did until I was 18. And not regularly being followed by security guards in stores, less likely to be arrested or incarcerated, having better access to healthcare and education. I earn far less pay than my colleagues who are men, but more than my colleagues who are women and also Black, Indigenous, Latina, and disabled. While I have had hardships, I have also had unearned privilege. It can be difficult to come to terms with this, but I work to not feel guilt or shame about it, and instead work to create change.

Your struggles and hard work are absolutely real and true. And you may have some privilege that kept it from being *even harder*. You have done nothing wrong. Society has kept other people from having the same privilege we have, and that is wrong.

A big piece of allyship is coming to terms with the privilege we have, recognizing that it may come with unfair advantages, and using our power to create positive change for people with less privilege. If you're reading this book, you have some amount of privilege. There is almost always someone with less privilege than us in this world. *What will you do with your privilege?*

It's our job as allies to understand our built-in privilege and use it to change the imbalances created through our history, systems, and culture. So that when everyone works hard, we all have equal opportunities to achieve the same level of success.

Let's Do This

As you read through the following chapters, some difficult feelings may arise. In my work with individuals and companies around the world, I've found that many people go through stages of grief, guilt, or shame as our awareness grows about historical and systemic inequity and injustice, as our ideas of success and opportunity shift and we realize that life is not the meritocracy that we were taught, as our understanding of the effects of oppression and injustice deepens, and as we realize we do have a role to play.

Part of allyship is sitting with this knowledge and exploring how different people experience social and institutional systems and structures. When we do this it's normal to experience stages of grief. I went through shock, denial, anger, bargaining, depression and finally acceptance . . . sometimes slipping back into anger and depression still! Shame and guilt can also arise. Perhaps we feel shame that our ancestors did some really awful things and we're benefiting from it, or shame that we didn't realize all this inequity and by not doing something we have been in some ways complicit. People with underrepresented identities may also feel shame or grief that while we are strong, somehow we are unable to move past the barriers and become the people we want to be.

It's OK to have all of these feelings. Sit with them, understand them, and move through them so that you can help change the inequities and be part of the solution now.

> *We can be the generation that changes this.*
> *Together. Let's do this!*

3

STEP 1: LEARN, UNLEARN, RELEARN

O ur work as allies often begins with unlearning what we know about success and opportunity. Like many people, I grew up being told that if you work hard that hard work pays off, you get what you deserve, you live your dream. But for many people that's not true: they have to work 10 times as hard to get to the same places, while working against many barriers put in front of them.

Our gender, race, ethnicity, disability, religion, age, sexual orientation, class, caste, geography, country of origin—all can give us more or fewer opportunities for success. Barriers to success and opportunity can come from:

▸ **Historical oppression.** While history is in our past, the effects of colonization, enslavement, human rights violations, and systematic discrimination continue to shape the present for many people. For some people, this oppression never ended.

▸ **Systemic inequities.** Because most of our systems were built during times of oppression, uncorrected inequities continue to persist in education, policy, justice, finance, healthcare, workplaces, and more. Historical oppression and systemic inequities also caused intergenerational trauma and a significant wealth and health gap.

▸ **Cultural marginalization.** People are marginalized by systems as well as culture, from the stories we tell and who tells them—through film, media, toys, games, books, advertisements, word of mouth, and other ways culture is replicated. This can shape how we see each other and how we see ourselves.

▸ **Personal biases.** Biases are often a thread from our past, learned instincts passed down through families, friends, and culture. When they emerge in our words and actions, they can be harmful, affecting someone's work, career, and ability to thrive. We explore biases more in "Step 2: Do No Harm."

The first step of becoming a good ally in the workplace is to become aware of oppression, inequities, and marginalization that our colleagues experience, understand our unique histories and cultures, and acknowledge them. By building deeper empathy for each other, we become more effective allies and can create stronger and healthier workplaces and communities together.

From a global and historical perspective, the number of groups that have suffered oppression and discrimination is staggering. In this chapter, we discuss Indigenous peoples across several continents, Black Africans and Black people in the United States, women across the globe, people from LGBTQIA+ communities, and people with disabilities. But this is only a partial list of the many people who experience oppression and discrimination.

Similarly, while this chapter includes a few examples of oppression, inequity, and marginalization, the extent of these abuses is far greater than we have space to explore here. I encourage you to keep learning about the experiences of people whose identities are different from your own, unlearning what you know about history, and relearning by opening yourself to new ideas and viewpoints.

Special note and trigger warning. We'll be diving into subjects that can be difficult and uncomfortable, and for some this may surface anger, shame, or trauma. You're not alone, many people experience these at one point or another. If these feelings come up as you are reading, please make sure you work through them. Take a moment to breathe, meditate, go for a walk, exercise, and/or talk these feelings through with someone you trust.

A New Chapter in Awareness

On May 25, 2020, George Perry Floyd Jr. was murdered by Derek Chauvin, a Minneapolis police officer. Darnella Frazier, a 17-year-old girl, filmed the murder that lasted more than nine minutes—and the video was shared around the world. This was not the first murder of a Black person by a police officer (a Black person is killed by a police officer in the United States at a rate of more than one person every other day), but this time something changed.[1] Just a few weeks earlier we learned that Ahmaud Arbery was jogging in his own neighborhood and was murdered by three White men, Travis McMichael, Gregory McMichael, and William Bryan. Before that, Breonna Taylor, an essential worker during the COVID-19 pandemic, was shot and killed in her own home by police when she had committed no crime.

Many people across the world were sequestered at home feeling anxiety and anger about a pandemic, with lives being lost each day and disproportionately, the lives of Black, Indigenous, and Latinx people in the United States. Almost one in four people in the United States were out of work. We were uniquely tuned in while sports teams stopped playing, and film and TV studios stopped releasing new content. George Floyd said the same words Eric Garner had said when he was killed by police in 2014: "I can't breathe."

There was a collective awakening like I have never seen. Despite the risks of COVID-19, people of all races and ethnicities protested in the streets for days, weeks, months, globally. On social media, many people became newly engaged with diversity, equity, inclusion, allyship, and social justice. My Black colleagues became overwhelmed with people who are not Black reaching out to them, asking if they were OK and how they could take action. My consulting colleagues and I were suddenly overwhelmed with inbound requests from companies seeking antiracism and allyship training, and other work addressing DEI—many companies for the first time were looking to address these issues. Just days before, most consultants like us were struggling to stay afloat with the disintegration of corporate DEI budgets during COVID-19 and the resulting economic downturn.

If you are new to this, welcome! I'm glad you're here, you give me hope and strength that we can create much-needed change together. Now that you are here, it's time to do the work of learning, unlearning, relearning, and then—above all—taking consistent action. I ask you to keep an open mind as you read these pages, and as you continue throughout your allyship journey—allyship requires some internal investigation as well as external activation.

We all have something new to learn; I'm still continuing to learn and grow as an ally. The journey truly never ends. Together, let's continue to unlearn, relearn, and create the change we wish to see.

History Has a Point of View

As a student at the School of Visual Arts in New York some time ago, I was required to take a couple of art history classes as part of my degree. I resisted it, I wanted to learn from contemporary artists and theorists, rather than linger on a history of art that was mostly focused on White men (what people at the time called the "White male canon"). The women I saw in typical art history classes were mostly on canvases, often nude, painted by men. I didn't want to spend another three months of my life learning about them.

Then I found a course on the history of women artists, which was all at once fascinating, validating, and completely angering. I learned about women who were painting at the same time as Vincent van Gogh, Pablo Picasso, Joan Miró, Wassili Kandinsky, and others who had influenced my early interest in art (before my work moved into installation art and video). I had never heard of Artemisia Gentileschi, Mary Cassatt, Berthe Morisot, Clara Peeters, Élisabeth Vigée Le Brun, Hilma af Klint, Augusta Savage, and so many others. Women weren't written about in history books or theory articles during their lifetimes—even as they were written about in diaries and letters as influencers—because usually art historians and theorists were men who didn't value their work. Art created by women was rarely purchased and shown by museums because usually curators were White men—and because women artists hadn't been canonized as leaders in their field by historians.

Women artists were quite literally written out of history. In fact, even at my school, women were written out of other art history classes and relegated to just this one course. Even in this course, we learned mostly about White women artists—the course did not explore the many Black, Indigenous, Latina, Asian, and Middle Eastern artists that were also written out of art history. (Plus, it most certainly did not discuss the structural barriers that historically kept more women with diverse identities from even studying and becoming artists in the first place.)

Fairly recently, museums have started to diversify their curatorial staff and rewrite art history to include women, Black, Latinx, Indigenous, LGBTQIA+, disabled, and other artists who were left out. It's an early and ongoing correction that has been decades in the making, due to the hard work of many people and organizations pushing for change.

How we tell stories, who tells those stories, who is the subject of those stories, and how they are portrayed—all of this matters. Stories sculpt our collective worldview, how we see ourselves and each other, how we understand success and opportunity, how we build our systems and processes, how we make decisions, and why we make them.

When our stories and histories are told from one point of view, key people and their stories are written out of history. Generally, we tell stories about what we know and whom we know, with a worldview we developed from people with similar identities to our own, passed on from generation to generation. We have to actively seek out new perspectives, new voices, and new experiences to change our worldview.

> *Imagine who has been written out of the history you have been taught. Who wrote your elementary and high school textbooks growing up? Who authors the history we read about today?*

Our Present-Day Historians Also Have Biases

Many people throughout the globe look to Wikipedia for quick answers about history. Wikipedia is run by the Wikimedia Foundation, a nonprofit that has notoriously struggled to increase the diversity of its editors. In 2011, most Wikipedia editors were from the "Global North," just 8.5 percent identified as women, and women overall made fewer edits than men. Women editors over the years have complained about biases and systemic inequities in Wikipedia policies, harassment among the editor community, significant gaps in historical records about women, and that articles written about women are more heavily scrutinized and more likely to be deleted.[2]

Wikimedia Foundation has been working to address editor diversity since 2011. Yet in 2019, still 64 percent of editors came from Europe and North America, and just 12 percent of editors were women—more than half of whom felt unsafe or uncomfortable on the platform.[3] With over 20 years of content developed, it will take a great and diligent effort to correct the impact of these systemic inequities and lack of diversity. This affects our collective history.

Our History of Oppression

> Within a few generations we had gone from being nearly one hundred percent of the population of this continent to less than one-half of one percent. We were all haunted.
>
> —JOY HARJO[4]

We have as a society done some very cruel things to each other historically, which can have a long-term effect lasting through generations into the present. When we learn more deeply about what our colleagues and neighbors might be going through and the barriers to opportunity that some people face, we can support each other to succeed in spite of those barriers. And we can help dismantle those barriers and work to heal from their impact.

Stolen Lands, Stolen Treaties, and Stolen Resources

In the 1400s, European people began to colonize lands and people at a global scale, in search for wealth and conquest. Colonialism told from the point of view of Indigenous people is a very different story than what I learned in our history books. From a Euro-centric perspective, Christopher

Columbus sailed the ocean blue to "discover" new lands, Diogo Cão "discovered" and explored the Congo, Vasco De Gama "opened" new trade routes to India, Hernán Cortés "conquered" the Aztecs, James Cook mapped lands from Hawaii to Australia and "claimed" them, and so the story goes. These men set out to explore and chart unknown territory, find gold and spices, and claim new lands for their kings, and later groups like the Pilgrims fled to freedom from persecution.

That's what my history books told me. Now I imagine my Indigenous and Black classmates reading these stories, and how they must have felt—*where were their ancestors in this history?*

What was left out of my history books was that Indigenous people lived here in North America for at least 15,000 years, developing rich, innovative cultures and traditions, and a deep relationship with the lands. Colonizers and conquistadores who arrived to "discover" this "new world" enslaved Indigenous people and claimed and exploited land that was not theirs to claim. In the Caribbean, the Taíno were the first Indigenous people colonized by Christopher Columbus. On the island now called Hispaniola (half of the island is now Haiti, the other half is the Dominican Republic), almost all Taíno people were killed by disease, war, and enslavement—the Taíno population went from 250,000 to 500 in less than 100 years.[5]

During the first 100 years of colonialism in the Americas, an estimated 56 million people died—more than 90 percent of Indigenous people in the Americas—due to disease, displacement, and war brought by colonizers and conquistadores. This was about 10 percent of the entire global population at the time.[6] My high school history textbooks definitely did not teach me about this genocide called "The Great Dying."

For those who survived, colonialism brought forced relocation and assimilation, which destroyed families, livelihoods, languages, and cultures. Colonizers made empty promises, most treaties were broken, and sacred Indigenous land to this day continues to be destroyed for resource extraction. It is a failure of how history is told that most Americans remember the names and stories of the few men who conquered the Americas, but not the names of whole cultures lost during this period of colonization.[7]

My home in San Francisco is on the traditional lands of the Ramaytush peoples in Yelamu. The Ramaytush Ohlone were colonized by the Spanish in 1769, forced to convert to Catholicism and live in overcrowded missions. By 1842, most Ramaytush Ohlone were killed, including all

Yelamu. From 15,000 people in 11 tribelets, just 15 people survived.[8] Only one Ramaytush family lineage continues today.

If you live on traditional lands of Indigenous people, please consider learning about them and acknowledging them in meetings, events, even websites. An acknowledgment can be as simple as: *I acknowledge we are on the traditional land of the Ramaytush Ohlone peoples in Yelamu. I honor and respect their Elders past, present, and emerging.* You can always go further toward a public commitment. Here is my own: *I recognize I benefit from living and working on their unceded ancestral homeland, and commit to working to redress the legacies of colonialism.*[9] Either way, don't stop at acknowledgment, support Indigenous people in working, speaking, and leading with you. We live on their traditional land, and Indigenous people deserve recognition, health, wealth, and power here.

Indigenous people continue to experience the effects of colonialism today. In the United States, home to 574 federally recognized Indian Nations, many people were forced onto reservations in geographically isolated areas far from their traditional lands, where the government built their homes (as part of the treaty agreements) with no running water or electricity, in areas where they cannot grow their own food, and where even now their land is still taken, burned, or mined. Unemployment rates on reservations are often very high, and access to healthcare and mental health services can be limited. And whether living on reservations, in suburbs, or in inner cities, one in three Indigenous people in the United States lives in poverty.

Deep institutional inequities exist in education, healthcare, and justice. Indigenous people in the United States are the most likely racial group to be killed by law enforcement, followed by Black people.[10] Indigenous youth are 30 percent more likely than White youth to be referred to juvenile court rather than charges being dropped.[11] Indigenous people are more likely to be stopped, searched, and arrested, and if convicted serve longer and more severe sentences.[12] Indigenous women are incarcerated at six times the rate of White women, Indigenous men at four times the rate of White men. Yet Indigenous people are twice as likely to be victims of violent crime, mostly committed by non-Indigenous perpetrators.[13]

Indigenous people experience similar patterns of historical oppression and systemic inequities globally. First Nations people in Canada experienced disease, war, relocation, Christianization, and forced assimilation. For over 100 years, children were forcibly taken from their homes and enrolled in boarding schools, often facing physical and sexual abuse, poor sanitation, disease, and lasting trauma. The last residential school closed in 1996. For 630 First Nations communities, many still don't have access to safe drinking water, experience significant health disparities and lower life expectancy, are more likely to be victims of crime, and make up over 30 percent of all people who are incarcerated (while they are only 5 percent of the total population). First Nations women in Canada are 42 percent of all incarcerated Canadian women.[14]

Throughout Latin America, home to 50 million Indigenous people from between 500 and 800 different cultures, Indigenous people faced similar oppression and today experience significant disparities in health, wealth, and opportunity, as well as land destruction and exploitation.

Aboriginal Australian and Torres Strait Islander peoples lived on their lands for at least 65,000 years before British James Cook landed in 1770, called it "New South Wales," and claimed it as property of King George III. An estimated 750,000 Indigenous people lived in the region, speaking over 250 languages.[15] Though many fought the colonizers, the Indigenous population declined to less than 74,000 by 1933. Similar to the United States and Canada, children from the Stolen Generations were taken from their homes and forced to assimilate.

In these few pages, there is no way to address 65,000 years of history, thousands of cultures, and millions of experiences of Indigenous people across many continents. Please continue your learning journey—there are many books and articles that can fill in the gaps in our knowledge about our history and the rich cultures of our neighbors, colleagues, and friends.

And then remember that awareness and acknowledgment are only the beginning: allies take action. Due to the results of colonization, there may not be many Indigenous people in your workplace, so your allyship for Indigenous people may start outside your workplace. There is a lot of room for allies to support Indigenous communities in their fight for rights, access, and opportunities—and repair hundreds of years of historical oppression across the globe.

[*How can you help Indigenous people gain equal access to wealth, health, and power?*]

FIGURE 3.1 **Photo of Cape Coast Castle's "Door of No Return" That People Passed Through Before They Were Put on Slave Ships[16]**

[Photo credit: user Sixthofdecember on Wikipedia]

Enslavement to Segregation to Redlining

> The slave went free; stood a brief moment in the sun; then moved back again toward slavery.
>
> —W. E. B. DU BOIS[17]

While people had lived in Africa for at least 250,000 years,[18] after a heightened period of invasion from the early 1880s to 1914, Europeans occupied and claimed almost 90 percent of the entire content.[19] Colonialism stripped African people from their Indigenous languages and ways of life, stole and enslaved people and took them to a new land, divided the continent, destroyed resources, and caused widespread deforestation and desertification.

Within Africa, millions of Indigenous African people were displaced to undesirable lands, forced into brutal labor and enslavement, imprisoned, and killed; many died of disease brought by colonizers. In the Congo alone, an estimated 10 million people (about 50 percent of the population) were killed during the occupation of Belgian's King Leopold II.[20]

Over 100 years, African people fought and regained their independence, starting with Egypt in 1922, until Zimbabwe in 1980 and Namibia in 1990. Yet colonialism had built artificial borders between people, destroyed economies and governing structures, and upended lives and cultures. After gaining independence, the effects of colonization lingered in the form of wars, authoritarian rule, and systematic segregation and discrimination like apartheid in South Africa, which lasted until 1994. African economies had become reliant upon export to Europe, resulting in cash crops, resource extraction, and environmental depletion.

> The iron entered into our souls.
> —CAESAR, a formerly enslaved man[21]

For more than 400 years, millions of African adults and children were taken from their homes by Europeans and forced into enslavement across North, South, and Central Americas; the Caribbean; Europe; and Asia. The first enslaved Africans sent to North America arrived in Hispaniola at the turn of the sixteenth century (the same island in the Caribbean where the Indigenous Taíno people had been colonized and enslaved, and faced genocide). Between 1501 and 1866, at least 12.5 million African people were forced into crowded ships and taken to the Americas. Nearly 2 million people died in captivity during the many months of forced overseas migration called the Middle Passage, where overheating, thirst, starvation, disease, violence, and suicide were common.[22] The absolute horror of being stripped of freedom, family, and home and shipped across the ocean in cruel bondage is suggested by the small sign displayed in Figure 3.1, which Africans passed through on their way to slave ships: "Door of No Return."

More than 472,000 African people were taken directly to North America, though hundreds of thousands of people were traded between North, Central, and South American and Caribbean colonies.[23] Through several generations, many millions of people were born and died enslaved by other people, experiencing severe cruelty on many levels.

From the time people were captured in Africa, Black people resisted, rose, and rebelled. Many people played key roles in the abolition of slavery in the United States, including Black writers like Ukawsaw Gronniosaw (aka James Albert), Phillis Wheatley, and Frederick Douglass; people who started rebellions like Nat Turner, Gabriel Prosser, and the captive Mende people on board the *Amistad*; people who fought in courts like Dred and Harriet Scott, Elizabeth Freeman (aka Mum Bett), Mary Ellen Pleasant, and Sojourner Truth; many along the Underground Railroad like Harriet Tubman and William Still; and the many people who fought in the Civil War.

Allies also played an important role: Quakers adopted the first anti-slavery resolution in 1688 forbidding members from owning slaves or taking part in the slave trade, and helped in the Underground Railroad. Indigenous Seminole communities in Florida, a diverse group of Indigenous people who were themselves refugees, offered a safe refuge for Black people who were free or escaped from enslavement. Several allies helped along the Underground Railroad like Laura Smith Haviland, Elizabeth Rous Comstock, and Levi and Catharine Coffin whose home was called "Grand Central Station." Writers and activists spoke out against slavery, like William Lloyd Garrison, Harriet Beecher Stowe, Matilda Joslyn Gage, Lucretia Mott, and Susan B. Anthony.

On June 19, 1865, in Galveston, Texas, the Union Army finally freed people enslaved across the United States—two and a half years after the Emancipation Proclamation was signed. This is the day we honor and celebrate as *Juneteenth*.[24] Yet life remained very difficult for freed Black people in the South who often worked as sharecroppers indebted to landlords, experiencing extreme poverty, severe racism, and black code laws that restricted their civil rights to compensation, voting, and owning property. Later Jim Crow laws legalized segregation across almost every area of society for almost 100 years: schools, transportation, restaurants, restrooms, public spaces, and other institutions were separate and unequal. Black people were systematically denied access to housing, healthcare, and insurance. Through a practice called "redlining," into the 1970s, governments and banks made mortgage decisions based on a person's address rather than qualifications and creditworthiness, a practice that continued with insurance, credit cards, and even the building and resourcing of hospitals, schools, lending institutions, and grocery stores.

Many decades since *Brown v. Board of Education* declared racial segregation in public schools unconstitutional, schools are highly segregated in the United States, where low-income Black and Latinx communities experience disparities in quality of curriculum and teachers, larger classroom sizes, and inadequate facilities and materials. Globally school segregation hurts us all, preventing opportunities to build understanding and empathy for each other, as well as forming barriers to learning, growth, wealth generation, and other opportunities.[25]

The Long Road to Women's Rights

> I raise up my voice—not so that I can shout, but so that those without a voice can be heard. Those who have fought for their rights: their right to live in peace, their right to be treated with dignity, their right to equality of opportunity, their right to be educated. . . . *We cannot all succeed when half of us are held back."*
>
> **—MALALA YOUSAFZAI[26]**

Women around the world have faced inequity and oppression throughout history and into the present day. Globally, women have fought and continue to fight for rights to own property, work and earn a living, divorce, get an education, and run for office, as well as for sexual and reproductive rights, freedom from violence and harassment, and more.

Women with intersectional identities often experience compounding barriers to opportunity. As an example: in the United States, while women earned voting rights in 1920, Asian American women weren't fully able to vote until 1952, and Indigenous women until 1962. Black women and Latinas—who were instrumental in the suffrage movement—couldn't fully vote until 1965 and 1975 respectively, decades after White women. One-third of people with disabilities still report difficulty voting, and voters in predominantly Black neighborhoods face continued disenfranchisement.[27] Around the world, women have slowly gained voting rights, though in some areas it can still be difficult or unsafe.

We still do not have a federal Equal Rights Amendment for women in the United States, after almost a century of activism since it was originally introduced. Over many years, states have been individually ratifying the amendment to their own state constitutions. And while the Equal Pay Act was passed in 1963, there is still significant pay disparity in many companies. Globally, women earn 31 percent less than men.[28] In the United States, women make 18 percent less than men, where Latinas, Indigenous, and Black women make significantly less.[29]

Gender equality is one of the United Nations Global Development Goals due to severe inequities: systemic discrimination, gender-based violence, sexual violence and harassment, intimate partner violence, lack of reproductive rights, forced marriage, kidnapping, trafficking, constraints on movement and travel, lack of financial freedom, disproportionate domestic work, and workplace inequities. Much has been written about gender inequality, I encourage you to learn more and become aware of the disparity women experience in your region and globally.

The LGBTQIA+ Fight to Live, Love, and Lead

> Each of us bears a responsibility to reject hate, whatever its form, whatever its justification.
>
> —GEORGE TAKEI[30]

The global LGBTQIA+ community is still fighting for basic rights to live, love, and lead—facing persecution, arrest, torture, domestic violence, hate crimes, medical abuse, bullying, harassment, unjust laws, cultural marginalization, and systemic inequities. In many countries, discrimination and persecution against LGBTQIA+ people are still legal.

In the United States until very recently people of the same gender were not able to marry, change their name, adopt children, own property together, or be out at work. More than one-third of the US LGBTQIA+ community experiences discrimination—a number considerably higher for people who are transgender (62 percent) and nonbinary (69 percent). This discrimination is experienced in public spaces, workplaces, schools, apartment communities, law enforcement, ability to rent or buy a home, travel, accessing and receiving medical care and other services, and more.[31] Transgender people are three times more likely to be unemployed, often don't have safe access to restrooms, experience anti-trans bias in health-care, are more likely to experience physical violence from law enforcement, and experience physical and mental health disparities.[32] Transgender and nonbinary people often cover their identity from family, friends, and coworkers—for fear of basic safety, discrimination, and microaggressions.

Awareness and public acceptance are beginning to change, with consistent activism, progress in legislation, and public figures coming out and speaking out—like Renée Richards, Harvey Milk, Ellen DeGeneres, George Takei, Laverne Cox, Janet Mock, Chaz Bono, Caitlyn Jenner, Pedro Zamora, Jason Collins, Elliot Page, Michelle Rodriguez, and Lana Wachowski. Allies have been cultivated in the LGBTQIA+ community for decades, with Jeanne Manford founding Parents, Families and Friends of Lesbians and Gays (PFLAG) in 1973. Allies like the nuns and doctors at St. Vincent's Medical Center worked as HIV/AIDS activists, researchers, and caregivers. Allies work together with the LGBTQIA+ community through public protest, raising funding and awareness, passing human rights legislation, fighting anti-LGBTQIA+ legislation, and winning key court battles.

Basic Disability Rights Are Still Unmet

> We have a moral duty to remove the barriers to participation, and to invest sufficient funding and expertise to unlock the vast potential of people with disabilities. Governments throughout the world can no longer overlook the hundreds of millions of people with disabilities who are denied access to health, rehabilitation, support, education and employment, and never get the chance to shine.
>
> **—STEPHEN HAWKING**[33]

People with disabilities—about 15 percent of the global population—have experienced laws legalizing lower wages, forced sterilization (up until very recently in many countries), lack of access to education, domestic abuse, physical and sexual violence, high rates of police violence (one-third to one-half of all people killed by law enforcement in the United States are disabled), forced detention, torture, bullying, harassment, abuse and experimentation in mental health facilities, denial of medical services, denial of the right to marry and have families, and denial of rights to housing and divorce. People with intersectional identities often face compounding barriers and discrimination, for example, women with disabilities are more likely to experience violence, abuse, and discrimination.

Workplace discrimination is one of the top human rights violations for people with disabilities, who experience major barriers in hiring. When landing work, people with disabilities are often offered positions below their level of expertise with inequitable compensation and benefits, and they are overworked and undervalued. These inequities contribute to a higher likelihood of poverty, affecting access to basics like medical care, as well as wellness, quality of life, and career opportunities.[34]

As we learned in "What Allyship Is and Why It Matters," people with disabilities earned basic rights in the United States through the Americans with Disabilities Act (ADA) just in 1990. Even those basic rights have not been given to people with disabilities in many countries—only 45 countries have antidiscrimination and other disability-specific laws.[35] In other words, discrimination is still legal. Marginalization and inequity for people with disabilities is common even with those laws in place, including mobility barriers for wheelchair, walker, and cane users in buildings and sidewalks; lack of accessibility in websites, apps, social media, images, videos, and other products for people who are Blind, Low Vision, Deaf, and/or Hard of Hearing; and lack of accommodation in education and workplaces for people with physical, mental, and intellectual disabilities.

When I started doing DEI activist work in 2014, people with disabilities were often left out of DEI conversations and solutions. Changing this has been incredibly important in my work, yet we still have a long road ahead. While the basic right to move and interact freely is slowly being met with accommodation laws, accessibility is still often an afterthought if a thought at all, and it is a long road yet to *inclusion* for people with disabilities.

There are many other communities around the world who have experienced historical oppression and systemic inequities.

[
Spend some time thinking about those communities:
Who are they? What can you learn from them?
How can you be a better ally to them?
]

Intergenerational Impact of Oppression and Systemic Inequity

> It struck me that perhaps the defining feature of being drafted into the black race was the inescapable robbery of time, because the moments we spent readying the mask, or readying ourselves to accept half as much, could not be recovered.
>
> —TA-NEHISI COATES[36]

Around the world, hatred and discrimination have taken the form of racism, sexism, ableism, nationalism, ethnocentrism, heterosexism, cisgenderism, classism, ageism, colorism, sizeism, religious discrimination (e.g., anti-Muslim discrimination, anti-Semitism), caste discrimination, bigotry, and more.[37] The generational ramifications can be severe.

Our history books and films often stop the story when people gain their independence, as if when colonialism or slavery ends, the oppression lifts. But systemic racism didn't end; Black and Indigenous people didn't suddenly have access to the equal housing, jobs, education, and wealth that were stolen from them for generations. People were still kept from these opportunities through Jim Crow laws, segregation, redlining, forced relocation and assimilation, lack of legal protection from discrimination, unfair and unjust law enforcement practices, and much more.

At the same time Black and Indigenous people didn't just heal from generations of extreme cruelty and enslavement and being stolen from their homeland. There is deep trauma in that, which does not just heal overnight; in fact, it can be passed on from generation to generation. And there is consequential impact from intergenerational positions of power—where decisions still have been and continue to be made without diverse people in the room, without taking into account diverse experiences and ideas.

When I was growing up, I saw what happened to Indigenous and Black people as history—it was a problem of my ancestors perhaps (though not really "my" ancestors, as mine came from the "north," I'd tell myself), but not my problem now. I did not recognize the repercussions of racism today, but racism is a present-day experience for many people. And it is a piece of all our experience, whether we are actively aware or not. My great grandfather was alive before slavery was abolished; my grandfather and father were alive during Jim Crow and redlining, and when Indigenous children were still being taken from their homes to be assimilated. During my lifetime, Black and Indigenous adults and children continue to be incarcerated at severely unequal rates, without equal access to education and high-paying jobs, disproportionately affected by COVID-19 and economic crises. We did not move from abolishment to equality in our four generations.

I am sure that some of the biases my grandparents and parents learned have seeped into how I think. And I am absolutely clear now that in four generations we did not fix all the inequities in our institutions. It takes both the will and the work to unlearn our biases and to undo discriminatory systems. The effects of what happened a few generations ago will continue to have an impact on all our lives—through our institutions, and through the way we treat one another—until we actively work to correct them.

There are two important interrelated effects of historical oppression: intergenerational wealth and health gaps.

Intergenerational Wealth Gap

Generations of Black and Indigenous people, women, and other marginalized people have been restricted from earning capital *by law*—reducing opportunities to earn wealth, and access quality education and housing. While those laws have changed in the last generation, the intergenerational impact has not been corrected. This inequity takes an exponential toll.

Due to years and years of disparity and discrimination, the net worth of White families in the United States is about 10 times that of Black families.[38] Indigenous wealth has not even been measured since 2000, when it was significantly lower than Black families. Women's net worth in the United States is just 32 percent of men's, and women also hold two-thirds of student loan debt. The wealth and poverty gaps are widening as well as for Black, Indigenous, and Latinx families—and especially for Black, Indigenous, and Latinx women.[39] While it improved in the 1980s and 2000s, this wealth gap is now as wide as it was in the 1960s.[40] The same gaps are also widening for people with disabilities, who face additional barriers to wealth generation—for example, 67 percent of Black people with disabilities are unbanked or underbanked, unable to build wealth or good credit.[41]

Globally, our wealth gap is widening for many people. This reduces upward wealth and health mobility through the schools we can attend—and as a result, job opportunities—as well as housing we can purchase and our access to healthy food, insurance, and healthcare.

Intergenerational Health Gap

There are significant health disparities in historically oppressed communities due to lack of health access, lower rates of insurance, biases in healthcare, diseases of poverty, and intergenerational trauma. Additionally, stress from the impact of discrimination and biases can affect long-term health and well-being.

Adults with disabilities are twice as likely as adults without disabilities to say their life has been harder because of discrimination; people who are LGBTQIA+ also report higher stress levels from discrimination.[42] By race and ethnicity, 40 percent Black, 36 percent Asian, 31 percent Indigenous, 27 percent Latinx, and 14 percent White Americans report discrimination as a major stress in their lives in the United States.[43]

Weathering is a term originated by Arline Geronimus to describe how continued discrimination can lead to premature aging and poor health outcomes.[44] People who experience discrimination are more likely to experience depression, anxiety, and psychiatric disorders, which can accumulate over time as someone continues to experience discrimination. Accumulated experiences of discrimination are also associated with physical health outcomes like cardiovascular disease, obesity, hypertension, inflammation, and other health indicators. These can reduce our overall quality of life as well as life expectancy.[45]

Discrimination can also affect self-esteem, life satisfaction, and feelings of control and well-being. As a result, there is also a link to engaging in higher-risk behaviors and coping behaviors like alcohol use and smoking, as well as participating in fewer health-promoting activities.[46]

Biases from medical professionals can lead to disparities in care as well, where research shows medical professionals can have less empathy when interacting with patients of another race.[47] As a result, Black and Latinx people have their pain needs met less frequently than White people, Black women are more likely than White women to receive a C-section, and Black and Indigenous women are significantly more likely to die from pregnancy-related issues.[48] One-third of transgender people report discrimination, abuse, harassment, or microaggressions in health-care settings.[49] People who experience regular discrimination are two to three times less likely to trust medical professionals, may delay seeking medical advice, and may be less likely to adhere to the advice.[50]

For these reasons and more, COVID-19 disproportionately affected people from historically oppressed communities around the world. Navajo Nation was one of the areas hit hardest by COVID-19 in North America. Many Diné people in Navajo Nation live in poverty, where nearly one-third of homes are without electricity or running water (despite treaties that promised this infrastructure when Diné people were forcefully displaced), and people often have to travel for hundreds of miles to access a grocery store or hospital.[51] Food deserts and lack of health services are a reality across reservations and in inner-city Black, Indigenous, and Latinx communities. On top of that, one in five Indigenous women, one in six Latinas, and one in ten Black women in the United States don't have health insurance, making it more difficult to obtain and pay for needed care.[52]

The health and wealth gap widened during the COVID-19 pandemic, with potentially devastating long-term effects. Black- and Latinx-owned businesses were hit harder, and women, Black, and Latinx workers were furloughed and laid off at disproportionate rates. This is not a trend in the United States alone; throughout the world COVID-19 exacerbated—and was exacerbated by—systemic inequities.

Intergenerational Trauma

The first time I heard the term *intergenerational trauma* was from a friend and DEI attorney, Michael Thomas. My company Change Catalyst co-developed an event called Inclusion 2.0 in 2016, about the intersection between wisdom, inclusion, and mindfulness. At that event, Michael spoke about "Intergenerational Trauma, Meditation and Inclusion." In just 10 minutes he captivated us all, and I never saw my work the same again.

Trauma creates physiological changes in your brain and your body's stress response, it can leave you emotionally distant from people you love, and it can reorganize your perceptions and imagination. "It changes not only how we think and what we think about, but also our very capacity to think," according to Bessel van der Kolk, who studies trauma.[53]

Groups of people can experience collective trauma when they are enslaved, colonized, forced to assimilate, interned, abused, bullied, systemically marginalized, and facing genocide. Groups can even experience a series of collective traumatic experiences over time. Eduardo Duran, who works with Indigenous cultures and the healing of trauma, describes the "soul wound" of trauma shared by a group of people as "historical trauma."[54] Joy DeGruy describes the residual impacts of generations of slavery as "post traumatic slave syndrome."[55] In her work in the 1980s and 1990s, Maria Yellow Horse Brave Heart showed that collective historical trauma can be accompanied by individual historical unresolved grief.[56]

If our ancestors personally or collectively experienced significant physical and emotional trauma, that trauma can be passed from generation to generation physically through fetal cells, as well as emotionally and culturally through family and community. Research on historical trauma and intergenerational trauma (aka transgenerational trauma) in Jewish, Black, Japanese American, and Indigenous communities has shown that we can pass down a lower sense of self-worth, dissociation, numbing and emotional detachment, survivor guilt and internalization of ancestral suffering, anger, depression, anxiety, hypervigilance, fear, and distrust, as well as physical health outcomes.[57] These can be exacerbated by regular experiences of discrimination and microaggressions.

This impacts our lives in many ways. When you see people who look like you being shot and killed by police officers regularly, it can be traumatic. When stopped by police, which is more likely to happen to Black, Indigenous, and Latinx people in the United States, the trauma is experienced again. Many people live through a physically and emotionally traumatic experience, even without complications in the moment.

When you experience daily harassment, bullying, or a world that is hostile to your identity, it takes its toll. When you have to apply to three times more jobs because you're more likely to be told "no" based on your identity, it takes its toll. When you're unable to obtain an apartment, mortgage, insurance, or bank account because of your identity, it takes its toll. When you have to worry about your safety regularly when in public spaces, it takes its toll. All of these can retrigger trauma.[58]

> Today, when I go somewhere, I'm afraid, and it's a fear that we all carry every day and you get so used to it that it's like it's part of you.
> —DANIELLE EWENIN, of the Kawacatoose First Nation in Canada[59]

If we don't work to heal this intergenerational trauma, we can continue to pass it on to the next generation and potentially cause harm to ourselves and each other. Some people navigate trauma through numbing—with alcohol, drugs, food, binge-watching, social media, and video games, for example. Other people navigate through masking: going through life wearing a mask that covers our true selves and experiences, or armor that protects us from further trauma. We can also internalize racism, sexism, and discrimination—believing the negative stereotypes, adapting our identity to fit the dominant culture, and marginalizing other people with underrepresented identities.

[*So how do we heal, and help each other heal?*]

Our Work to Collectively Heal

> What if we rushed towards our own accountability and understood it as a gift we can give to ourselves and those hurting from our harm? What if we understood our accountability, not as some small insignificant act, but as an intentional drop in an ever-growing river of healing, care and repair that had the potential to nourish, comfort and build back trust on a large scale, carving new paths of hope and faith through mountains of fear and unacknowledged pain for generations?
> —MIA MINGUS[60]

We are still unraveling the cultural, political, and economic systems that once colonized and enslaved people and continue to create inequity and exclusion. The correction is ongoing and hard fought, and allies have a big role in this correction. There are many ways we can build resilience and healing, including:

Pass legislation. Support and press for basic human rights, land rights and protection, Indigenous self-governance, environmental equity and climate justice (environmental destruction and climate change are often most harmful to historically oppressed people), affordable healthcare, and services that reduce barriers to upward mobility. Also encourage and support funding for correcting institutional inequities, recommitting to failed treaties, and improving public health and community healing. Many have called for reparations for colonization and enslavement too.

Share your learning and growth with your community. Be public about your values around correcting systemic inequities and improving social justice. Acknowledge historical harm, and commit to correct it. Share with friends, family, and community that you are working to create change. Individuals, governments, corporations, and brands can make supportive public commitments and correct systems and messaging that cause harm. This can be very powerful.

Correct systemic inequities. We still have severe inequities across education, housing, banking, policing and incarceration, workplaces, and industries. Listen to what people need to heal and correct inequity, and take action with them. There are many opportunities to make a difference, like protesting, petitioning, policymaking, writing legislators, generating awareness, using your connections, and voting with your dollars. (If you protest as an ally, listen to the organizers and follow their lead. If you're from a majority group, don't instigate violence, and work to keep protestors with underrepresented identities safe—many allies put their bodies between protestors and police to keep protestors safe.) We'll address workplace inequities throughout the remaining chapters.

Use your power as a consumer. Brands listen to consumers, so use this power to advocate for your values around inclusion. If a brand is not representing diverse people or messages in their ads, if they're perpetuating biases and stereotypes, if they are exploiting people or the environment along their supply chain—let them know you expect better. Also support businesses owned by people with underrepresented identities.

Activate intergenerational allyship, advocacy, and activism. Raise children and grandchildren who actively work against inequity and for justice, diversity, inclusion, and equity. Talk with them about our history and current injustice, share your own exploration and learning as an ally, enroll them in working with you to create change. Buy books and toys that represent diverse experiences and cultures. Advocate for more inclusive learning (better history books!) in their schools. Travel so that children experience diverse cultures and perspectives. Provide opportunities to build interracial friendships at a young age—through schools, playgrounds, and programs with diverse children. These relationships have been shown to reduce prejudice in children.[61]

Build intergenerational resilience and healing. While oppression may shape our opportunities in life, it does not define us. If you have experienced trauma, know that you have the power to heal from within, and to break the intergenerational cycle of trauma with *intergenerational healing*.[62] A growing body of research shows effective methods for healing individually and across communities. These include mindfulness; psychotherapy; connecting with community and cultural traditions; emotional support from family, friends, and colleagues; and reclaiming the body through yoga, Tai Chi, Quigong, massage, or other embodied practices.[63]

There are many more ways to create change, including supporting and voting for diverse public officials, donating to and volunteering for organizations fighting voter suppression and other inequities, doing your jury duty (Black and Indigenous people need allies in the courtroom, as they are disproportionately incarcerated), and listening to and supporting initiatives generated from the community.

Collectively, we can work to heal and repair our global society so that it is fair and just for everyone, breaking the cycle of discrimination and intergenerational trauma. While inequities continue to permeate our institutions and our culture, we have the power to change them.

Cultural Marginalization

> It's important for not just me but women of color, trans women, and people who are marginalized to be telling stories of themselves. It's important for us to be behind the lens.
>
> **—PETRA COLLINS**[64]

People are marginalized in many ways by society, including at the cultural level, where our collective storytelling can either reinforce stereotypes or break them, and can actively include diverse voices and perspectives or continue to perpetuate one type of voice. We all have the power to reduce cultural marginalization.

Cultural marginalization can begin at birth, where we assign our babies a sex and gender, and give them toys, books, and experiences that help frame how they see the world and themselves. In the same way our history has a point of view—and can shape our worldview—so do journalism, education, entertainment, video games, television, films, novels, toys, magazines, fashion, and advertising. Each of these industries has a lack of diversity in their creators and in their stories.

My career began in the film and television industry, which is now starting to come to terms with its lack of diversity and a sexualized environment where harassment and abuse have been prevalent. From 2007 to 2019, just 5 percent of film directors were women, 13 percent were people of color, and less than 1 percent were women of color.[65] Large studios have very few women and people of color at decision-making levels like producers and executives, film critics are mostly White men, and many people have called attention to the significant lack of diversity in the Academy of Motion Picture Arts and Sciences. This translates into who tells our stories, what stories are told, and which stories are recognized and amplified.

Overall cast diversity is better, but still has room for significant improvement: 34 percent women, 34 percent people of color, 2 percent disabled people, and 1 percent LGBTQIA+.[66] Representation is only a portion of inclusion, however—people with underrepresented identities often have fewer lines, are portrayed as stereotypes, and/or are one-dimensional characters lacking depth. This problem was so prevalent, the cartoonist Alison Bechdel wrote a comic strip about it in the 1980s, which has since turned into the "Bechdel test": to pass the test, a film must feature at least two women, who talk to each other about something besides a man. It seems simple, yet only 58 percent of films have passed the test out of more than 8,000 films.[67] Other versions have been proposed, like the "Ava DuVernay test," where "African-Americans and other minorities have fully realized lives rather than scenery in White stories."[68] On top of the lack of opportunities for actors who are trans and disabled: characters who are disabled and trans are often portrayed by actors who are not disabled or trans.

The video game industry has similar issues, where women characters are fewer and often sexualized. When women characters or avatars are available in games, they are often "premium" characters and more expensive to purchase. There is low diversity among creators (81 percent White, 71 percent men), and the gamer community in general can be an unsafe environment for women. In 2014, #Gamergate called attention to the industry's culture of harassment and general mistreatment of women, yet it has been slow to change. At the same time 61 percent of gamers believe more diversity in game content is important for the future of gaming.[69]

The publishing industry is very slowly coming to terms with its lack of diversity. In 2015, Corinne Duyvis started the hashtag #ownvoices to highlight the importance of books written by a person from a marginalized or underrepresented identity, about a protagonist with the same identity.[70] Between 2015 and 2019, race and ethnic diversity in the publishing industry did not markedly change, with 76 percent of people identifying as White—even higher in editorial staff (85 percent). The industry is predominantly women (about 75 percent), yet the number of women decreases in executive roles (about 60 percent), showing that even in an industry dominated by women, men rise to positions of power at higher rates.[71]

In 2019, just 13 percent of books released in the United States were written by Black, Latinx, and Indigenous authors combined, despite being 32 percent of the population. Black, Latinx, and Indigenous character portrayal was higher at 18 percent. Just 3 percent of characters were LGBTQIA+ and 3 percent disabled. For contrast, significantly more characters (29 percent) were animals or other characters like trucks, monsters, etc.[72] Children's books can also perpetuate stereotypes of many types, from girls being princesses, to boys hiding emotions, and Black and Latinx kids living in poverty. One study of Australian, Singaporean, and Turkish math textbooks found just 9 percent of textbooks did *not* include gender bias.[73] Children's toys and the toy industry have similar issues.

Journalism has been notorious for severely overrepresenting Black people as violent and criminal, and White people as victims. Black people are disproportionately portrayed as living in poverty and reliant on government programs, with Black men as absent fathers.[74] White police officers are overrepresented, Latinx people are overrepresented in pieces addressing immigration and social problems, Muslims overrepresented when reporting on terrorism, where Asians are often portrayed as the model minority.[75] Historically, Asians have been positioned as model minorities in the West, creating a hierarchy and subsequent division among groups with underrepresented identities, while simultaneously erasing the diversity of Asian identities and experiences.

> I love watching "Hidden Figures" with my daughter. And not just for being able to see what it is like in this particular movie, with Black women who are navigating racism, finding paths forward, and excelling in their field. And not just for my daughter, but also for my son to see what excellence looks like. . . . Exposing them to all sorts of stories, whether it is Black women excelling or Muslim women excelling: what does success look like and how do we achieve that together?
>
> **—MUNA HUSSAINI**[76]

The stories we consume shape how we see each other and ourselves. And when they erase some people's stories entirely, and perpetuate stereotypes and other biases, they can shape our own biases and worldview. For marginalized people, these stories can deepen feelings of being on the margins of society, excluded, and isolated. When we don't see role models who look like us, this can affect decisions in our careers, how we show or cover our identities, as well as our confidence and self-esteem. Each of us takes these biases with us into our homes, neighborhoods, and work-places—shaping how we interact with one another.

Take a critical look at the films, television, games, magazines, and books you come across over the next few weeks—ask yourself if they are lacking diverse voices and storytellers, perpetuating stereotypes, and/or leaving out perspectives.

[
*Who are the makers of the stories you
and your family are consuming?*
]

Actions You Can Take to Learn, Unlearn, and Relearn

In addition to the ways we can all contribute to intergenerational healing discussed earlier, here are a few ways that you can be a better ally by continuing to learn, unlearn, and relearn:

Read a book that gives you a new perspective of history from a different point of view. Wherever you grew up, chances are good that your history books left out a piece of your local and global history. *What's missing?*

Become more aware of who is creating your entertainment and how people are portrayed. Pay attention to who is authoring the articles you're reading, directing that film or TV show you're watching, creating the video game you're playing. Perhaps try something new, a story told from someone with an identity that is different from your own. Recognize when systemic inequities, cultural marginalization, and personal biases appear in stories. And if you notice that stories are perpetuating stereotypes or lacking diversity in general, consider advocating for more diverse voices by sending a letter to the editor, studio, or publisher. It can make a difference if we all do this.

Go outside your comfort zone and network to learn more. New learning can be uncomfortable, especially if you were socialized to not talk about race or other identities. We have to unlearn that. It's time to talk about race, ethnicity, gender, disability, age, religion, sexual orientation, and other aspects of identity. We become more comfortable by getting to know people who are different from us. Three-quarters of White people in the United States don't have friends who are not White.[77] If this is you, you're not alone, but it's time to change that—attend events created for diverse people, follow new people on social media (this has helped me a great deal), listen to new podcasts, talk to people at events who you might not normally talk to (not about their identity, about their work or life), get to know your colleagues.

Consider how you can help colleagues, friends, neighbors, children, or grandchildren to learn, unlearn, and relearn. Share what you're learning and your path of allyship, share this book and other resources you find. Have conversations about inequity and inclusion, about race, ethnicity, gender, disability, age, religion, sexual orientation. These are often stigmatized conversations, but the more we discuss them, the more we can shed light on the issues and focus on solutions together.

Don't expect people with underrepresented identities to educate you about them—be mindful that while it's your job to learn, it's not their job to teach. Generally, people with underrepresented identities are already facing extra burdens of microaggressions and inequities, and have to work harder to succeed. My big rule of thumb is that if you can learn it on the internet or in a book, don't ask someone to explain it to you—it's an unfair and unnecessary burden. Always ask someone if it's OK to inquire about their identity—some people are very happy to share, where other people may decline.

Remember that many people want to be asked about and respected for their skills and expertise, rather than their identity alone. There are tons of books, websites, magazines, documentaries, and articles. Go to a good website and find a list of great books written by Black, Indigenous, Latinx, disabled, or LGBTQIA+ authors and start reading.

Keep Moving Forward

These may be difficult pages to read through. I admit they were also difficult to research and write. I encourage you to take a moment here to reflect on what you've learned, how it makes you feel, what comes up for you.

But then please don't get stuck here in this awareness—awareness is only the beginning of allyship. Take time if you need to, to breathe a deep breath, go for a walk, meditate, exercise. And then come back, and let's get to work. We each have the power to create change. That's what this book is about.

For all of the reasons in this chapter and more: where talent is universal, opportunity is not. Not yet. It's our job as allies to learn, unlearn, relearn our collective history and its effects, ensure we are not perpetuating harm ourselves, advocate and work to repair and correct inequitable systems, and lead the change to a better future for everyone. Small steps are fine to begin. The world changes when you and I take one step at a time to make our communities and workplaces better for us all.

EXERCISE

In this section we explored the importance of learning, unlearning, and relearning—specifically focusing on the history of oppression, and the resulting systemic inequities and cultural marginalization. What new commitment will you make, based on what you've learned in this section?

I commit to: _____

_____

_____

_____

_____

_____

_____

_____

STEP 2: DO NO HARM— UNDERSTAND AND CORRECT OUR BIASES

4

> I've learned that people will forget what you said, people will forget what you did, but people will never forget how you made them feel.
>
> **—MAYA ANGELOU[1]**

We all harm people without intending to. People have been harmed throughout history due to historical oppression, systemic inequities, and cultural marginalization. Much of this harm continues today, and can surface through our individual words and actions—and our *non*-actions. As allies, we must learn the ways we might be harming people without realizing it, acknowledge the impact of this harm, and correct our actions.

Correcting Our Biases

Biases are mental patterns or shortcuts that influence our perception about something, someone, or a situation. We learn them from our families, friends, teachers, media, and throughout our culture. While we might not be aware of our biases, they can perpetuate oppression, inequity, and marginalization.

Because they are learned responses, biases can be unlearned. As allies, we must learn to interrupt our *unconscious* biases by making them visible and becoming deeply *conscious* of what we say and do. This requires some effort and time to unlearn and unravel what has been ingrained in our consciousness over our lifetimes, but it gets easier over time.

Our biases appear in many ways, from the small nonverbal cues we give through facial expressions and body language, to assumptions we make about people we are hiring or promoting, to the way we design events, physical spaces, reviews, benefits, programs, products, or services. All of these can have real consequences on whether or not someone is hired, promoted, or able to access other opportunities; or whether they feel safe and like they belong in their workplace and in the world.

Due to biases, investors are more likely to invest in attractive men, attractive people are more likely to be employed and earn more, résumés with African American sounding names receive fewer callbacks, people with disabilities are seen as unhirable, a motherhood penalty and fatherhood boost results in compensation disparities, Black women are often "invisible" where their presence and statements are less likely to be remembered than their White peers, leadership roles are seen as masculine, and applicants with women-sounding names are rated lower for competence, hirablity, and mentoring potential.[2]

Biases can influence how we see and interact with each other in the office and outside the office. Walking into stores and restaurants with my husband who is Black, I see White women holding their purses tighter, security guards following him through the store, cashiers looking harder to be sure he hasn't stuck anything in his pockets. He's a successful entrepreneur and leader in his field—though *no one* should be treated as a criminal because of the color of their skin. He doesn't get to just walk into a room, he walks into a room and has to take into account how his skin color affects people.

My husband is also my cofounder, and when we're in important partnership meetings, often people assume he is the CEO because he's a man, or the inverse: they won't even talk with him because they see him as my assistant. Our biases can be so quick, and yet they can harm someone's sense of worth, safety, respect, and belonging.

Table 4.1 provides some examples of biases that show up in the workplace.

TABLE 4.1 **Examples of Workplace Biases**

Bias	Definition	Example
Identity bias	Bias against or for someone's gender, race, ethnicity, disability, religion, age, class, caste, political views, geographic origin, body size, or thinking style; or parents, immigrants, LGBTQIA+, veterans, people who have been incarcerated, etc.	• Assigning admin tasks to women. • Not interviewing someone with a disability because you don't think they will perform well. • Believing people with a particular gender, race, or thinking style are better leaders. • When hands are raised at an event or in a meeting, you call on men first. • Passing over someone for promotion who is transgender or nonbinary, perhaps you don't believe they would excel in customer-facing or management roles.
Stereotyping	Also called perception bias, this is a type of identity bias: an assumption and often derogatory belief about a particular group of people.	• Assuming someone who is Asian, Latinx, or Indigenous can't speak English well. • Assuming Asian people are good at math or engineering, while women who are not Asian are bad at them. • In job performance reviews, describing an assertive woman as "aggressive" and an assertive man as "confident." • Believing a Black person is not a good fit for leadership because they are "angry" or "overly direct."

(continued)

TABLE 4.1   **Examples of Workplace Biases** *(continued)*

Common Biases in the Workplace

Bias	Definition	Example
In-group/ out-group bias	Also called affinity bias, the tendency to warm up to people like you. This often leads to in-group favoritism and out-group discrimination. An in-group could be an identity, school, neighborhood, hometown, sports team or type of sport, fraternity or sorority, or other affiliation.	• Taking a chance on someone from your in-group, while requiring someone from your out-group to pass tests to prove their skills. • Looking for talent in your own networks, from schools and communities that you identify with. • When hiring, evaluating for "culture fit" or pattern matching to your current team: looking for similar patterns in education, personality, and other attributes.
Halo effect	The tendency to think everything about a person is good because you like them. This often combines with affinity bias: being more likely to warm up to someone like you, and thinking everything about them is good. The opposite is the "horns effect," where someone makes a mistake in the past, and you believe they are incapable of succeeding in the future.	• Enjoying a colleague's company outside of work, and choosing them for a promotion because you have a special connection with them and your instinct says they'll succeed. • Someone you like makes a mistake and you brush it off as circumstance, where someone you don't know well makes a mistake and you hold them accountable. • A brand creates a product you really like, and you expect all of their products to be good products. • Someone who is attractive is often perceived as more intelligent, trustworthy, successful, healthy, and competent than others.
Confirmation bias	The tendency to seek information that confirms preexisting beliefs or assumptions.	• Social media algorithms are designed to show us information the platform believes we will like, usually confirming our beliefs and attitudes. This can make us believe most people have the same beliefs as our own, and make it challenging to have constructive conversations about opposing beliefs. • Asking one-sided questions to get answers confirming what we want to hear—this can play a role in reference checks, conducting investigations, quality control processes, interviews, or when seeking feedback.

(continued)

TABLE 4.1   **Examples of Workplace Biases** *(continued)*

Common Biases in the Workplace

Bias	Definition	Example
Groupthink	Also called conformity bias, consensus bias, or bandwagon effect,[3] the tendency for people in a group to desire harmony within the group and therefore find a decision that minimizes conflict, rather than a decision that achieves the ideal outcome.	• In a workplace culture that is not psychologically safe, members of the group may not feel safe to contradict ideas or offer alternatives. • This can happen when a team is rushed. In 1986, the NASA team was working so hard together to meet the launch deadline for the space shuttle *Challenger*, they didn't listen to engineers warning there could be a problem based on the outside temperature. Tragically, the consequence was that the shuttle disintegrated just after flight.[4]
Attribution bias	The tendency to attribute behaviors to personality traits or identity rather than circumstance.	• When someone is having a bad day and is unpleasant, assuming they have bad character. • If a person has a large body size, assuming they have a problem with overeating or laziness rather than, for instance, a medical condition.
Negativity bias	The tendency to recall negative or unpleasant memories more readily than positive ones.	• Receiving a mostly good performance review, but lingering on one or two pieces of negative feedback. This can exacerbate feelings of impostor syndrome. (More about impostor syndrome in "Step 4: Advocate for People.") • Having a great day collaborating with colleagues, and then experiencing a microaggression that significantly affects the rest of our day. • If someone gives a bad first impression, we may continuously recall that impression despite many positive interactions since then.

(continued)

TABLE 4.1 **Examples of Workplace Biases** *(continued)*

Common Biases in the Workplace

Bias	Definition	Example
Self-licensing	Also called self-bargaining, the tendency to do one "good" thing and feel you are off the hook for doing more good things, and/or that you have license to do something less good.	• A company puts out a social justice statement in support of a group and donates money to a nonprofit, but doesn't change their habits that are harmful to the same group (e.g., inequitable hiring or products that perpetuate stereotypes). • Having one Black friend and still making racist comments, or mentoring one woman while harassing or bullying other women. • Performative allyship can be a result of self-licensing. (More about performative allyship in "Allyship Is a Journey.")
Anchoring bias	When your perception relies heavily on the first piece of information you learned about a person.	• In salary negotiations, you might anchor to someone's previous salary and value them with this number in mind. Often people with underrepresented identities are underpaid, so this bias can perpetuate inequity. • You perceive someone by how they are introduced—if they are introduced in a biased way, you can take on that bias about them.
Status quo bias	Also called loss aversion bias, a preference for things staying the same. Change is weighed against the perceived loss of giving up the status quo. System justification bias goes further: defending the systemic or cultural status quo even when it's unfair or unjust.	• Having good camaraderie on the team, and weighing a new hire against whether they'd play well with the team. • Being comfortable with your own leadership style, and being reluctant to mind your microaggressions because it would change how you lead. • Believing a business is doing well, and that changing how you do things—e.g., increasing diversity—is an unwanted risk.
Just-world bias	The tendency to believe that the world is inherently just and actions have predictable, appropriate consequences.	• A belief in meritocracy: that people achieve success based on effort, talent, and ability alone. • It may take someone with just-world bias longer to come to terms with unfairness, injustice, and inequity. As a result, someone might blame a victim of injustice, deny the need for or validity of DEI work, or even deny major historical injustices.

(continued)

TABLE 4.1   Examples of Workplace Biases *(continued)*

Common Biases in the Workplace

Bias	Definition	Example
Experienced regret	Also called choice switching: when a good decision leads to a bad outcome, it can lead you to decide against the good decision next time ("once bitten, twice shy").	• I've seen this play out in several workplaces where one "diversity hire" doesn't work out, and the recruiter, team, or company is afraid to hire more people with underrepresented identities. • You promote one woman to a leadership role who doesn't succeed in that role, and you come to the conclusion that women just weren't meant for the role.

Several other biases can show up and influence DEI in the workplace, including: selection bias (being more aware of something when our attention is called to it), empathy gap (underestimating the influence or strength of your own or someone else's emotions), time-saving bias (underestimating time that could be saved or lost by doing or not doing something), bias oversight (believing other people are more biased than you), authority bias (attributing greater intelligence or accuracy to an authority figure), social comparison bias (favoring people who don't compete with your strengths), ambiguity effect (avoiding options where an outcome is unknown), self-serving bias (attributing your successes to internal factors, while attributing failures to external factors like your team or an individual), and automation bias (a bias toward technology and the automation of systems).

[*Do some of these biases sound familiar to you? Which ones stand out for you?*]

Actions You Can Take to Interrupt Your Biases

> Rather than being defensive, allies actively seek out critique, not only to be effective allies, but also as a means to realizing their own full humanity.
>
> **—KEITH E. EDWARDS**[5]

It takes 0.1 second to make a first impression.[6] While this rapid judgment was essential when we were relying on those instincts for survival thousands of years ago, it's less helpful to us now when often based on incorrect assumptions and biases. The speed is so rapid, we can't stop them in the moment. But we can do a few things to interrupt our biases:

Pause, humanize, and empathize. Before saying or doing anything, give yourself time to disrupt your response. Then work to humanize and empathize, being fully present with the human in front of you. Be curious about them, and allow your impression of them to unfold as you learn more about them. The more time and real information you have to establish an impression, the more accurate it will become.

Practice this over time, and teach yourself to stop listening to first impressions, stop letting them guide you, stop allowing yourself to judge people. Replace judgment with curiosity.

Prime yourself and your team to be aware of biases before going into a meeting or embarking on a project. For example, if you're about to interview a candidate, remind everyone beforehand that you value diversity of experience and to be cognizant of your biases. If you're working on a project together, remind everyone up front that you want to build a truly inclusive and equitable solution and ask everyone to keep this in mind.

Create a culture that values DEI growth, where it's normal to acknowledge and counter biases. When you catch yourself making a biased statement or decision, talk openly about it, and share how you'll counter the bias. Develop team or company norms where you and your colleagues hold each other accountable for checking biases, welcome feedback, regularly question how biases are showing up in your projects, and support each other in your growth.

You can also create processes and systems to counter biases and hold yourselves accountable. "Step 4: Advocate for People," includes systemic interventions you can put into place to interrupt both biases and microaggressions.

Using Self-Regulation

In decision-making, we often rely on our intuition, especially in a time crunch. But as we know, our intuition is built by norms, stereotypes, and heuristics (rules of thumb) that can be inherently biased. To make less biased and more inclusive decisions, we have to go beyond our intuition. Following these steps can help:

1. Pause. Take a breath and a step back. *What have I learned about biases that I can apply to this situation?*
2. Become aware of your intuition. *How am I showing up in this moment? What is my intuition telling me right now about how to approach this situation?*
3. Ask yourself why. *Why am I thinking about approaching this situation in this way? What assumptions am I making?*
4. Acknowledge any implicit biases and interrupt them. *How might biases be influencing my approach to this?* If you can, put a name to any biases that are showing up.
5. Reframe your response in a less biased way. *What else do I need to do or learn, so I can develop a less-biased approach? How can data help me make a more informed choice? Can I put together a diverse team to create a more inclusive solution? And once I have what I think is a less-biased solution, how can I test the solution with diverse people?*
6. Then respond in an inclusive way. *Am I using inclusive verbal language as well as body language? Am I approaching people and situations with empathy? Am I modeling a growth mindset* (we'll discuss this in "Step 6: Lead the Change")?
7. Reflect, forgive, and improve. Embrace any discomfort, forgive yourself for the biases you had, and work to improve. *Did the outcome feel more inclusive? Are there ways I can make future decisions like this less biased by improving systems and processes?*

Reducing biases in decision-making takes a little time and effort, but it can lead to a powerful result. If you keep practicing this, it can become second nature. Make sure to use this framework for decisions made with or about people with *overrepresented* identities as well as people with *underrepresented* identities—our goal is to correct biases so we are not privileging some people while marginalizing others. We'll discuss how to work with teams to improve decision-making processes in "Step 6: Lead the Change."

Make sure you also understand and reverse your biases toward yourself. We acquire biases toward ourselves from what people say about us and our own stereotypes of who we are. This can get in the way of our own successes and reduce our ability to show up for other people as allies. Spend some quality time thinking about what biases you hold against yourself. These could be stereotypes you still hold on to, hurtful feedback that doesn't serve you, a limiting belief or something you tell yourself every day because you always have. Let go of those biases and allow yourself to be your own unique self, ready to surprise you and the people around you.

My Own Struggle to Correct My Biases

Like many people, I grew up learning that gender is "boy or girl," "man or woman." But what I learned isn't reality, it is an artificial gender binary system. In reality, people identify along a gender continuum where some people are nonbinary and/or gender nonconforming.

It can take time and effort for new learning to become instinct. I have friends and colleagues who are nonbinary and use *they/them* pronouns. Early on, I felt a bit confronted by it because I didn't fully understand it. So I worked to better understand. I was fortunate to take some incredible gender studies courses in college that opened my mind to the intellectual understanding, and then I gained a deeper understanding from people's lived experiences in books, articles, lectures, and friendships. I also follow nonbinary people on social media to listen to their perspectives.

I can never truly know someone's unique experiences and my learning isn't complete, but I have worked hard to develop a deep understanding of what gender nonbinary people with different intersectional identities might experience. Yet even with that empathy and understanding, my brain still wants to categorize my nonbinary friends in a binary system (i.e., *he* or *she*). First-impression biases can be deeply ingrained. I am a work in progress as I change how my brain recognizes gender so that *they/them* roll off my tongue. My team corrects each other, and we hold each other accountable for using a person's correct pronouns. I also practice using nonbinary people as examples in presentations and stories, pay attention to pronouns people use to describe themselves, and research people's pronouns (on social media, for example) to ensure I get them right.

Disrupting this bias and reprogramming my brain is not easy, but it's important. I'll get there, one self-correction and apology at a time.

We all have biases, it's what we do about them that sets us apart. Biases are more likely to occur when facing time pressure, fatigue, nervousness, discomfort, and other stressors, so ensure you are using interventions especially during these times.[7]

What About Unconscious Bias Training?

Unconscious or implicit bias training (UBT) can help you learn your individual biases, but it won't change DEI across your workplace much, if at all. It's a bit like if I stopped writing the rest of this book. It will help you be a bit of a better human to know about your biases, but to really create the change we all need, we need you to be an advocate and to lead much-needed change too. We have to go beyond learning to action, and UBT doesn't take us there alone.

About 50 percent of our inbound client inquiries at Change Catalyst are from companies who did UBT and it didn't create the change they wanted. They've usually spent their budget on rolling out UBT across their organization, and now their employees are either angry nothing is changing, or fatigued and ready to move on from DEI because it's been a lot of work and budget for little gain. Training needs to go further and deeper.

A 2019 meta-analysis study analyzing evidence from 492 studies on UBT interventions, found "little evidence showing that change in implicit measures will result in changes for explicit measures or behavior."[8] Our work and the work of many of my colleagues have confirmed this: while UBT can help people learn, it does not consistently change behavior.

People need the tools to know how to take action once they've learned about biases. UBT can be powerful at the right time, with the right trainer—*if* it is not a "check the box" training but a program that includes UBT, allyship, and specific departmental training. And it must be rolled out in tandem with systemic change.

Additionally, people taking the training have to truly want to learn (they have moved beyond initial awareness and are ready to take action). A very public instance of how UBT can go wrong: in 2017, James Damore attended UBT at Google, and was so turned off by it that he wrote a 10-page manifesto professing UBT and DEI are discriminatory and "compassion for the weak." He said we should have "respect for the strong" and not "lower the bar," because women are inherently and biologically inferior to men when it comes to engineering roles. It was circulated throughout the company, causing significant division and trauma. Google fired Damore for advancing harmful stereotypes, and he went on to be a public figure speaking out against DEI on conservative talk shows.

If you do conduct UBT, don't make it mandatory, accompany it with training that teaches people how to change their behavior, reward and hold people accountable for that behavior, develop processes that help people reduce biases in decision-making, and above all, make sure you are investing more time and resources into reducing systemic inequities.

We want an easy fix, but change takes more work than a one-off training. It also takes more work than a technology fix. . . .

Can Technology "Fix" Biases?

While there are apps available for hiring teams that can remove names, education, and other common indicators that typically provoke bias, these do not fundamentally correct the problem. Humanizing and empathizing are one of the keys to reducing our personal biases, yet when people rely on technology to correct their biases they don't do the work to correct their own behavior. This normalizes biases, communicating that it's OK to have biases because technology will just filter them. It can also cause automation bias, and worse, algorithms for job recruitment can be biased themselves—these applications are still new, programmed by humans with biases, and artificial intelligence learns from historical data that can be biased.[9]

Removing someone's name and experience in the hiring process also strips away someone's identity, where we *want* our teams to recognize their colleagues' unique identities and work to ensure people with those identities belong. Biases play a role in many workplace decisions beyond looking at résumés: interviews, job offers, performance reviews, promotions, project assignments, and so on. We want to change *behaviors*, where people correct their own biases, and value and seek out diversity as a *culture add*.

The problem is that we do not value people with some names the same as others. It's time to fix that by teaching ourselves to value difference.

EXERCISE

The next time you encounter a person with an underrepresented identity that is different from your own, note your initial reaction (or nonreaction). In the office, it can be a first handshake, a lunch, or a presentation they give. Outside the office, it could be an encounter on the train, on the sidewalk, or in a store.

Note your initial impressions and your verbal and nonverbal communication in that situation. *What assumptions did you make? What did you say, how did you hold your body, how did they react? Did you approach them differently than you would someone with an identity like your own? And how might you approach a situation like that in the future in a way that interrupts some of your biases?*

Here's what I learned and want to work on next time:

_____

_____

_____

(continued)

_____

_____

_____

Now use those learnings for your next encounter with some-one new. *How did you approach that person differently? How did it feel? Were you surprised or did you learn something new?*

It may have been uncomfortable, that's what happens when you try something new. Keep working on disrupting your first impressions. Be open, and allow someone to present themselves to you in the way they want to be identified, free from any assumptions or biases you unfairly place upon them.

Showing Empathy

> It is important to cultivate genuine relationships with people of diverse backgrounds. We have to practice the muscle of empathy in small ways, and in small conflict, so that when a huge issue comes up, a huge issue around bias, that muscle is exercised and you are ready to respond.
>
> —DR. NAJEEBA SYEED[10]

The best allies I know listen, learn, and act with empathy. Empathy requires self-awareness of your own presence and perspective, curiosity, openness to someone else's perspective, and courage to respond and show your empathy for them and their experience. Psychologists Daniel Goleman and Paul Ekman outline three types of empathy:[11]

▸ **Cognitive empathy** is perspective-taking: we intellectually under-stand someone's experiences.

▶ **Emotional empathy** is directly feeling: we emotionally understand someone's experiences.
▶ **Compassionate empathy** combines both: we understand, feel, and respond to someone's experiences. This is so essential as an ally.

Let's break down what compassionate empathy looks like. Figure 4.1 shows a model we use at Change Catalyst, building on the work of Theresa Wiseman.[12]

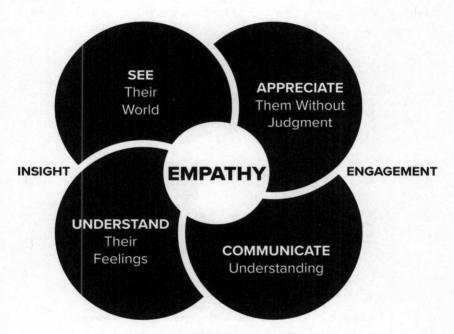

FIGURE 4.1   **The Elements of Empathy**

Compassionate empathy is a combination of insight and engagement. Gaining *insight* includes seeing the other person's world and understanding their feelings, cognitively and emotionally. Insight is just half of empathy. The other half is *engagement*: appreciating their unique experience without judgment and communicating this understanding. We often leave out engagement, but it's not enough to *think* about someone, you have to *interact* with them to show empathy.

Begin by seeing the person's world, which may be quite different from your own. Listen to them with empathy: be fully present and receptive, allowing the other person to fully show up. Your eyes, ears, mind, and heart are open, and you're not formulating a response until that person has been truly heard. Approach the conversation with open curiosity, and work to see their world as they see it. Listen to understand their unique feelings and experience—it may be quite different from how you might feel in a similar situation. Through self-awareness, recognize when you might be projecting your own ideas onto their experience, and reopen to a new perspective.

FIGURE 4.2   **Find Commonalities and Value Differences**

When we first meet people, and even when we've worked with people for some time, we usually look for what we have in common. But to have empathy—and to be a good ally—we must value and appreciate what we don't have in common. Our individual experiences are what make us who we are. When we approach each other recognizing and highly valuing both what we share *and* what we don't share, we enter a new level of understanding and connection. Figure 4.2 succinctly conveys this concept.

Then appreciate the person without judgment and communicate understanding. Empathy is different from pity or sympathy. As we build empathy, we build a relationship—we learn what someone is experiencing, then we access our own feelings to connect with them. We will never be able to "walk in their shoes," but we can appreciate their experience and let them know we see them and hear them, and we care. Showing empathy doesn't have to be complex—in the medical industry, physicians are taught to show empathy by wincing when their patient feels pain, for example.[13]

If empathy doesn't come natural to you, it can take some effort at first. Fortunately, Wiseman and several others have found that the more you practice empathy and put forth "empathic effort," the better you become at it, and the more it can over time become a way of being.[14] Having this compassion, and compassionate action, for each other can make us happier.[15] Practice this with your colleagues, your friends, and your family.

> *Where might you have an opportunity to show empathy for someone in the next couple of days? Look for those opportunities, and take them.*

Believing Versus Gaslighting

> To be an Indigenous woman in this country is to intimately understand both interpersonal and systemic gaslighting.
>
> —EMILY RIDDLE (NEHIYAW ISKWEW)[16]

Thinking back to the time I was experiencing microaggressions daily as an executive, there were a few key moments that really struck me. One of them was after a C-suite meeting, where I showed my colleagues our high turnover rates and lower engagement numbers for women in our firm. It was a week after I'd informally brought up the issue to the team for the first time. My goal was to discuss the data together, so we could address it and still become a great firm for women—which was one of our business goals.

As we came out of the meeting, a colleague of mine in the C-suite whisked me over to a corner of the room and said, "You've got to stop with this 'woman thing.'" He told me it was all in my head—even though I had literally just finished showing that it was in the data. He said it was ridiculous, to stop discussing it, and to "suck it up."

That hit hard. He was telling me it was a problem with me, not with the way I was being treated nor the way other women were being treated. I'd recently had some other negative experiences at the company that had deeply worn me down. So after that moment, I did stop talking about it and started working on solutions on my own to reduce turnover and improve engagement. (See the sidebar in the Introduction: "When All You Can Do Is Create Change Covertly.")

Gaslighting in the workplace can be either conscious or unconscious, and can take the form of denying or discrediting someone's experience, minimizing the impact or trauma from inequity, blaming someone for being mistreated or abused, and convincing someone experiencing microaggressions—and/or other people around them—that a person's experience is all in their head. Over time, this can be very damaging, severely affecting someone's self-esteem and making them question their reality.

Due to extensive gaslighting of women during the #MeToo movement, people started using the hashtag #believewomen to counter it. Gaslighting can happen in the workplace, in the doctor's office, at home, in the criminal justice system, and other areas of life. Medical gaslighting, for example, can occur when a doctor minimizes, ignores, mistreats, or misdiagnoses a patient.

If we're gaslighting unconsciously or unintentionally, it often means we haven't been listening with empathy, and we haven't been working to value someone's unique experiences. Perhaps we're comparing their experiences to our own, or envisioning how we might act in a similar situation. That's not compassionate empathy. If we haven't had a similar experience, it could be because we have been privileged not to have that experience, or we haven't experienced the trauma of having similar past experiences.

People who are being gaslighted might hear people say they are "difficult," "overly sensitive," "dramatic," "angry," "insecure," "just not a good culture fit," "thin-skinned," "taking it personally," "taking it the wrong way," "irrational," "too emotional," "overreacting," "reading too much into it," "not really listening or understanding," "imagining things," "making it all up," "the only one who feels this way," and more.

With compassionate empathy, we believe people when they tell us what they are experiencing, even if it's different from our own experience. If you find yourself resisting what someone is saying, take a moment to investigate that. *What are you resisting, and why? Is there something you need to learn more about to better understand someone's experience? Or is their experience bringing up an emotion you don't want to feel?* Everyone's experience is their own; make sure you are not denying their experience.

5

STEP 3: RECOGNIZE AND OVERCOME MICROAGGRESSIONS

> Microaggressions are linked to a wider sociopolitical context of oppression and injustice (historical trauma) that results in a soul wound passed on from generation to generation of those who understand their own histories of discrimination and prejudice. . . . Each small race-related slight, hurt, invalidation, insult, and indignity rubs salt into the wounds of marginalized groups in our society.
>
> **—DERALD WING SUE[1]**

Microaggressions are everyday slights, insults, and negative verbal and nonverbal communications that, whether intentional or not, can make someone feel belittled, disrespected, unheard, unsafe, othered, tokenized, gaslighted, impeded, and/or like they don't belong. While smaller aggressions than bullying, harassment, macroaggressions, or flat-out abuse, they can reinforce inequities and their effects can be traumatic and long-lasting. Also called microexclusions, microaggressions can be rooted in our biases and lack of understanding or empathy. And similar to biases, the key is to develop our empathy skills and become intentional so that we recognize the microaggression forming and stop it before it happens. In this chapter, we'll learn how to recognize and overcome microaggressions, so we don't unintentionally harm people with our own words and actions. In "Step 5: Stand Up for What's Right," we'll learn ways to interrupt microaggressions when we see them.

The term *microaggressions* was first described in 1970 by psychiatrist Chester Middlebrook Pierce as "subtle, stunning, often automatic and non-verbal exchanges which are 'put-downs' of Blacks by offenders."[2] It's now used to describe these actions against someone from any marginalized group.

Psychologist Derald Wing Sue has built decades of work on microaggressions and racism, and defines three forms of microaggressions:[3]

▶ **Microassaults**—slurs, name-calling, avoidant behavior, privileging, discriminatory actions.
▶ **Microinsults**—diminishing or demeaning someone's identity or accomplishments, implications of negativity or abnormality, rudeness.
▶ **Microinvalidations**—minimizing or ignoring someone's feelings and statements, invalidating someone's citizenship or identity, denying racism or oppression, denying privilege exists.

In Sue's work studying the effects of microaggressions across race, gender, and sexual orientation, he found the accumulated effect of microaggressions over time can be significant:

When a marginalized group member encounters microaggressive stressors, four pathways may show their negative impact:
(1) biological: there may be direct physiological reactions (blood pressure, heart rate, etc.) or changes in the immune system;
(2) cognitive: it may place in motion a cognitive appraisal involving thoughts and beliefs about the meaning of the stressor; (3) emotional: anger, rage, anxiety, depression, or hopelessness may dominate the person's immediate life circumstance; and (4) behavioral: the coping strategies or behavioral reactions utilized by the individual may either enhance adjustment or make the situation worse.[4]

Roberto Montenegro, who studies the biological effects of discrimination, has shown that chronic exposure to microaggressions can turn into "microtraumas"—not only emotionally but also physically.[5] Christina Friedlaender has shown the cumulative harm from microaggressions "can include stress, anxiety, depression, high blood pressure, insomnia, substance abuse, eating disorders, social withdrawal, suicidal ideation, and post-traumatic stress disorder."[6]

Each individual microaggression can be harmful in the short term, and as microaggressions accumulate daily, they can take a significant toll on someone's life and career in the long term. People with underrepresented identities encounter microaggressions *on top of* the stress everyone has in work and outside of work, which is an unfair disadvantage in our work and in our lives. As allies, it's our job to understand what "microaggressions" are, and make sure we don't do them.

The following pages include several examples of microaggressions. This isn't meant to be a be-all checklist of what not to do, I've provided it to paint a picture of what some daily microaggressions might look like, and how you can reframe your approach and work toward eliminating your own microaggressions.

You may see some things here that you do or have done. At one time or another, all good allies find ourselves making a mistake. It's our job as allies to listen, learn, unlearn, relearn, make mistakes, apologize, and keep learning. There are lots of people whose lives we can change if we improve how we show up for them in the present and the future. So forgive yourself for what you may have done or said. Especially if you've done it recently, you might go back to that person or group and apologize. And then keep working hard to not do it in the future.

Verbal Microaggressions

Language matters; it can make the difference between shutting someone down and lifting them up. Table 5.1 shows common verbal microaggressions and some ideas to consider. (Keep in mind that language is always changing, so it's important to check in with people to ensure terminology you're using works for them.)

TABLE 5.1   **Recognizing and Overcoming Verbal Microaggressions**

Common Verbal Microaggressions

Avoid these microaggressions	Consider this
Interrupting: • Interrupting someone while they are speaking. • Talking over someone's words. • Not allowing someone to finish their thought.	People with underrepresented identities are more likely to be interrupted. Men are three times more likely to interrupt a woman than another man.[7] Interruptions can be verbal and nonverbal—if we are thinking about what we're going to say next, we might be saying something with our body that tells someone we aren't listening and want to talk. Take a step back and listen with empathy; respectfully allow someone to finish their complete thought.
Taking up more than your share of airtime: • Dominating the conversation. • Not creating space for someone to speak. • Speaking on panels or at events that don't have diverse speakers.	A study from Brigham Young and Princeton Universities found that given a mixed population at the table, men take up 75 percent of the conversation in a meeting.[8] Be aware of who has taken up airtime, create openings, and genuinely invite people to share their thoughts. Say no to panels without diverse speakers; suggest someone with an underrepresented identity in your place.
Assuming someone is foreign because they present as being from a minority ethnic or racial group: • "You speak good English" when they were born in an English-speaking country. • "But where are you *really* from?"	These statements are othering—they can make someone feel like an "alien in their own land" and like they don't belong. If you're interested in their hometown, ask "Where did you grow up?" If they want to tell you their ethnicity or race, they will.
Assuming someone is not intelligent until they prove otherwise: • "Wow, he's really *articulate*." • "She *actually* really knows her stuff." • "You're a credit to your race." • Assuming someone with a disability is not intelligent and talking in a condescending way at them.	These statements reveal your bias about someone's intelligence based on their identity. Like several microaggressions, they imply this person is an exception to the rule (e.g., that Black people aren't normally articulate). Give someone a deep compliment about their expertise and skills instead. See the sidebar: "What's Wrong with Saying Someone Is 'Articulate'?"

(continued)

TABLE 5.1   Recognizing and Overcoming Verbal Microaggressions *(continued)*

Common Verbal Microaggressions

Avoid these microaggressions	Consider this
Not doing the work to know someone's name: • Calling someone a common name from their culture: "I can't remember their name, it's like *Raj* or something." • Not learning how to pronounce someone's name: "That woman with the name I can never pronounce." • Mixing up the names of two Black people who work at your company. Or two people who are Latinx, Asian, Arab, and/or women.	Someone's name is a key piece of their identity and does not take much effort to learn. Learn, practice, and remember their name. It's OK to ask someone how to pronounce their name; when you do, write it down phonetically for yourself so you remember. Mixing up people's names can be a form of invisibilization.
Negating someone's identity: • "I don't see race," "I'm color-blind," "We are all one race: the human race." • Asking someone of mixed race, "What *are* you?" This is dehumanizing, no one should be referred to as "what" vs. "who." • Telling someone of mixed race what race they are, "No, you're White—you look White. You're totally White." • "You don't act/look like a normal" Black/Asian/disabled/etc. person. • "Tone down your appearance" or "Don't bring your 'lifestyle' to work." • Incorrectly identifying someone's race, ethnicity, or disability. • Providing the wrong type of accessibility for someone's disability (e.g., giving a braille document to someone who is Deaf). • Centering your identity, culture, communication style, etc., as the norm, and everyone else as abnormal or inferior.	While often well-intentioned, "I don't see race" or "I'm color-blind" can be experienced as "I'm erasing or ignoring a part of your identity." Not seeing race or color is also a privilege that many people don't have because society treats people differently based on visible identity. Instead learn and acknowledge someone's unique identity, culture, tradition, history, and experience, as well as the unique oppression and systemic barriers they may face as a result. Remember to value difference. Rather than centering your identity and culture as the norm, recognize that each identity and culture is equally normal, valid, and valuable. Do the work to learn about identities different from your own.

(continued)

TABLE 5.1 **Recognizing and Overcoming Verbal Microaggressions** *(continued)*

Common Verbal Microaggressions

Avoid these microaggressions	Consider this
Disparaging someone's language: • Calling an Indigenous language a "foreign language." • "You don't sound Black." • Asking someone from a racial or ethnic minority group, "Why do you sound White?" (Michelle Obama writes about being asked this as a child in her neighborhood in Chicago.[9])	These can be a form of cultural gaslighting and/or erasure, making someone feel like their internal identity is incongruent with what it "should" be. Avoid these phrases and sentiments and instead work to ensure someone feels they belong.
Implying someone was hired because they have unfair advantage as someone who has an underrepresented identity: • Calling someone a "diversity hire" or otherwise implying they were hired because of their identity versus their expertise. • Insisting on "reverse discrimination."	This can be very belittling. Our hiring processes have embedded biases in them that have actively excluded people with underrepresented identities over many years. *Finally* companies are starting to correct this inequity, which means they are bringing in qualified candidates from diverse backgrounds. You probably wouldn't say "he's a White male hire" in a derogatory way, even though our systems have been biased toward White men for years. Catch yourself if you're thinking this; recognize and support someone's unique skills and expertise.
Diminishing someone's accomplishments: • Questioning someone's expertise. • Asking to see someone's badge at your company if they don't look like they fit in. • Treating a person of color as the hotel or event staff at a conference rather than an attendee or speaker, or a restaurant valet rather than a customer. • Assuming a veteran has no skills other than to use a gun or act aggressively: "She worked in the military so she has a fighting instinct, but what else can she do *really*?" Perhaps she led a large team under high-stress situations to debug military-grade technology, for example.	These are often first-impression identity biases. People from underrepresented identities generally have to prove their expertise and skills over and over again throughout their lives, even when they have achieved leadership positions. Even Edward Enninful, *British Vogue* Editor-in-Chief and the first Black editor of the magazine, has been told to use the garage entrance as he entered his own office. Pause, catch yourself, and interrupt these biases before you say or do something that can cause harm.

(continued)

TABLE 5.1 **Recognizing and Overcoming Verbal Microaggressions** *(continued)*

Common Verbal Microaggressions

Avoid these microaggressions	Consider this
Dismissing someone's experiences with systemic inequity and marginalization: • "Everyone can succeed, if they work hard enough." • Insisting on a meritocracy. • "Don't play the race card." • "I'm not a racist" said in defense of someone pointing out a microaggression.	This is a form of gaslighting. There is a large body of research showing people with underrepresented identities are discriminated against and marginalized. Listen to and believe someone's experiences.
Stereotyping: • Assuming a woman who wears a head scarf is not intelligent, liberated, or speaks English. • Saying someone who is a Gen Xer or baby boomer "won't get it" because they are older. • Saying "of course you're good at math" to an Asian person.	These are based on stereotypes and identity bias. Pause, humanize, and empathize to catch yourself before you do or say something harmful.
Misgendering someone: • Assuming someone's gender identity based on your perception of how they look. • Dismissing a person's pronouns.	This can be especially harmful for people who are transgender, nonbinary, and/or gender nonconforming. Don't assume someone's pronouns—look them up (often people include their pronouns on social media) or ask them when you first meet them. For example, "I use *she/her* pronouns—what are your pronouns?"
Referring to an artificial gender binary or grouping everyone using terms referring to men: • "50/50 gender balance" • "ladies and gentlemen" • "boys and girls" • "you guys," "mankind"	Binary terms exclude people who are nonbinary and gender nonconforming. Work to de-gender your language. Try "everyone," "you all," or "y'all." Replace "50/50 gender balance" with "gender parity."
Deadnaming: • Using the name someone was assigned at birth before they changed their name. • Saying someone "used to be a man/ woman/she/he."	Transitioning is an external presentation of an internal identity, where a person may never have identified with their sex assigned at birth. If someone has transitioned, do the work to relearn their gender. If they have changed their name, use their new name.

(continued)

TABLE 5.1   **Recognizing and Overcoming Verbal Microaggressions** *(continued)*

Common Verbal Microaggressions

Avoid these microaggressions	Consider this
Outing someone: • Asking someone who is transgender and/or has a disability to identify themself publicly. • Talking about someone's disability, gender, or religion publicly without their permission (potentially outing them).	When someone comes out as transgender or having a disability, it can be a very difficult process to navigate and they may do it in phases. Coming out in a private conversation is very different from coming out publicly. People from some religions have been severely persecuted and may not want their religion public. Let people tell their own story, however and to whomever they would like to tell it.
Explaining *for* someone: • "What she's trying to say is . . ." • Explaining a concept to someone who is an expert in the field.	Often this is based on stereotypes and identity biases, assuming someone is not intelligent or experienced. (Sometimes called "mansplaining" or "whitesplaining.") Instead, assume someone is experienced and intelligent. Allow someone to explain their ideas themselves, find out who they are and their expertise, and only explain a concept to them if they want to know more.
Making a joke about someone's identity: • Joking about someone's sexual orientation, race, ethnicity, gender, religion, or other aspect of their identity. • Jokingly calling a Muslim a "terrorist," a Jewish person "cheap," a Black woman a "Welfare Queen."	Also based on stereotypes and identity bias, jokes can be incredibly harmful—and considered harassment. Often racist, sexist, ableist, heteronormative jokes are told by someone who is uncomfortable with a particular identity. Explore your biases and your discomfort, and self-regulate.
Taking credit for someone else's idea: • Taking another person's idea in a meeting and running with it without giving that person credit. • Giving the wrong person credit for an idea.	Often a person with an underrepresented identity shares an idea that is dismissed, and later it is repeated by someone else and championed. This can negatively impact their career. Listen to people's ideas, and give them due credit.

(continued)

TABLE 5.1 **Recognizing and Overcoming Verbal Microaggressions** (continued)

Common Verbal Microaggressions

Avoid these microaggressions	Consider this
Objectification, exoticization, and inspiration porn: • Treating people with disabilities as inspiration: "the way you overcome your disability is so inspiring." • "Rags to riches" stories of poor people and immigrants overcoming obstacles against all odds. • Exoticizing people or cultures, treating people as objects rather than humans. • Tokenism—using one or a handful of people to create the impression of diversity, or asking them to represent all people from their culture or identity.	These can be dehumanizing, reinforce stereotypes, and objectify a person for the benefit of others. They show up in film and television, video games, talk shows, books, toys, media, and workplaces. The fashion and advertising industries have notoriously exoticized and treated models as objects. Stella Young discusses "inspiration porn" in her TEDxSydney talk, "I'm not your inspiration thank you very much."[10] Instead of seeing disability as a weakness or something to overcome, recognize disability as someone's proud and powerful identity. Instead of using people's stories, looks, and identities for your own benefit, make a difference by humanizing and fixing systemic barriers for people with underrepresented identities.
Racist or prejudiced sayings: • "Indian giver," "sold down the river," "no can do," "long time no see," using master/slave terminology, "you people," "that's so gay," "powwow," "vision quest," "spirit animal," "open the kimono"	There are many phrases we still use that have deeply racist backstories or are considered cultural appropriation (discussed later in this chapter). Catch yourself before saying them; find alternatives for each of these phrases.

(continued)

TABLE 5.1 **Recognizing and Overcoming Verbal Microaggressions** *(continued)*

Common Verbal Microaggressions

Avoid these microaggressions	Consider this
Ableist sayings: • "Blind to," "blinded by," "turn a blind eye," "blind spot," "double-blind study/review" • "Deaf to," "turn a deaf ear to," "falling on deaf ears" • "Crazy," "insane," "loony," "loony bin," "lunatic," "mad," "madman," "madhouse," "maniac," "nuts," "psycho," "psychopath," "whacko," "daft," "so ADD," "bonkers," "deranged," "mental," "mental case" • "Lame," "deformed," "cripple," "crippled," "crippled by" • "Moronic," "retarded," "imbecile," "idiot," "stupid," "cretin" • "Feeble-minded," "dumb," "spaz," "midget," "mouth breather"	Many common phrases are derogatory and rooted in ableist ideas that disability is negative, less than, abnormal, and deviant. Catch yourself, self-regulate, and find alternatives. Educate yourself about ableism beyond language as well. Activist Lyda X. Z. Brown writes: "Ableism is not a list of bad words. Language is *one* tool of an oppressive system. . . . Ableism is systematic, institutional devaluing of bodies and minds deemed deviant, abnormal, defective, subhuman, less than. Ableism is *violence.*"[11]
Centering disability language around ableist ideas of disability: • "Differently abled," "handicapped," "handicapable," "*the* disabled," "special needs," "specially abled" • "suffers from _____," "wheelchair bound," "confined to a wheelchair"	This language often centers the norm around people *without* disabilities to make them feel more comfortable, while othering people *with* disabilities as abnormal, pitiful, and/or inspirational. Generally, people prefer "people with disabilities" (person-first language), "disabled people" (identity-first language, or the social model of disability), or their specific disability like Autistic, Deaf, and Blind. Rather than "wheelchair bound"—because no one is bound or confined to their wheelchair—try "wheelchair user" or "someone who uses a wheelchair."

When we tell a disabled person that we don't consider them to be disabled, what it is doing is perpetuating the stigma that being disabled is a bad thing. And when we don't use words like *disabled* or *disability*, it is saying we think it is a bad word, and there is shame around it.

—TIFFANY YU[12]

What's Wrong with Saying Someone Is "Articulate"?

When I train executive teams about microaggressions, this is often the most discussed microaggression. In a leadership workshop I led, a Black executive explained it this way: "It's a back-handed compliment," she said. "What are you really telling me here? You're conveying that you are surprised, and that I am an exception to how you see Black people. That I can speak well, as compared to other Black people? It's not within the normal realm of compliments, and it doesn't make me feel good. It happens all the time, and it's draining." If your intention is to pay someone a compliment, do your work as an ally to use a phrase that they will receive as a compliment.

Actions You Can Take to Reduce Your Verbal Microaggressions

Have you witnessed some of these verbal microaggressions? Have you experienced some of them? If you're a person with an underrepresented identity reading this, I'm sure you could easily think of at least 10 more.

Have you said some of these phrases? Most of us have. Do the work to do no harm:

Break yourself of verbal habits that can cause harm. Choose a few micro-aggressions to work on, and catch yourself before or as you're saying them. You can ask your team, family, and friends to help catch your microaggressions as you learn. If you catch yourself after saying them, work on apologizing and correcting yourself.

Learn the language people use to describe their identities. Know how to pronounce their name, how they describe their disability or religion or ethnicity, and understand their pronouns (*he/him, she/her, they/them,* or something else). This really matters to people. Language around identity is personal and always evolving. So if you don't know, just ask.

Nonverbal Microaggressions

> People's emotions are rarely put into words, far more often they are expressed through other cues.
>
> **—DANIEL GOLEMAN[13]**

Facial Expressions

Many microaggressions are nonverbal, so they can be subtle. When I was an undergraduate student at the University of Washington, one of my many work-study jobs was on a psychology research study. We used Paul Ekman's foundational work in the 1970s on microexpressions to study parents' interactions with their children.[14] The study primed parents with specific facial expressions to show their kids, and mapped how those expressions affected their kids' success on individual tests and collaborative projects.

I used a lot of what I learned studying facial expressions and Ekman's Facial Action Coding System in my work as a documentary filmmaker. A documentarian is mostly a silent interviewer, so nonverbal feedback can be a very powerful tool in moving an interviewee where you want them to go—and giving them encouragement if they are feeling impostor syndrome, shyness, or uncertainty.

Our facial expressions can convey our feelings and thoughts. Seeing another person's facial expressions can change how we show up. When someone is experiencing fear, nervousness, or what Ekman calls perceived "threat-to-self," it makes a big difference whether you show them contempt or enjoyment, confusion or understanding, disinterest or interest. When I'm on stage speaking in front of an audience, I look for people in the audience to grab onto, who are genuinely listening, encouraging me, and giving me nonverbal feedback. This can affect presentations, meetings, performance reviews, interviews, and other times when someone perceives there is a lot at stake.

Ekman's work is used by countless researchers as well as the Federal Bureau of Investigation (FBI), Transportation Security Administration (TSA), Central Intelligence Agency (CIA), Dalai Lama (on work around compassion and emotions), and graphic animation studios (Ekman was an advisor for the Pixar movie *Inside Out*).

Body Language

> When the body closes, the mind follows.
> —ALLAN AND BARBARA PEASE[15]

A close counterpart to facial expressions is body language. A few key pieces of body language to keep in mind in avoiding microaggressions are closed body language and dominant power positioning. We might have closed body language or specific facial expressions due to a disability, a cultural norm, a cold room, a bias, or a reaction to something outside that moment altogether. Become aware of how you might make people feel inadvertently, and change it if you can.

Closed body language includes crossed arms, folded hands, crossed legs, turning your body away from someone, putting your hands in your pockets, looking down at your phone or the table, and putting your open computer between you and another person. These can literally put a barrier between you and the other person, whether that person is sitting or standing across from you, or they are giving a presentation in front of the room or on stage. When your body language is closed, you may be showing a person that you are closed off to the ideas or experiences they are sharing. And you might actually be more closed off to what they're saying. Looking away, disinterested, tired, or otherwise occupied also can be felt as a significant microaggression.

Dominant power positioning includes hands on hips, hands behind your head, legs open wide while sitting (taking up lots of space), or one leg crossed perpendicular to the other over your knee. This can also include putting your arm on someone's shoulder or wheelchair, standing over them while they are sitting down, or moving too far into their personal space.[16] All can imply dominance over the other person, be very off-putting, and shut them down.

Avoidance

> When you are connecting with people with disabilities . . . you don't have to have all of the answers. Just the confidence to start the conversation.
>
> **—VICTOR CALISE**[17]

As shown in Table 5.2, microaggressions can also be nonverbal and passive: when we fear saying or doing the wrong thing, we might avoid someone altogether. This avoidance can have long-term effects on someone's life. The first time I learned about avoidance was in 2016, while talking with Victor Calise, Commissioner of the New York City Mayor's Office for People with Disabilities. Earlier that year we held our Ability in Tech Summit to address DEI for people with disabilities in tech. I shared with him that for our career fair portion of the event, tech companies repeatedly said they "couldn't" come because their teams had not been trained on how to talk to people with disabilities, or they didn't know how to accommodate them. Victor told me avoidance is commonly experienced by people with disabilities—and since then I've recognized it happening with Black, LGBTQIA+, and Muslim colleagues and friends, as well as people with other marginalized identities.

Avoidance can also occur *as a result* of microaggressions. Due to discrimination, microaggressions, and lack of accessibility or inclusion—or the anticipation of these—people with underrepresented identities often avoid social situations. A 2018 Australian study found 31 percent of disabled people engaged in avoidance behaviors because of their disability.[18]

> *Who are you avoiding out of fear or lack of knowledge? What can you do to change that?*

TABLE 5.2 **Recognizing and Overcoming Nonverbal Microaggressions**

Common Nonverbal Microaggressions in the Workplace

Avoid these microaggressions	Consider this
Invisibilization and exclusion: • Ignoring someone's presence in the room, in a conversation, or in a public space. • Not inviting someone to a meeting when they should be there because of their expertise and role. • Having non-senior-level people or non-"VIPs" sit against the wall versus sit at the table. • Seeing or treating two Black women as interchangeable.	Invisibilization is a form of othering: "I don't see you or recognize you." This could happen in meetings or events, where no one introduces themselves to a person with an underrepresented identity. Or walking past someone and pretending they don't exist. This happens to me often in my own neighborhood in San Francisco, the heart of the tech industry: men will literally run into me because they don't see me, or expect me to move out of their way. Be mindful of inclusion in meetings—invite people to be in the room where decisions are made, with a powerful position at that table. Ensure everyone is introduced to one another. Pause, humanize, and empathize.
Not paying attention: • Looking at your laptop or cell phone or otherwise multitasking while someone is speaking. • Talking aside to someone else when a person is sharing an idea or experience. • Closing off your body or communicating disinterest when someone is speaking.	Give people your full attention. Put down your phone, close your laptop, and pay attention. Practice empathetic listening. Use open body language and facial expressions that connect with the speaker, show you are truly listening and care what they have to say. If someone is new to a group or company, the only person like them in the room, or just nervous, this can make a huge difference. And you may also find that you remember more about what they say.

(continued)

TABLE 5.2   **Recognizing and Overcoming Nonverbal Microaggressions** *(continued)*

Common Nonverbal Microaggressions in the Workplace

Avoid these microaggressions	Consider this
Touching without permission: • Touching someone's wheelchair, leaning against it, or pushing it. • Patting the head of a little person and/or a woman. • Touching a Black woman's hair or a Muslim woman's headscarf. • Rubbing a pregnant woman's belly. • Putting your hand on someone to quiet them.	Each of these can be belittling and offensive; it's not OK to touch someone without their permission. A wheelchair user often sees their wheelchair as an extension of their body—don't lean on, push, or otherwise handle it without permission. (Same for canes and walkers.) As an ally, consider opening the door for them if it's not automatic, and removing any obstacles from their path.
Racist, sexist, or ableist nonverbal actions: • Referring to sign language by waving your hands in a nonsensical way. • Using an animal reference (e.g., monkey, ape, cougar) when referring to a person. • Calling the police when you see a Black person in your neighborhood, or calling security when at your workplace. • Crossing to the other side of the street when you see a Black man coming toward you on the sidewalk, locking the door when you see a Black man walking near your car, grabbing your purse when you see a Black person near you. • Using cat or cougar gestures, or gestures about their body, when describing a woman.	These are demeaning and derogatory actions that must be eliminated from our society—they are harmful to us all. Refrain from calling security or the police because someone looks suspicious—this is a bias that puts Black people in harm's way far too often and needs to be unlearned. Recognize and reverse your biases when you assume someone is a criminal or doesn't belong. If you tense up when a Black man walks down the street next to you at night, recognize yourself tensing up and change it, show warmth and kindness instead. Pause, humanize, and empathize.
Visual storytelling: • Featuring stories, pictures, or other examples that don't show diversity, tell inappropriate jokes, reinforce stereotypes, or are slights. This might be in slides, websites, presentations, social media, advertisements, etc.	Filter all your work with a DEI lens. Always consider the diversity, accessibility, and inclusion of written language, images, and other visual expressions.

(continued)

TABLE 5.2   Recognizing and Overcoming Nonverbal Microaggressions *(continued)*

Common Nonverbal Microaggressions in the Workplace

Avoid these microaggressions	Consider this
Other facial expressions and body language: • Rolling your eyes or otherwise dismissing or mocking someone. • Giving a "knowing" side look to someone about someone else. • Embodying dominant power positioning.	Become aware of how your body and facial expressions make someone feel. *Is someone closing their own body language in relation to yours? Are you encroaching into their personal space?* Once you begin to recognize this, you might also be able to see other people do this too, and interrupt it. See the earlier "Facial Expressions" and "Body Language" sections.
Avoidance: • Not interviewing or approaching someone because you "don't know how" or "don't know how to accommodate." • Avoiding the seat next to a person with a marginalized identity, or sitting further away than normal in a conversation or an interview. • Asking different questions in a job interview because you are afraid to ask them, or assume you know the response. • Not giving someone proper feedback to grow.	See the earlier "Avoidance" section. Don't let fear be reason or excuse for exclusion. Do the work to learn how to speak with, interview, or accommodate someone. Make sure you are providing quality feedback to people who need it to grow in their work. (We'll also discuss providing quality feedback in "Step 5: Stand Up for What's Right.")

(continued)

TABLE 5.2   Recognizing and Overcoming Nonverbal Microaggressions *(continued)*

Common Nonverbal Microaggressions in the Workplace

Avoid these microaggressions	Consider this
Cultural appropriation, exploitation, and denigration: • "I love the culture, I'm wearing ____ to show my appreciation" (e.g., cornrows, Kente cloth, bindi, headdress, war paint, kimono, sombrero). • Brands using stereotypical tropes, cultural icons, or historical figures as mascots, logos, and/or brand names. • Sampling or popularizing music from another culture without recognition or compensation. • Wearing blackface, brownface, or yellowface. • Speaking with someone else's accent or dialect (e.g., "blaccent"). • Art, dance, or writing that replicates or borrows heavily from another culture without attribution, permission, or cultural context. • Casting actors or models to play historical or cultural figures from an identity that is not their own (e.g., White actors playing Asian or Black roles, cisgender actors playing transgender roles). • Toys, games, videos, or movies that popularize and monetize cultural figures and traditions without permission or correct cultural context.	Avoid wearing, practicing, or making money from aspects of another culture's identity—unless you have been given permission to do so, and provide historical context and attribution. Sometimes this also takes the form of exoticization or exploitation of another culture or religion. Instead, support the makers, keepers, and educators of tradition and groups working to reclaim their history and culture. See the "Cultural Appropriation Versus Cultural Appreciation" section later in this chapter.

> Crucial to how we feel is being aware of how we are feeling in the moment. The sine qua non of that is to realize that you are being emotional in the first place. The earlier you recognize an emotion, the more choice you will have in dealing with it. In Buddhist terms, it's recognizing the spark before the flame. In Western terms, it's trying to increase the gap between impulse and saying or doing something you might regret later.
>
> **—PAUL EKMAN[19]**

Actions You Can Take to Reduce Your Nonverbal Microaggressions

In addition to the considerations in Table 5.2, there is other work to do no harm:

Prime yourself. In advance of a meeting or other interaction, prime yourself ahead of time to genuinely feel the emotion you want to present to someone. Microexpressions happen in an instant, just like first impressions. Ask yourself ahead of time: *How do you want to show up for this person? What do you want to learn from them, how do you want them to feel?* For example, if you want someone you are interviewing to show their best self in the interview, prime yourself first with thoughts of welcoming, compassionate empathy, and inclusion.

Seek to become more self-aware in the moment. Be aware of what your facial expressions and body language are conveying. *Are you conveying the message you want to convey?* If not, change it if you're able to do so. Sometimes when I'm listening to someone give a presentation in a meeting when the room is too cold, I find myself frowning or crossing my arms because of the cold. Obviously, a frown is not what I want to convey to the speaker! So I quickly put on a sweater, remove the frown, and work on giving positive, encouraging facial expressions, even nodding.

Practice empathetic listening. We teach our kids "whole body listening" and then somehow forget it as an adult. If you want to show someone you are listening and care about the conversation you're having, open your body to the person you're listening to: if you're physically able to, face the person speaking, unfold your arms and legs, and put your feet flat on the floor. Try leaning into the conversation a bit to show that you're listening. It will make a world of difference in how you both show up for each other.

Learn more about body language and facial expressions. You might check out Paul Ekman's work on facial expressions or Allan and Barbara Pease's work on body language. These have made a big difference in how I show up in groups and one-on-one conversations.

Environmental Microaggressions

In addition to verbal and nonverbal microaggressions, there is what Derald Wing Sue calls environmental microaggressions: "demeaning and threatening social, educational, political, or economic cues" that are "manifested on systemic and environmental levels."[20] These include mascots, advertisements, media images of racial injustice and police brutality, inaccurate and belittling portrayals of someone's identity in films and television, and lack of representation in magazines, novels, textbooks, videos, and other media. Table 5.3 shows some of the ways environmental microaggressions can manifest in our workplaces.

TABLE 5.3   Recognizing and Overcoming Environmental Microaggressions

Common Environmental Microaggressions in the Workplace

Avoid these microaggressions	Consider this
Leadership is not diverse and inclusive: • Leadership team is not diverse. • Microaggressions and inequities are allowed to occur without people with authority intervening. • *Diversity, equity,* and *inclusion* are terms used by leadership in a hollow way, without true action taken (e.g., public statements made but no real internal work).	A lack of leadership diversity shows people you may not value people like them as leaders, and there is likely a glass ceiling for people with underrepresented identities. Not focusing on DEI as a leadership team communicates to people with underrepresented identities that you don't care about their needs. Work on DEI as a leadership team. See "Step 6: Lead the Change" and "Step 7: Transform Your Organization, Industry, and Society."
Accessibility and accommodation are not inclusive: • The accessible entrance to the building is down a dark alley far from the main entrance and requires you to buzz in and wait for someone to answer. • Signage, shelves, food, and supplies are at a level too high for people who use wheelchairs, Little People, or people of short stature. • Every time someone with a disability wants to attend an event or meeting, they have to ask for accommodation. • The company website doesn't include basic accessibility features.	These show accessibility is ignored or an afterthought rather than a key priority, and can make someone feel undervalued and othered. Design with accessibility in mind from the beginning, with input from people with diverse disabilities. If you know someone with a disability is joining a meeting or event, make sure accessibility is in place before they have to ask. This is true inclusion.

(continued)

TABLE 5.3   **Recognizing and Overcoming Environmental Microaggressions**
(continued)

Common Environmental Microaggressions in the Workplace

Avoid these microaggressions	Consider this
DEI is not a priority in the culture: • Leadership cares about DEI, but managers don't prioritize it. • Asking people with underrepresented identities to fix DEI, often without compensation. • Not acknowledging the impact of environmental microaggressions and discrimination people experience outside the workplace. • Company website, marketing, or advertisements show a lack of diverse representation. • DEI is addressed through Black History Month and Women's History Month events, and/or ERGs, but not systemically and culturally. • The company is only prioritizing diversity for women: "We'll get to the other groups after we get gender right." • Company holidays are not inclusive. • The company doesn't take into account caregiver schedules (e.g., hosting events in the evenings or expecting people to stay late at work). • Food and beverages offered are not inclusive (e.g., halal, kosher, vegan, vegetarian, gluten free, nondairy, nut free, and attention to any other cultural dietary needs).	Prioritize DEI across the organization, from the top to bottom and throughout the middle. Hold leaders accountable for creating change, and address DEI for all underrepresented groups. Go beyond events to real, systemic change. Ensure your brand and messaging reflect DEI. Offer flexible holidays so people can take off the holidays they celebrate, consider flexible hours to accommodate parents and other caregivers, and remote options for caregivers and people with disabilities. See "Step 7: Transform Your Organization, Industry, and Society" for more ideas. Recognize when people are experiencing microaggressions and systemic inequity outside the workplace, and have safe conversations about them.

(continued)

STEP 3: RECOGNIZE AND OVERCOME MICROAGGRESSIONS

TABLE 5.3   Recognizing and Overcoming Environmental Microaggressions
(continued)

Common Environmental Microaggressions in the Workplace

Avoid these microaggressions	Consider this
Microaggressions in the physical space: • The only place in the office to privately pump breast milk is in the broom closet or bathroom stall. • There isn't a place in the office to pray, meditate, or have quiet time. • There is no safe all-gender restroom for people who are trans, nonbinary, and gender nonconforming. • There are fewer women's restrooms in the office, located only on every other floor. • Meeting rooms are all named after men and/or reflect only one cultural identity. • Images of successful people or quotes on office walls are not diverse. • Physical space is difficult to navigate for wheelchair users; event space lacks accessible seating.	Design for inclusion in the physical space, gather input from diverse people, design with "edge cases" in mind: *Who is this space for? How do we ensure people of all identities feel welcome?* Offer a Mother's Room, Prayer Room, and quiet space for people to meditate or take a technology break. Provide single-stall or all-gender restrooms that are safe for people who are trans, nonbinary, and gender nonconforming. Also make sure Muslims have single-stall (or gendered) restrooms to prepare for prayer. All décor and meeting names should be diverse and inclusive.
Technology is not inclusive: • Conference phones or event microphones don't pick up women's voices well. • Voice-activated technology doesn't pick up people's accents. • Accessibility technology is old and outdated. • Online events or meetings use technology that isn't accessible.	I've spoken at several events where microphones picked up men's voices well but not women's voices, or in meeting rooms where a woman has to move the phone close to her so it will pick up her voice. Voice-activated technology often doesn't pick up accents well. And many offices and events use technology that is not accessible, where disabled people cannot participate. Each of these is othering and a barrier to participation. Keep in mind that inclusion in technology matters.

The Impact Is the Key

Each individual microaggression can be harmful in the short term, and as microaggressions accumulate daily, they can take a significant toll on someone's life, career, and family in the long term. People with underrepresented identities encounter microaggressions *on top of* the stress everyone has in work and outside of work, which is an unfair disadvantage in our work and in our lives.

Often when people learn about microaggressions, they focus on the intent: "that's not what I *meant*," "I didn't *intend* them to feel that way," or "they took it the wrong way." Unintentional harm is still harm: the impact is the key. Microaggressions are experienced and felt, regardless of your intent.

We must move from unintentional harm to intentional allyship. We don't always know the historical context and cumulative effect of someone experiencing the microaggressions again and again; we have to trust their experience. If it matters to the person we're working with, it matters to us as colleagues and as allies.

Cultural Appropriation Versus Cultural Appreciation

When I was a child, my sister, father, and I were part of a YMCA program called "Indian Guides and Indian Princesses." The goal of the program was to bring fathers closer to their daughters and sons. However, the activities included designing your own "Indian" leather headbands with feathers, building igloos in the snow like the "Eskimos,"[21] singing "Indian" songs, and creating handmade "God's Eyes" and "spirit catchers." These activities were usually led by White men, reading how to do them from a handout. We took on individual Indigenous-sounding names, had a name for our "tribe," elected a "Chief," and in our overnight camping expeditions we even held "powwows." The program and activities were racist, culturally appropriating Indigenous traditions, spiritual practices, and livelihoods.

We had no right to appropriate the names, rituals, attire, activities, and housing of Indigenous people. Each was taken out of their Indigenous cultural context and brought inside our White urban middle-class neighborhood as our own. I'm ashamed I participated in a program and activities that did this.

Perhaps it would have been different if the program had focused on learning from Indigenous people about their culture, language, and experiences—respecting them, valuing them, and appreciating their unique worldview. But we didn't, these activities weren't created so that we could appreciate Indigenous culture, they were created to bond with family members over a quaint "Indian" activity that othered and belittled Indigenous people as primitive and historical.

Apparently, the program was initially developed by Harold Keltner, a White man, and Joe Friday, from the Ojibway Nation, in the 1920s.[22] Over the years, it evolved away from its arguably more authentic roots and into a program full of stereotypes, cultural appropriation, and racist tropes. In 2001, the YMCA renamed the program "Adventure Guides" or "Adventure Guides and Princesses."[23] With a quick internet search, it looks like many of these programs still have very similar programming today.[24]

Cultural appropriation (also called cultural misappropriation) is inappropriate, unauthorized adoption or co-opting of language, music, hairstyles, attire, fashion, art, traditions, culture, and history of another culture. The appropriator is usually someone from a majority or dominant culture who co-opts from a marginalized culture, often removing an object, culture, or tradition from its original context and placing it in the context of the dominant culture. Individual acts of cultural appropriation are generally nonverbal microaggressions. A brand's acts of cultural appropriation are environmental microaggressions.

Appropriation of Indigenous culture permeates most regions where Indigenous people were colonized and is seen by many people as an extension of continued colonization.[25] For instance, the Kansas City American football team is called the Chiefs, where celebrities bang on a drum as the crowd, with many wearing "war paint" and headdresses, does the "tomahawk chop." Fans of the Atlanta Braves baseball team adopted the "tomahawk chop" as well, hoisting foam tomahawks.

After the murder of George Floyd on May 25, 2020, several companies had an internal reckoning with their lack of DEI internally, as well as the cultural appropriation and racism within their brands. After nearly 100 years, Dryer's Grand Ice Cream retired the brand name "Eskimo Pie"; B&G Foods reconsidered its racist Cream of Wheat mascot; the Washington football team retired their racist "Redskins" name and logo; Quaker Oats retired the 130-year-old Aunt Jemima brand and logo based on a racist stereotype; and Conagra reviewed its "Mrs. Butterworth's" brand, Mars its "Uncle Ben's" brand and logo, Colgate-Palmolive its "Darlie" toothpaste, and Nestlé its "Red Skins and Chicos" line. The band "Dixie Chicks" rebranded to "The Chicks," New Orleans' "Dixie Beer" rebranded, and Land O'Lakes removed the Indigenous woman from its branding in April 2020, with many more brands hopefully to follow.[26] These brands are racist and sometimes sexist, appropriating, stereotyping, and perpetuating notions of enslavement and servitude. There is a museum in Michigan dedicated to racist memorabilia like these.[27]

As a general rule, avoid wearing, practicing, or making money from aspects of another culture's identity unless you have been given permission to do so. If you admire and respect a culture, learn from that culture, purchase items directly from that culture, and attribute the work to the people you learned and purchased from. You also have a powerful voice that can help create change—if you see someone or a brand who is culturally appropriating, tell them so. And protest with marginalized people when they are fighting to reclaim their cultural icons.

There is a lot to digest in this and the previous chapter (Steps 2 and 3), but it's critical that we understand and correct our biases, and that we recognize and overcome microaggressions in the workplace and in our lives so that we do no harm.

Together, we're unlearning a lifetime of learning.

EXERCISE

In Steps 2 and 3, we explored working to do no harm by correcting our biases, showing empathy, and minding our microaggressions. Reflecting on what you've learned, what are three things that you will commit to doing differently?

1. I commit to: _____

_____

_____

2. I commit to: _____

_____

_____

3. I commit to: _____

_____

_____

What is the first step you will take to achieve these commitments? By when will you do this?

As a first step, I will: _____

_____

_____

_____

_____

_____

_____

STEP 4: ADVOCATE FOR PEOPLE

6

> If you have a voice, use it. If you have legs, stand up. If you have feet, step up. If you have each other, fight together.
>
> —JANNA CACHOLA

(RE) learning and doing no harm are incredibly important foundational acts of allyship. And to deeply correct inequity and build inclusion, we also need to take action as advocates. An *advocate* uses their power and influence to support a person or group of people. This is a crucial continuation and deepening of allyship, where we move from unintentional harm to intentional good.

Our work as advocates is to help build equity and inclusion, often through small acts that can make a big difference in someone's life. Our actions can include helping ensure our colleagues have a seat at the table and their voices are heard, intervening if harm does occur, building confidence and courage if someone has lost theirs due to discrimination and microaggressions, taking on the burden of educating other people about allyship, and mobilizing people, teams, and companies to take action for positive change. It requires continuing to build your knowledge and stepping forward to take action on someone's behalf.

Exclusion Can Change You

As an advocate, it's helpful to recognize the impact of continued inequities and exclusion in the workplace, so we know how and why to advocate for people when they need it.

Tokenism

> For years I thought NASA only hired me because they needed women.
>
> **—MAUREEN ZAPPALA**[1]

Tokenism is a symbolic gesture or appearance of diversity. It's not inclusion; it's a minimal gesture of diversity without doing the work to achieve true representation and it can make someone feel like they are token*ized*. Many people with underrepresented identities regularly experience being the "only" in the room. Navigating through spaces as the only woman, the only queer Black woman, the only Latinx person, the only Deaf person can be exhausting—because it takes additional energy, and the chances of experiencing biases and microaggressions are higher.

As the only person like you in a space, you may feel undervalued, treated differently, like an "other" where you don't quite fit in. You may be asked to represent viewpoints of your entire race, ethnicity, gender, disability, religion, age, or other aspects of identity. You may find yourself feeling like you need to be perfect in order to best represent all people with your identity. This can be a heavy burden to carry on top of your daily work.

Stereotype Threat

> The stereotype threat that many of us feel: if I mess up, then I mess up for everyone behind me. It is so much pressure. . . . It was locking me in. I needed that ally, who was a White male, to call that out. But I also needed something that was incredibly special in that moment: I needed him to listen to me, and he did.
>
> **—DAISY AUGER-DOMÍNGUEZ**[2]

Stereotype threat is a risk or fear of confirming a negative stereotype about your identity. With stereotype threat, a person experiences a physiological stress response, combined with consistent intellectual monitoring of their performance, and an emotional regulating of their own negative thoughts. As a result of this additional physiological, intellectual, and emotional response, they have less cognitive capacity to perform the task at hand.

In the first study confirming stereotype threat in 1995, Claude Steele and Joshua Aronson demonstrated that stereotype threat can undermine intellectual performance in Black students.[3] Similar studies have shown gender stereotype threat can impact math and science performance, and age stereotype threat can impact memory, cognitive, or physical performance. Research has shown similar effects of stereotype threat among immigrants and people with disabilities.[4]

Covering

When a person doesn't feel safe, or like they belong in a space or culture, they will often *cover* their identity or a portion of it. Many people will cover an aspect of their identity to avoid bias, microaggressions, or discrimination. Erving Goffman introduced this term in 1963, using the example of President Franklin Delano Roosevelt. FDR was paralyzed from the waist down from polio, yet hid his disability from the public as much as possible. Secret Service agents would block the view of his wheelchair, he held on to advisors or family members as he walked with a cane, he held on to lecterns in front of audiences to appear standing, and entered a room and sat behind a table before other people entered so they wouldn't focus on his wheelchair.[5]

In a study spanning 10 different industries, Deloitte found that 83 percent of people from the LGBTQIA+ community cover a piece of their identity, as well as 79 percent of Black people, 66 percent of women, and 63 percent of Latinx people. Even 45 percent of straight White men cover either their appearance, affiliation, advocacy, or association. The majority of people who cover feel it's important to their long-term professional advancement, yet also feel it is detrimental to their sense of self-worth.[6]

Code Switching

> It's exhausting, but I wouldn't go as far to call it inauthentic, because it's an authentic part of the Black American experience. . . . Code-switching does not employ an inauthentic version of self, rather, it calls upon certain aspects of our identity in place of others, depending on the space or circumstance. It's exhausting because we can actually feel the difference.
>
> —DIONE MAHAFFEY[7]

The term *code switching* comes from linguistics, originally used to describe the alternation of language by a bilingual or multilingual person. In the United States, this might show up as people speaking African American English Vernacular (a dialect of English) at home or with friends, and switching to Standard American English while at work or in other predominantly White environments.[8] A person who code switches often speaks one language at home and in private spaces, and another at work or in public spaces. Code switching can also show up in someone speaking a mixture of two languages like Spanglish (Spanish and English), Taglish (Tagalog and English), Hinglish (Hindi and English), and other hybrid or mixed languages.

Code switching has evolved to also include switching between the ways someone presents themselves in different sociocultural settings—this can include verbal language, body language, clothing, hairstyle, and other attributes. People code switch to fit in, survive (to literally survive in encounters with law enforcement, or to keep their job in the workplace), persuade an audience, show solidarity or affection, share group identity, or reflect social status.

Impostor Syndrome

> I am always looking over my shoulder wondering if I measure up.
>
> —SONIA SOTOMAYOR, US Supreme Court Justice[9]

If you're told your whole life that you're not good enough, regularly experiencing microaggressions that question your expertise, you might begin to believe. A person experiencing *impostor syndrome* diminishes or doubts their expertise, experience, skills, and accomplishments—believing that they are not up for the task at hand and even feeling like a fraud—despite evidence of high achievement.

The term was coined by Pauline Clance and Suzanne Imes in the 1970s.[10] Even Albert Einstein felt impostor syndrome: "The exaggerated esteem in which my lifework is held makes me very ill at ease. I feel compelled to think of myself as an involuntary swindler." Eighty percent of women and 58 percent of men experience impostor syndrome at least once in their lives.[11]

I have experienced impostor syndrome regularly before speaking in front of large audiences, and even as I write this book. Despite decades of experience and expertise in my field, I still have to work to shake the feeling that I don't know enough, I'm not experienced enough, I'm not an expert—as if I've been "faking it 'til I make it" for decades, never internalizing that I've "made it." Much of my life I have worked in spaces where my experience and expertise have been questioned as a woman, consistently having to prove myself over and over. These experiences can cause and reinforce impostor syndrome.

People from underrepresented identities tend to feel this more frequently as we internalize messages from microaggressions and discrimination experienced throughout their lives. We may avoid taking a promotion or stretch assignment, speaking up when we have a great idea to contribute, accepting a public speaking opportunity, applying for a job—and fear may hold us back from being our best when we do. Dr. Adia Gooden has found that we also might overwork to prove ourselves, procrastinate because it feels overwhelming to start or finish a project, and blame our successes on luck.[12]

Impostor syndrome, bias, and discrimination go hand in hand. For example, women apply to fewer jobs than men, and only when they meet

100 percent of the qualifications (versus men who apply when they meet 60 percent of the qualifications). This could be due to impostor syndrome, being socialized to follow the rules, not seeing examples of successful people like us in those roles, and that we are statistically less likely to be interviewed with fewer qualifications due to biases of recruiters and hiring managers.[13]

Emotional Tax

> A history of trauma trains you to always be ready to shut down and step back. Many don't realize the work you put in to step forward and stay present.
>
> **—THEMA BRYANT-DAVIS[14]**

As a result of an *emotional tax* from microaggressions and biases, a Catalyst study found Black men and women feel they have to be "on guard" in the workplace, where they often feel unsafe and are less likely to speak up about important or difficult issues at work.[15]

A single incidence of a microaggression can lead to an immediate 25 percent decline in an individual's performance on a team project.[16] Many studies have shown people who experience regular microaggressions in the workplace experience anxiety, depression, anger, fear, skepticism, fatigue, hopelessness, disengagement, and cognitive disruption—the psychological energy it takes to endure workplace microaggressions can detract from tasks at hand.[17] We've learned that discrimination and microaggressions can contribute to lower self-esteem. This can affect participation, engagement, creativity, energy, efficacy of presentations and collaborations, as well as performance, productivity, well-being, and overall career success.[18] Here's how the emotional tax might show up:

▶ **Lower engagement.** If someone is not feeling safe, respected, or supported in their workplace, they are much less likely to be engaged. This may be reflected in a company's engagement surveys.

▶ **Lower productivity.** Due to cognitive and emotional disruption from discrimination and microaggressions, a person can find it more difficult to do work tasks.

▶ **Numbing, distancing, and stepping back from opportunities.** When not safe or engaged, a person may distance themselves from the team and culture, and avoid situations where they might experience microaggressions.

▶ **Increased turnover.** If someone doesn't feel safe or like they belong, they are likely to seek a different workplace or a different industry.

▶ **Fatigue, burnout, and physical and mental health outcomes.** The emotional tax can wear a person down over time and can impact short- and long-term wellness.

▶ **"Failing up."** A person might earn a leadership position due to hard work and expertise, only to find they are not succeeding in that role. Microaggressions can have high stakes in leadership roles.

Each of these can take a lot of energy, and we are missing out in the workplace if our colleagues are not showing up as their authentic selves. But where exclusion can change someone, allyship can too. Now that we know some of the impacts of biases and microaggressions, and are working to interrupt them in ourselves, it is time to learn ways we can intervene and advocate as allies.

Becoming Someone's Champion

> Where allyship really matters to me is when somebody actually takes my side. . . . There are so many folks who have taken my side, there are so many places where I think to myself, "you did not need to stick your neck out for me in that specific way." And maybe it is big, maybe it is small, maybe it is public, maybe it's not, but for that person it's still sticking their neck out.
>
> —IRMA OLGUIN JR.[19]

Earlier, I shared our Change Catalyst research showing that the top actions people want from their allies are to trust them, give them confidence or courage, and mentor them. Following in fourth place is recommending them for a new opportunity, followed by taking action when someone harms them, amplifying their voice and ideas, and recognizing their work and accomplishments.[20] These are all acts of advocacy.

"Give me confidence or courage" is a countering of the impact of oppression, inequity, and marginalization. People who experience impostor syndrome, stereotype threat, tokenism, and even covering and code switching could use a boost in self-esteem. "Trust me" is a countering of the lack of trust people often experience in their lives, especially people from marginalized groups. *Trust me* to do the job well given my experience and skills, to have the capacity to learn new expertise, and to manage people if given the opportunity. Research shows that when employees perceive that their supervisors trust them, their workplace self-esteem grows—which in turn impacts their overall task performance, job satisfaction, and well-being at work.[21] *Trust me* to succeed, and *mentor me* to help ensure that I do succeed.

When people recall their most impactful experiences with allies, often it is a time when someone took a risk for them, took a chance on them, went out of their way to support them or champion them. We spoke about biases in "Step 2: Do No Harm," including affiliation bias. We tend to be champions of people with whom we share affiliations, whether we share a common school, neighborhood, employer, fraternity or sorority, children's school, religion, or culture. Yet people who are from marginalized and excluded groups often don't have those networks of affiliation. So it's time to rethink who we are champions for, and look for opportunities to champion people outside our affiliations. The following are some ways you can be someone's champion:

Help a person navigate their new workplace and role. If someone is new to a role and a company, it can be difficult and time-consuming to navigate through the new culture, systems, and processes. Share your time with them to help understand how to access workplace programs (like ERGs, benefits, and professional development opportunities), systems (like technology, culture, and company norms), and processes (like performance review processes, how to get promotions and raises, and how to submit time off).

Invite, encourage, and support new leaders. People from underrepresented backgrounds are statistically excluded from leadership roles, with very few of us making it to the top of organizations. As you rise in your career, keep sending the ladder back down and supporting people as they climb that ladder. Use your influence, open your networks, and lend your power so that people have opportunities to rise. Refer people for jobs, promotions, new projects, education, and leadership opportunities.

You might make space for people to step into opportunities by sharing your own platform—ask someone on your team to present a piece of a new project instead of presenting the whole project yourself, take a chance on someone for a new leadership role, even consider stepping back a bit so they can step forward. And then continue to support them so that they succeed in that new role. If there are no leadership opportunities currently in your workplace, create a succession plan for current staff to become leaders when an opportunity arises.

Mentor and sponsor people. These terms are often used interchangeably but there are important distinctions.

A *mentor* educates and guides someone throughout their career. You can become a mentor formally through mentorship programs, which are often structured around a specific topic and time-based. Or informally, by meeting for coffee (physically or virtually) once a month or a few times a year, and making yourself available during key moments throughout someone's career. A mentor can help with career strategy and vision, help develop specific skills needed for career advancement, or offer advice in navigating a key career move.

A *sponsor* backs someone with their power, position, and networks. As a sponsor, you personally invest in and advocate for someone's career advancement. You make key connections for them, advocate for them even when they aren't in the room, give their work greater visibility, and stick up for them in difficult situations.

When focusing on DEI, many people and organizations default to mentorship, which sometimes comes from a bias that people aren't getting opportunities due to their lack of skill and expertise. However, as we know, often people aren't getting opportunities due to systemic barriers and lack of access.

Mentorship assumes someone needs help with building their skills. Sponsorship assumes they already have the skills and just need help opening doors so they can use those skills. For an intern or junior person, mentorship might be life changing. A junior manager with a mentor is 21 percent more likely to reach the next level in their career as someone in the same position without a mentor. Someone who is ready to move forward further in their career often needs a sponsor who can open networks they don't have access to, or use their influence to help them gain recognition, build their reputation, and land a new job, promotion, or raise. A manager or executive with a sponsor is 53 percent more likely to progress to the next level in their career than someone in the same position without a sponsor.[22]

The Power of the Network Effect

When there is an intergenerational impact on opportunity—where generations of parents and grandparents have been excluded from opportunity—often people don't have the networks and affiliations that can open doors to access education, jobs, industry resources, and other key areas that help propel careers. And even with access to those networks, often we are the only person in the room like us. Allies can open doors to these networks, introduce us to people in the room, help us feel like we belong there, and elevate our status to rise in that room.

In addition to opening our network to people who need it, part of allyship is recognizing the limitations of our own network and working to expand it. This can impact our empathy and understanding, and can have real consequences in the workplace. For example, recruiting efforts often initiate from the existing networks of company leaders and recruiting teams—especially when hiring quickly. That can mean hiring teams are missing key networks to connect with untapped talent. When the limitations of our networks are combined with messaging and branding that doesn't attract untapped talent, companies often struggle to diversify their talent pool. To diversify your talent pool, work to diversify your affiliations, widen your network, go outside of your traditional sphere, and build new connections.

We also tend to gravitate to people like us to mentor and sponsor. Research shows that women and men have an equal number of mentors. Yet because women often have other women as mentors, and unfortunately fewer women are in senior levels of organizations, women's mentors tend to be less senior and therefore have less influence in their industries. The seniority of a mentor can impact someone's career more than a person's gender—affecting promotion, compensation, and overall career advancement.[23] Men are 46 percent more likely than women to have a sponsor, so more work needs to be done to build sponsorship opportunities for women.[24]

Get involved in your workplace ERGs or affinity groups. If your company has ERGs and they are open to allies, get involved as an ally. ERG meetings and events are great places to listen, learn, and grow your empathy and understanding. But don't stop there, offer your time to help advance their mission and projects. If you're an executive, consider offering your power and influence to become an executive sponsor. These groups are often notoriously underfunded, so regardless of your position, you can advocate for them to receive the funding they need to do their work well.

Fund and partner with advocacy programs. If you're in a position to donate to an organization personally, that can be very beneficial to an advocacy organization. If you have a corporate budget, consider sponsoring an existing program, partnering on a project with an advocacy organization, or hiring them on a project where their expertise can mutually benefit both organizations.

One of the big issues we often see in our tech industry ecosystem is that corporations with money will develop *new* programs that compete with advocacy organizations who have been doing the work for years. Before you create a new program (e.g., events, internships, apprenticeships, code schools, mentoring, and other advocacy programs), do the research and see if there is an existing program that you can partner with for mutual benefit.

Volunteer. Volunteering is a great way to give back and open the doors of opportunity. You can volunteer to speak at a local middle or high school, volunteer for afterschool programs, or open your workplace doors for tours and events that inspire youth to enter your industry and see it as an opportunity for them.

There are likely lots of advocacy programs focused on DEI in your field—donate your time and expertise to an organization that can use it. Often these organizations need marketing, sales, public relations, accounting, legal, research, data analysis, project management, and business help—give them a steady number of hours or work in a project-based capacity. Do your research to find them and then reach out and list specific expertise and hours you can offer them.

You can also volunteer your time to an internal program at your workplace focused on DEI. Open your networks, give your time for behind-the-scenes tasks that need filling, do whatever they need to accomplish their goals. Be open to serve in whatever capacity is needed—DEI work is not all glorious work, and allies can really help with the work that just needs to get done.

Help build allies. To create the change we wish to see, we need a critical mass of allies in our workplaces and across industries. Use your power, influence, knowledge, and passion to normalize allyship. If you are a person with power and privilege—especially a leader—it's easier for you to bring more allies to the table. So use your influence to create change. Talk about the need for allyship and your journey as an ally, model allyship, and build norms in the culture around allyship.

EXERCISE

Spend a moment thinking about how you might be a better advocate for someone:

- Do you know someone who doesn't have the confidence they should, given their experience and expertise?
- Is there someone who is new to your team who might use support in navigating their new position?
- What about someone in your life who could use a mentor or a sponsor, who could use your influence or networks to broaden their opportunities?
- Do you know someone who is incredible at their work, and could use someone with your influence to advocate for their promotion or another new opportunity?
- How might you help someone along their own path of allyship?

I commit to: _____

_____

_____

_____

_____

7

STEP 5: STAND UP
FOR WHAT'S RIGHT

> When you are doing something that is right, you just do it and take care.
>
> —ALICE NKOM[1]

As we've discussed, microaggressions come in a variety of forms and can have a variety of harmful impacts. They can be incredibly deflating and depleting, and can affect health and happiness of the individual or the group on the receiving end far beyond the microaggression moment. In "Step 3: Recognize and Overcome Microaggressions," we learned that microaggressions come in the form of microassaults, microinsults, and microinvalidations. We can counter these with microaffirmations, micro-interventions, microsupport, microassurances, and microvalidations.

Microaffirmations

> I am in a position where I can be a voice for the disabled community, but I am not the only voice. My responsibility is to bring others alongside with me. To bring another voice that is a different perspective that I just can't bring. I will never be able to bring a Black disability perspective. I will never be able to bring a trans disability perspective. I will bring other people along for that.
>
> —KR LIU[2]

Many trainings and articles about microaggressions focus on how to intervene in the moment. It's crucial that we normalize calling people into conversations about microaggressions and how they can be harmful—and we'll go into ways to do this in the next section. At the same time, there are several other important ways to support people who experience microaggressions, systemic inequities, and other barriers to opportunity.

In contrast to microaggressions, *microaffirmations* are little ways that you can affirm someone's identity, recognize and validate their experience and expertise, build confidence, develop trust, foster belonging, and support someone in their career growth.[3] These can help mitigate and disrupt the harmful effects of historical oppression, systemic inequity, cultural marginalization, and personal biases. The following section provides a number of microaffirmations you can practice.

Take a Moment Out of Your Day to Learn

Get to know people, and pay active attention to their words and ideas. Show genuine curiosity and compassion about the lives and work of your team members and colleagues. Build relationships with them so you can better collaborate together, and advocate for each other. When they are speaking, listen and be fully present. When they are sharing their ideas or experiences, make sure you show compassionate empathy.

Mirror the language someone uses to describe their own identity. Listen and learn how someone pronounces their name and describes their identity; recognize what pronouns they use. Then mirror the language they use to describe themselves—it shows them you're paying attention and that you care about them. (Thank you to Jeannie Gainsburg for sharing this concept with me.[4])

Acknowledge important religious and cultural holidays and life milestones. Keep an eye out for key moments that might be important in someone's life, and recognize them. You might send a quick note to wish someone a lovely Diwali if they celebrate it, or make a note on your workplace intranet—or a public statement—to share about Indigenous People's Day, Transgender Day of Remembrance, National Coming Out Day, Black History Month, Juneteenth, Ramadan, Lunar New Year, Disability Employment Awareness Day, Pride Month, Yom Kippur, Holocaust Remembrance Day, International Women's Day, Hispanic Heritage Day, Deaf History Month, and so on. Also birthdays, births, graduations, congratulations, and weddings can each be nice moments to send a quick note. Make sure you are checking in during harder life moments, too, like deaths, illness, and other key life moments.

Provide Feedback

Provide regular, quality formal and informal feedback. Women, and especially women of color, tend to receive less quality feedback that can help them make any needed course corrections and develop as leaders.[5] This can be due to stereotypes and/or avoidance, where managers are uncomfortable or fearful of how someone might receive feedback. When women do receive formal feedback, it is often about their communication styles (e.g., "too aggressive," "not assertive enough," "your speaking style can be off-putting") rather than actionable developmental feedback about skills ("deepen your knowledge about ____, which will help you ____").[6] Lacking quality formal feedback can impact promotions, raises, and bonuses. And without quality informal feedback, someone doesn't have an opportunity to improve performance between reviews, which can make a big difference in career advancement and overall success.

Establish ahead of time what behaviors and skills demonstrate proficiency and leadership in a role, tie progress and feedback to team and business goals, use the same feedback criteria for everyone in that role, and develop a plan with each person to improve their skills and navigate career progression. Also give people quality feedback on presentations, projects, leadership moments, and other intermittent milestones.

Provide both positive feedback and constructive criticism. When I was in film school working with actors, one of my directing teachers taught us to always give an actor two to three pieces of specific positive feedback before providing negative or constructive feedback. It can make a big difference in their next performance: you build their confidence, help them learn what does work, and then ask them to try something new.

Provide subtle feedback in presentations and idea sharing. Even on a video call or in a meeting when you're not speaking, your facial expressions and body language can be an important source of feedback. Make sure you are fully present when someone is sharing, and think about the message you're conveying nonverbally. You can nod, show you are thinking and taking in their ideas, indicate you want to know more, let them know you're confused by one of their points, and so on.

Actively Include People and Recognize Their Expertise

Work hard to ensure participation from everyone on your team. Solicit ideas and feedback on projects. If you're leading a meeting or a project, explicitly invite participation from everyone, and if someone has not contributed, invite them to share their thoughts either in the moment or afterward.

When someone isn't participating, take notice and support them. A person who is feeling marginalized or excluded, tokenized, or like an impostor may sideline themselves—by not speaking up, not contributing, not showing up. In the remote workplace, people might turn off their video because they aren't engaged, don't have a good home environment to show on video, feel excluded, and/or are burned out from inequities and exclusion (the "emotional tax" we discussed in "Step 4: Advocate for People"). Check in with them to see if and how you can support them.

Acknowledge expertise and skill. People with underrepresented identities often find their expertise and skills are regularly questioned and held to higher standards. Make it a point to acknowledge people's expertise and skills, and solicit their expert opinions and ideas. In one study, nearly two-thirds of women and people of color in engineering reported having to prove their expertise repeatedly, compared to 35 percent of White men: their expertise was questioned, their successes were discounted, they were often pressured to let White men take the lead, and they were disproportionately asked to do office housework.[7] Knowing these biases exist, recognize when someone's expertise and ideas are being questioned and counter that by acknowledging their expertise and giving them opportunities.

Recognize people's achievements. One of the best ways to share with your colleagues, team members, and the world that someone is accomplished is by recognizing their achievements. This could be small ways, like recognizing someone's integral work on a project, or larger public awards and achievements.

Invite someone to speak. If you've been invited to give a speech or presentation, ask if you can bring an expert colleague with you to the stage. Or consider stepping back and recommending someone who isn't often asked to speak. As someone who has done this for years across many events, I have learned that if someone is experiencing impostor syndrome, or if they are dealing with a lot in their life, they may say no or not respond the first time. Try again and let them know why you want their expertise. If you're asking someone to share their expertise at a corporate event or an event that makes a profit, make sure they are paid equitably for their expertise.

Amplify their voice. Use your platform to amplify someone else's ideas and story—this might be in marketing, communications, presentations, reports, verbal storytelling, vendor management and procurement, product and service design, or some other way your platform can elevate new voices and ideas. Make sure you credit those voices and ideas, elevate their status, and share your influence.

[
What new microaffirmations will you incorporate into your work over the next couple of weeks?
]

Microinterventions

> A tremendous ally is someone who has compassion for your displacement, lack of inclusion, or lack of equity, and they speak up and advocate for you whether or not you know it. It goes beyond helping you self-advocate, to the point of someone advocating for you.
>
> —DANNY ALLEN[8]

In "Step 3: Recognize and Overcome Microaggressions," we discussed how to recognize and overcome microaggressions in ourselves. Microinterventions are an important piece of allyship, where we are taking action to recognize and interrupt microaggressions when other people commit them. As an advocate working to intervene, we want to find ways to stop microaggressions before they start, intervene when microaggressions happen, and treat the impact of microaggressions after they happen.

To reduce microaggressions, you have the option to intervene with systemic interventions and direct interventions. You may choose one or both methods depending on your power, safety, and/or presence:

▸ **Systemic interventions.** Preemptively intervene with education, processes, and systems to reduce the possibility a microaggression will happen. And create a system and processes to address microaggressions and treat the impact when they occur.
▸ **Direct interventions.** Directly intervene in the moment a microaggression occurs, to disarm and reduce harm, and educate the

microaggressor. If you don't feel safe to intervene in the moment, you aren't present when a microaggression occurs, or you don't realize a microaggression has occurred until too late to intervene in the moment, there are still several ways you can directly intervene after a microaggression has occurred. Also recognize and treat the impact of microaggressions through direct intervention.

Systemic Interventions

Systemic interventions focus on education, systems, and processes that reduce the possibility that microaggressions will occur, and provide a framework for addressing microaggressions and their impact if and when they do occur. Here are some ideas for developing systemic interventions:

Create a culture that values DEI. Develop and normalize company values that address safety and belonging. Work to hire diverse people who share DEI values—interviews, reference checks, and offsite interactions can help illuminate which candidates are supportive of DEI. Reinforce your DEI values through short- and long-term strategies, authentic messages and action from leadership, integration of DEI metrics into business goals, quality events and training, and programs, policies, and processes that address DEI.

Develop company policies and processes that can reduce microaggressions and biases. Help develop inclusive policies and processes for conducting meetings, hiring, compensation and promotion, performance reviews, events, ideation and innovation, product and services development, and other areas.

Every organization should have explicit codes of conduct, antiracism, and antisexism policies. Ensure these are culturally intelligent—incorporating the broad, intersectional needs of diverse employees; they are well socialized throughout your company; and they are enforced. Your policies and processes should extend beyond the incident—*how can you also recognize and counter the lasting impact of microaggressions and other acts of exclusion?* Design solutions with a diverse group of people with underrepresented identities, including experts in DEI.

Ensure your company is not creating environmental microaggressions as well, by developing policies around safe and accessible all-gender restrooms, mother's rooms, prayer rooms and single-stall or gendered restrooms for prayer preparation, inclusive language and visuals in office decor, accessible and inclusive office spaces for people with disabilities, and events held at inclusive and accessible times and locations with inclusive food and beverages. Marketing and product teams should also ensure their work has an equitable and inclusive lens.

Develop DEI learning opportunities. Help people to learn about and explore allyship, empathy, and inclusive leadership through training and other learning and development resources. As we learned earlier, training on biases and microaggressions doesn't work in isolation. However, holistic training can be very effective if part of a larger program strategy that addresses DEI at the systemic level.

Develop informal learning opportunities as well. Encourage people to take genuine interest in others and to learn about each other's unique stories and experiences through events, safe facilitated conversations, and even informal "watercooler" settings. Bridge the empathy gap.

Normalize advocacy on your teams. Work together to call out unintended biases and microaggressions, and collectively learn about what may cause harm. Share this book with your team, discuss each chapter together, and consider doing the exercises together.

If you are someone from an underrepresented background, telling your story might help someone learn about biases and microaggressions, and how they can harm. It also might help someone with an underrepresented identity know they are not alone. This has been hugely powerful in the #MeToo and Black Lives Matter movements, where women and Black people have used social media and internal office channels to tell their colleagues about their stories.

And all of us can help someone else see what's possible as an ally by telling our story of learning and growth—and even sharing our mistakes. As an example, artist Laura Park found out about the death of 15-year-old Latasha Harlins in an old news story. Latasha was shot and killed by Soon Ja Du, a convenience store owner who had assumed she stole a bottle of orange juice. Soon never went to prison. "I hadn't meaningfully considered the amount of privilege I have—the privilege to be shocked," Laura wrote. She used her platform as an artist to share her learning and activation as an ally. She published her personal exploration and plan for allyship in a full-page spread in the *New York Times*. "How can I divest from systemic racism? How do I invest the amount of privilege I hold in anti-racism . . . ? The assignment I've given myself is to put it in my life—on my schedule. In my day. To make time and space."[9]

Moving Through the Initial Fear

The next section on direct interventions is often one of the most difficult pieces of allyship for people I've trained. It requires presence, curiosity, and courage. So let me tell you a little story first.

Just a few years ago, decades into my adult years, I started riding motorcycles for the first time. When I was growing up, I never dreamed of riding motorcycles—in my mind, based on what I learned from society and family, it was dangerous and something outside the realm of what women do. But then I met Wayne, who is now my husband, and rode on the back of his motorcycle . . . and eventually realized I was done riding on the back and wanted my own.

I took a class where I passed the test for my motorcycle license, but I don't know why they let people go from taking a weekend class using cones in a middle school parking lot, to having a license to ride in the real streets and highways of San Francisco! The first time I rode on the highway, I got on the highway by mistake about two days after I bought my first Ducati Scrambler. The fear was real.

It was the fear of getting into an accident, as well as the chaos of fast city traffic just before rush hour. Combined with the fact that on a motorcycle there are many additional things to worry about. Each limb has a different role: your right hand controls the front brake *and* the throttle, your left hand controls the clutch, your left foot controls the gear shifter, your right foot controls the back brake, and your body and arms together control steering. All of that is a *lot* to think about, and in the beginning it is very mechanical as you think about every action separately. All while navigating traffic on two wheels. It was scary, but I made it safely.

So here is what I've learned: it gets easier. Way easier. Now I don't even think about what all my hands and feet are doing, I just do it. I trust myself, and I trust the bike. I took an intermediate course that made a big difference in my riding, and I practiced, practiced, practiced. I am smart and wear protection, and I trust my educated instincts. Figure 7.1, where I'm standing on my motorcycle (it's not moving!), symbolizes my achievement.

FIGURE 7.1   I Overcame My Fear of Riding a Motorcycle
[Photo Credit: Erick Davidson, @erickd]

I have worked hard to get past fear. I believe fear is the biggest barrier for learning to ride motorcycles and learning to be a good ally. Fear of taking risks, fear of doing something wrong. Instead of holding my breath out of fear, I am learning to breathe through the fear. I breathe into the curves and they are so much smoother. If I come up against an obstacle, often the worst thing I can do is let fear control me and slam on the brakes—I breathe and take it in, move around the obstacle, and then keep going.

Sure, there is some risk in being a good ally. (But not nearly the risk there is in riding a motorcycle!) When you're feeling fear, I encourage you to breathe into it. Ask yourself what you're fearful of. If it helps, list what could possibly go wrong, and work through what you would do in each of those situations. Usually it isn't that bad. Honestly, what we should be fearing most is what happens if we don't step up as an ally. Because generally, there is a lot more harm when we don't step up as an ally, than when we do.

Direct Interventions

If you are in the presence of a microaggression as it is occurring, you can make a big difference by intervening. With direct interventions, we move from bystander to what people call upstander: standing up when you see something that is harmful or belittling. This can be the most difficult way to intervene, but often the most impactful, because you are recognizing and validating a person's experience when they are confronted by a micro-aggression, stopping it from continuing to create harm, and educating the microaggressor as well as any other people in the room.

Direct interventions are much easier and more effective if you are focusing on inclusion as a company, and you have actively enrolled your team in working together to eliminate microaggressions. Consider implementing some of the systemic interventions we discussed earlier in addition to these direct interventions: for example, go through allyship or antimicroaggression training together, work to enroll and hold each other accountable for reducing microaggressions as a team, and develop values, rules, and processes that you can point to when intervening.

The following sections offer some methods for direct microinterventions, as well as some scripts you can practice. A few general things to think about:

Resolve to stand up against expressions that can be harmful. We discussed several examples of verbal microaggressions in "Step 3: Recognize and Overcome Microaggressions." If you see or hear these, do something, say something. Follow the guidelines in the next section.

Interrupt interruptions and airtime inequity. When you notice that a few people are dominating a conversation or someone is being interrupted, do something or say something to give everyone the airtime they deserve.

Echo and attribute. Often people with underrepresented identities' ideas are dismissed and then brought up by someone else later and championed. Other people may receive credit for their ideas. To counter this, echo the words of the person who initiated the idea in the first place, and attribute the idea to them. This can change someone's career over time: giving credit on projects can lead to promotions and leadership opportunities, for example.

Recognize and address nonverbal microaggressions. Nonverbal micro-aggressions can often create inequitable power dynamics. If people are not paying attention, ask them to pay attention. If someone is physically hovering over another person in a way that is shutting them down, find a way to get them to move: invite them to a whiteboard, hand them coffee, ask the group for a quick break. If a person pushes someone's wheelchair without permission, pats a Little Person on the head, or touches a Black woman's hair—educate them on why that can be offensive.

Remove environmental microaggressions. If you see microaggressions manifested in the physical or virtual space, call attention to them and work to dismantle them: racist mascots; sexist presentations or presentations that lack diverse representation; lack of a mother's room or prayer room in the office; lack of a safe all-gender restroom; lack of diverse representation on the company website, or in product, marketing, and advertisements; or company events that are not at inclusive times, aren't accessible, don't offer inclusive food and beverages, or don't have diverse representation.

Take action as an ally around important environmental microaggressions happening outside the workplace that might affect your colleagues: racial injustice, issues around women and LGBTQIA+ rights, immigration issues, violence against religious minorities, and so on. Usually environmental microaggressions are addressed by people from underrepresented identities alone—and there is real power in allies noticing and doing something about it as well.

Actions You Can Take to Respond to a Microaggression in the Moment

If you are working to intervene in the moment, there are different ways to respond depending on someone's intent:

- ▸ If someone's intent is *not* to harm, you have an opportunity to pause, name and disarm the microaggression, educate the micro-aggressor, and treat the impact. While good intention in no way negates the harm caused by a microaggression, it is an indicator that someone may be open to education.
- ▸ If someone's intent is to harm, education may not help. Pause, name and disarm, and treat the impact. Focus on ensuring the

safety and well-being of the person experiencing the microaggression. If someone intends to cause harm, there may be something deeper happening that needs to be addressed—consider reporting this person to people operations or human resources (HR).

When you can't determine intent, assume good intent (which is usually the case). And whether or not harm is intended, if you don't feel safe, work with a colleague or supervisor on an intervention.

Table 7.1 shows this general framework for responding to a microaggression.

TABLE 7.1   How to Respond to a Microaggression

Intent of the Microaggression	Microintervention Action				
	Pause	Name and Disarm	Educate	Report	Treat the Impact
Not to cause harm	✓	✓	✓	*	✓
To cause harm	✓	✓		✓	✓
In either case, if you don't feel safe . . .	Work with a colleague or supervisor to determine the best interventions together.				✓

If someone continues to use microaggressions after repeated microinterventions, you may consider escalating it to a supervisor.

Start with a pause. If you decide to intervene in the moment, pause the action right away. I learned this from my colleagues Tiffany Jana and Michael Baran: "Most [subtle acts of exclusion] continue to occur because subjects and observers get stuck trying to figure out what to say, and by the time they have some ideas, the moment has passed and they just let it go." When you observe a microaggression, all you have to remember in that moment is a simple phrase to pause, which gives you time to collect your thoughts about what to say next. Come up with whatever phrase works for you—such as "hold on," "pause please," or "can we stop for a moment, please?"[10] Derald Wing Sue and Lisa Beth Spanierman suggest using the term "Ouch."[11] If you're doing this work as a team, consider agreeing on a term you can all use.

If someone experiencing a microaggression has already paused and intervened on their own behalf, support them, demonstrate they are not alone in recognizing the microaggression and its harm, and back them up if needed.

Name and disarm. Explain why you paused the action. Naming what happened shines a light on microaggressions that are often invisible and can help the person experiencing the microaggression feel recognized. Microaggressions can have significant power, and the situation can be pretty toxic—as an ally you can help diffuse that power disparity. You can do this by disagreeing, interrupting, redirecting, describing the potential impact, or describing your own thought process or experience as an ally.

Educate. When working to educate, appeal to the person's values and beliefs, build empathy, help them understand the difference between good intent and harmful impact, and let them know how their words and actions can create harm in the moment and over time through accumulations of microaggressions. You could also share with everyone in the room that you all benefit from an environment without microaggressions: improving team health and happiness, increasing engagement levels and productivity, providing opportunities for growth and leadership.

We don't want to punish or shame anyone. Shame is not a good motivator for change, it can often backfire and turn people away from change. Show empathy, assume good intent, and give the microaggressor space to take in new information without being judged or criticized.

Behavior change takes time. Don't expect someone to immediately change their ways in the moment, but you can start the process of change and continue to support their growth. As Sue and Spanierman write, "Over the long run, microinterventions plant seeds of possible change that may blossom in the future."[12]

Report. If the intent was to harm, education may not be effective. Rather than continuing the discussion beyond disarming, consider reporting the incident to a supervisor and/or HR. If you are a supervisor, get to the root of the issue to see if it can be corrected—check with your company HR procedures to be sure you're following them. In some cases, there may be some deep racism, sexism, ableism, or other prejudice that you are not able to correct, which could cause harm to the team in other ways as well. In this case, consider whether or not this person should be a part of the team.

Similarly, if someone shows a pattern of microaggressions where they are continually causing harm to people despite direct interventions, a solution needs to be reached through HR, coaching, and/or systemic interventions.

Treat the impact. We don't talk enough about this final step: treating the impact of the microaggression. Impact is incredibly important, because as we have learned, microaggressions can have significant short- and long-term effects on someone's health and work. We'll spend more time on how to do this later in this chapter.

The many things to think about can feel overwhelming at first, as you're working through the mechanics, wondering if you're really seeing a microaggression, and worrying about saying or doing the right thing. Most of the time, when we are bystanders and don't work to intervene and treat the impact, we are causing the most harm by aligning ourselves with the microaggressor and allowing harm to continue to happen. So gather the courage to do *something*—whether it's in the moment or after the fact.

Use your instincts to determine the extent of your action in the moment. You may decide to skip the education piece—perhaps you'll be shaming someone by actively pausing a whole group and trying to educate them, or there is a power differential and you don't have the power to fully intervene, or you don't feel safe. If so, perhaps postpone the education piece until you can meet one-on-one or escalate to a supervisor or HR, and just work to diffuse the situation in the moment. You can do this by changing the subject and moving the group's attention away from the microaggression, or by giving the floor to someone who has been interrupted or has had their idea taken from them.

If the microaggression is a racist, sexist, ableist, heterosexist, or other discriminatory comment or action—that is absolutely not OK in the workplace, and as allies we need to put a stop to it. If you choose not to intervene in the moment, do find a way to intervene afterward. Allies intervene to stop the cycle of harm.

Table 7.2 includes several sample scripts for intervening.

TABLE 7.2 **Intervention Scripts to Stop Harm from Microaggressions**

Direct Microintervention Scripts

Sample Script	Example
Interrupt interruptions: "_____ hasn't had a chance to get a word in, let's hear them out." "I'd really like to hear what _____ has to say." "We've heard a lot from just a couple of people in this conversation, does anyone else on the team have thoughts or ideas? I'd love to hear them." Pause after saying this—a little extra silence is OK and gives people time to gather and share their thoughts.	You're in a meeting and someone is being repeatedly interrupted. "I'd really like to hear what Sam has to say. I know they have been trying to say something for a while, let's hear their thoughts." You're in a meeting and realize there are a few people from underrepresented identities that haven't said a word, while people with overrepresented identities have dominated the conversation. "I am noticing that several folks haven't had a chance to speak yet. Serena, Sam, Leigh—do you have ideas about this? If so, I'd love to hear them."
Echo and attribute: "Yes, I'm so glad you're bringing back to _____'s idea here. That would really have an impact, what a great project for them to take on and lead." "Right—I remember when _____ brought that up a while ago, I love it. _____ did you want to share what you had in mind?"	In a meeting a week or two ago, Sally had an idea for a new product that was questioned and then pretty quickly dismissed. In the meeting today, Gerard has a new idea that is remarkably similar, and people on the team are liking it. "Right—I remember when Sally brought that up several days ago, I love it. Sally, I know you put some work into this, but didn't get fully heard—did you want to share more about your idea, or perhaps talk about it more in our next meeting?"
Call people in to give their full attention: "Hey everyone, I know we've had a long day but let's really focus on this presentation. _____ has a lot of expertise, and this is important." "I'm noticing that we are not fully present here, can we take a moment to put down our phones and let go of other distractions?" "Hey team, we've been at this for a while. Let's take a five-minute break. When we come back, please arrive with video on ready to give your complete attention."	Ruchika is new to the team and giving one of their first presentations in front of the group. You realize very few people are paying attention and Ruchika is stumbling a bit. During a break in Ruchika's thoughts, you might say, "Ruchika, excuse me, I just want to pause a moment because I'm noticing we're not all fully present for you. I know we've had a long day, everyone, but let's really focus here. Ruchika has a lot of expertise, and this is important."

(continued)

TABLE 7.2   Intervention Scripts to Stop Harm from Microaggressions *(continued)*

Direct Microintervention Scripts

Sample Script	Example
Shine a light on unfairness: "We seem to be questioning _____'s expertise a lot, but we know she is an expert in her field. I am confident she will lead this project to success. Let's move on." "I noticed you said _____ about Amy and _____ about Jack. They are doing similar things, but you've described Jack in a positive light for it while doing the opposite with Amy. Can we go back and reevaluate?"	After interviewing a few candidates for a senior role, your team is debriefing the candidates. When comparing candidates' answers to an interview question, a Black woman's response is referred to as confrontational while an Asian man's response to the same question is described as confident and headstrong. "I noticed you said Raquel's response was 'confrontational' while John's response was considered 'confident.' They both disagreed and made valid points, but you've described John in a positive light while doing the opposite with Raquel. Can we go back and reevaluate?"
Ask for clarification: "Could you say more about what you mean?" "I'm not sure I understand, can you say that in a different way?"	In the tech industry, often people brush off someone's opinions or discount their expertise because of a technical hierarchy: "Whatever, they're not technical they don't get it." You could interject: "Could you say more about what you mean?" This gives someone an opportunity to catch their mistake and rephrase.
Separate intent from impact: "I suspect you didn't realize this, but when you _____, it can be hurtful/offensive because _____. Instead you could _____." "I'm sure you didn't intend this with what you said, but here's how it might impact someone _____."	When I was on a global executive team, we were discussing hiring more women at the company, and a principal said, "Yeah, I'm OK hiring women but I don't want to lower the bar." There were several women in the room at the time. I could have said, "I suspect you didn't intend this, but that statement can be offensive because it sounds like you're implying women are not as qualified as men."

(continued)

TABLE 7.2   **Intervention Scripts to Stop Harm from Microaggressions** *(continued)*

Direct Microintervention Scripts

Sample Script	Example
Share your process: "I noticed you _____. I used to say/do that too, but then I learned _____." "I'm learning that by saying _____, it can be harmful because _____. You might try _____ instead." You can also say you were not comfortable with a statement rather than putting the focus on the person experiencing a microaggression: "What you just said made me uncomfortable. I have learned that many Black people find it offensive when someone says _____, because _____. I know you care about being an inclusive leader, so as a suggestion you might rephrase and say _____."	Say you're talking about the importance of diversity in your company, and someone says, "I don't see color, I treat everyone the same." You might say: "I used to say that too, because I thought it was a compliment. But then I learned that it can negate someone's unique identity and experience." You might add: "Also, diversity is important at this company. We want to have diverse people with unique experiences at our company—there's an important business case for this. So seeing and valuing someone's unique identity is important."
Disagree, and challenge stereotypes: "I don't find that funny because _____." "I don't agree with what you said because _____." "That is a negative stereotype of _____ (group of people). I think it's really important when we're focusing on inclusion to be aware of stereotypes, and make sure we are evaluating individual skills and expertise."	I have a friend, Isis Anchalee, who started her engineering career at a company that featured her in a hiring ad for their company. Many people on Twitter and other social platforms got angry and said they hired models not real engineers. Even after they learned she was an engineer, they said that she didn't *look* like an engineer. A reply could be, "That is a negative stereotype of women, that they can't be engineers. People of every identity can be good engineers. Isis is a skilled engineer whose expertise should not be questioned simply because she's a woman." Isis and her colleagues actually started a hashtag after that moment, which went viral globally: #ilooklikeanengineer.
Refer to rules or values: "That is against our meeting guidelines, where we stated _____." "That's against our values, or our antiracism, antiharassment, or antibullying policy, which states _____."	Someone in a meeting tells a joke about a disabled person, and a few people laugh. You could say, "I want to bring us back to our core values as a team, and one of those values is _____. I would really appreciate it if we could all hold true to these values, and that our words reflect them."

(continued)

TABLE 7.2 **Intervention Scripts to Stop Harm from Microaggressions** *(continued)*

Direct Microintervention Scripts

Sample Script	Example
Redirect, protect, and address one-on-one: "Can I take the conversation in a different direction? I have a project I'm working on and could use some ideas _____." "OK, let's move on. _____ I want to schedule a one-on-one to talk about this further." "How about we talk about the next item on our agenda? I have something I want to share with you _____, can we schedule some time together today or tomorrow?"	If interventions don't work in the moment, or if you're not feeling safe to intervene, steer the conversation in a new direction. You can address it privately afterward, or work with your supervisor or colleague to come up with a solution to address the microaggression together. "How about we talk about the next item on our agenda?" And privately to the microaggressor: "I have something I want to share with you, Robert, can we schedule some time together today or tomorrow?"

EXERCISE

These are just a few examples of the many ways you can work to intervene when a microaggression occurs. Spend a moment reading through Table 7.2 and the microaggressions listed in "Step 3: Recognize and Overcome Microaggressions," and create your own version of the scripts that you can use when microaggressions come up in your workplace. When you have these ready, it is much easier to intervene in the moment. Then put your scripts into practice.

Intervening Through Collective Action

Sometimes this work feels challenging because we believe we are alone in this process. Microinterventions are often much easier when we have a partner or a group of people working together through collective action. When Barack Obama took office as president of the United States, just one-third of his top aides were women. They often found they were being left out of important meetings or when in those meetings, they weren't being heard. So they started to amplify, echo, and attribute each other:

when one woman said something, another would echo the idea and attribute it to her, forcing recognition for her contribution. President Obama took notice and began calling on more women in the meetings.[13]

> *Think of a common microaggression you've observed in your workplace. Whom could you work with to intervene through collective action?*

Actions You Can Take to Directly Intervene After the Microaggression Moment Has Passed

If you decide not to intervene in the moment, you aren't present when a microaggression occurs, or you don't realize a microaggression has occurred until too late to intervene in the moment, you can still intervene after a microaggression has occurred.

If you're still in the meeting, you can say something like, "You know, something happened earlier that didn't sit well with me." Describe what happened, and then use one of the scripts to disarm and educate.

You can also talk with the microaggressor privately. It's often best to begin by appealing to their values, for instance, "I know you care about inclusion, so I was hoping you might be open to some feedback that I think could help." Or simply ask if they are open to some feedback. Then describe what happened, and discuss the impact of microaggressions—especially how this microaggression may have impacted a person or group. Use one of the scripts to educate, for instance, "I understand you didn't intend this, but here's how it might impact someone ____. As someone who is committed to inclusion, you might reframe by saying, ____."

Often someone will get initially defensive as they work through the issue. Be ready for them to say that they didn't intend to, for example. The sidebar "How Do I Respond When Someone Says . . ." provides some talking points to address this argument. An ideal outcome from this conversation would be for them to have a plan to learn/relearn and avoid future microaggressions, and to genuinely apologize to the person or group for their mistake.

How to Respond When Someone Says:
"But I Didn't Intend It That Way" or "Aren't We Being Too Sensitive?"

When someone learns about a microaggression that they have committed, often they will respond defensively. Their sense of reality is being questioned—a reality that has been illuminated through their bias and resulting microaggression. This unlearning and relearning can be a difficult and uncomfortable process.

Questioning the harm is often a first response: "But I didn't intend it that way," or "Aren't we being too sensitive?"

- First, I'm glad you didn't intend harm—that's the first step. If you are not intending to harm someone, it's your job to make sure your words don't harm them. When you learn that your words have created harm, it's important to apologize, listen to why, and learn to use different words and actions.
- The impact is key. Just like in an argument with a friend or family member, if you say or do something that hurts someone, even if you didn't intend to hurt them, you still have to do the work to repair the relationship. Intent can help people forgive, but you still have to rebuild trust and respect.
- This is not about being too sensitive, this is about a real need to correct the continued oppression and inequity that can come through in the little things we say. Our words and actions can be harmful. (We have been discussing the real, life-changing impacts of oppression, inequity, marginalization, and microaggressions throughout this book—refer to statistics and research if it's helpful.)
- If someone is shutting down at work due to repeated microaggressions, that affects us all. It affects productivity, profitability, innovation, and our collective happiness at work.

The worst harm from a microaggression can come from denying someone else's harmful experience by centering it on your own intent. Trust people's unique experiences. Use your curiosity to build compassionate empathy. Really work to understand what they are going through—not what you are going through, or what you imagine you would go through in a similar situation. What matters is what *they* are going through and what *you* do about it as an ally.

Recognize and Treat the Impact

Most trainings, books, and tools that discuss intervening do not include this last crucial step to repair the harm: we must recognize and treat the impact of microaggressions. We know microaggressions can be incredibly depleting and can affect health and happiness. The effect often lasts far beyond the microaggression moment.

Check in privately with the person who experienced the microaggression. Genuinely listen to how they are doing. Validate their experience. Let them know you hear them, appreciate them, saw what happened, and that you were not OK with it.

Microaggressions can be exhausting and impact someone's courage, confidence, and self-esteem. Additionally, when a microaggressor is confronted, often they will attempt to deny and invalidate the harm a microaggression can cause. This gaslighting (see "Step 2: Do No Harm") can be very harmful, causing someone experiencing the microaggression to feel further belittled, question their own experience, blame themselves, and/or internalize the microaggression to the point where they may believe it to be true.

Make sure they know they are a valuable and valued member of the team, you value their skills and experiences, and that their ideas are important and needed. Continue to show this through your actions for weeks, months afterward. Microaffirmations and becoming someone's champion (see "Step 4: Advocate for People) can be a great way to improve confidence and self-esteem, and continue to address the effects of microaggressions beyond the immediate impact.

Have a conversation about what support they could use from you. And if appropriate, ask them if you can improve the way that you intervene in the future to better support them. Often someone experiencing microaggressions could use time to heal—time away from work and away from the microaggressor. If you're a supervisor, allow them this time.

After a microaggression or series of microaggressions, you may also consider helping a microaggressor rebuild trust with the person or people they have harmed. This happens over time, often with education and/or coaching for the microaggressor, an apology, and a psychologically safe environment to have open communication.

Ensure everyone's safety and well-being, and work to ensure it doesn't happen again. People want allies to have their backs; they want them to be trustworthy and follow through on promises. Work to create systemic interventions as well as continued direct interventions, so that your colleague has a safe and happy work environment, where they can focus on their work. *How can you advocate for them and with them so that microaggressions stop?*

Also consider what else you might need to do to counter the effects. *Did the microaggression affect an opportunity, for example—and if so, can you help them gain new opportunities?*

EXERCISE

Practice putting microinterventions into practice with the following scenarios.

Practice Scenario 1: In a brainstorming meeting, you observe that an individual is talking considerably more than everyone else in the room. Sometimes they are even interrupting people, particularly women.

- *Once you notice, what do you do?*
- *What if they continue to interrupt, what would you do next?*
- *What might the impact of this be on the people who have been interrupted?*
- *How would you go about treating the impact of these microaggressions?*
  - *What would you do immediately?*
  - *What would you do (if anything) following the incident?*

(continued)

After you're finished, you might select another microaggression from "Step 3: Recognize and Overcome Microaggressions" and answer the same questions.

Practice Scenario 2: After a Black team member gives a presentation, you hear someone on your team tell him, "Wow, you were so articulate!"

The Black team member tells the person it was not an appropriate comment. In response the person says, "That wasn't my intention at all. Why are you so sensitive?" The Black team member is clearly uncomfortable and stops responding.

- *How might you intervene in this situation? Get specific about what you would say and do.*
- *How would you go about treating the impact of this microaggression?*
  - ▸ *What would you do immediately?*
  - ▸ *And what would you do (if anything) following the incident?*

Practice Scenario 3: Your company has just hired a new senior leader who is Latina. In a team meeting, someone on your team rolls their eyes when they hear the news. You notice this.

- *What do you do in response?*

Then they tell you, "Of course she got the job."

- *How do you respond?*

You learn this person believes the new hire got the job because she is Latina.

- *Now how do you respond?*
- *What could the impact be on the new hire, even if they weren't in the room?*
- *What might you do to mitigate any potential impact?*

Here we're working to stand up for what's right as an advocate for each other. We're not saviors and this is not charity. We're helping correct years of oppression and marginalization by listening and learning what people need, intervening when they could use an ally, standing beside them, supporting them, and championing them. The next step is to lead the change, working with people with underrepresented identities to correct inequities.

STEP 6: LEAD THE CHANGE

> Leadership is about empathy. It is about having the ability to relate to and connect with people for the purpose of inspiring and empowering their lives.
>
> **—OPRAH WINFREY**[1]

We have a legacy of inequitable and marginalizing systems, processes, and cultures in our companies, across our industries, and throughout our society—passed down through the generations before us. And it takes all of us working together to correct them, so that we all have the opportunity to work, lead, and thrive in stronger, happier workplaces and communities.

In our research, we found many allies are motivated to do this work to become better leaders—whether leading the change for ourselves, our businesses, our colleagues, our friends and family, or the next generation. We become better leaders by becoming inclusive leaders: growing our empathy and courage, refining our individual work to be more inclusive, building team norms around DEI, and collaborating to create more equitable and inclusive systems, processes, and cultures.

You can lead the change from wherever you are in your career—this chapter is for us all, whether we're managers, directors, executives, or just beginning our careers. The following pages include individual actions for becoming better leaders, actions for team leaders, actions teams can take together (consider working together as a team to address these), and actions that can be taken by anyone on a team. It's not meant to be a checklist so much as a lifetime menu. Work to build your capacity for change: one or two steps now, then a few more when you're ready, and continue to take additional steps over time.

Lead with Empathy and Allyship

> Any leader has to be, in my opinion, an Ally in Chief.
> —KATE JOHNSON[2]

Empathy is a crucial leadership skill—people with empathetic colleagues and leaders report more effective collaboration and creativity, higher team morale, and better performance. Demonstrating empathy for each other also increases employee engagement, job satisfaction, retention, customer satisfaction and loyalty, business growth, and profitability.[3] Yet we are often missing empathy in our workplaces—72 percent of CEOs say the current state of empathy in the workplace needs to change.[4] That same study found 96 percent of people in the tech industry feel their colleagues have difficulty demonstrating empathy.[5] Considering the impact tech products have on the world, this lack of empathy could have a negative impact on many of our lives.

If showing empathy doesn't come easy for you, it's OK—it can be learned.[6] As a young girl, I grew up in a family that didn't really discuss or show feelings for each other. That made it really difficult for me to have or show empathy for other people. I approached people intellectually rather than emotionally, and often missed opportunities to be present emotionally for friends and family when it really mattered. In my late teens and early twenties, I actively worked to cultivate my empathy through reading, learning how facial expressions and body language convey emotion, getting to know myself through writing and later meditation, asking questions of myself and others, and deeply listening. Over time, the awkwardness of sharing emotions gave way to a genuine passion for understanding my own emotions and those of others—and it turned into a career of empathy-building through filmmaking, social marketing, behavior change, change management, and DEI. I now train and coach leaders to build empathy in themselves and across their teams.

Meet yourself where you are and work to grow and show your empathy. And keep in mind that when we have conflict or are interacting with people different from us (people we may view as our out-group), our empathy tends to reduce—which means we may have to remind ourselves to expand our in-group and step into our empathy in these situations. We also have to work harder to tap into our empathy when we're stressed or on a deadline.[7] Building your empathy muscle will not only help you become a more effective ally, but it will also help you become a more effective leader.

In "Step 2: Do No Harm," we looked at how to show empathy. The following are some ways to continue your journey to lead with empathy and allyship:

Grow your self-understanding, build new relationships with people not like you, and demonstrate empathy toward them. Good allies know themselves well, which helps them listen, learn, and act with empathy. You can grow your self-understanding through coaching, therapy, journaling, meditating, or other practices that generate self-awareness and mindfulness. Spend time with people from different backgrounds and identities and really get to know them and understand their experiences—through travel, social media, working on community projects, attending events, scheduling informal meetings, or some other way. And the best way to show your empathy is to take action as an ally: listen with empathy, communicate your understanding verbally and nonverbally, and then use your empathic learning to take action on someone's behalf.

Build your emotional and cultural intelligence. Emotional intelligence (shortened EI or EQ for emotional quotient) is a term that dates back to the 1960s from psychologist Michael Beldoch.[8] The idea was made popular by Daniel Goleman, who describes it as a combination of *personal competence*: self-awareness and self-management or regulation of your own emotions, plus *social competence*: awareness of other people's emotions and the ability to manage and build relationships. Goleman found that EQ accounts for 58 percent of performance in most jobs, and 67 percent of the abilities necessary for leadership performance.[9] I've worked with several leadership teams that have focused on EQ growth as a team, and they tend to be more self-aware, open to new ideas, collaborative, and solution-focused when it comes to DEI and allyship. They lead with empathy.

Cultural intelligence (CI or CQ) adds an additional dimension of understanding cultural contexts, and working effectively across different cultures in the workplace. While much of CI work focuses on global cross-cultural teams, it's equally important to do this whether you have a local, regional, or global workforce that is diverse across gender, race, ethnicity, disability, age, religion, sexual orientation, and other identities, as well as geography. You can work on EI or CI by reading or individually working with an executive coach, and/or through group training and coaching.

Develop a growth mindset. Psychologist Carol Dweck has shown in her research that our mindset about learning and intelligence can shape our creativity, empathy, achievement, and career success. Someone with a growth mindset believes that anyone can develop intelligence and skills through hard work, dedication, and opportunities to learn. With a growth mindset, leaders embrace challenges, learn from criticism, persist in the face of setbacks, put in effort as a path to mastery, and find inspiration in the success of others.

Leaders with a fixed mindset, in contrast, believe intelligence is static and inherent—they tend to avoid challenges, ignore feedback, give up easily, see effort as worthless, and feel threatened by others. They also view other people as fixed, which can reinforce anchoring and confirmation bias, stereotypes, and other biases about them.[10] *Do you have a fixed mindset about yourself, or someone on your team?* Work to have a growth mindset about yourself, as well as others—be open to challenges and opportunities, and open the door to opportunities for other people to learn and grow.

Develop inclusive leadership skills. There are several models of inclusive leadership you might explore—one that has had a lot of traction with several of my clients is Deloitte's "six signature traits of an inclusive leader":[11]

1. **Commitment.** Develop personal values that include DEI, and stay true to those values by committing to action. These values might

relate to fairness, respect, kindness, justice, and a belief in the value of diversity for your team and business.

2. **Courage.** Show vulnerability and humility, acknowledge your personal strengths and weaknesses and work on them, and admit mistakes. Also, be brave as an agent of change, take responsibility for challenging the status quo, do the work to create needed change, and hold yourself and others accountable.

3. **Cognizance.** Become self-aware of your biases, and mindful of situations where you're most likely to be biased (e.g., when you're fatigued or stressed). Self-regulate to ensure biases don't influence your decisions and processes. Be mindful of fairness across your individual and company policies, processes, and structures. Assess fairness in outcomes (like compensation, promotion, attribution, and recognition equity), processes (ensuring transparency, consistency, accuracy, and inclusion), and communication (using respectful, authentic, transparent, and inclusive explanations).

4. **Curiosity.** Be open to different perspectives, and tolerate ambiguity. Have a thirst for learning and understanding: fill the gaps in your knowledge, open yourself up to new ideas and experiences, and engage in respectful listening and conversation without judgment. Accept that uncertainty is inevitable in the search for personal growth—don't get caught up in the fear of uncertainty, instead use your courage to remain open to change.

5. **Cultural intelligence.** Seek to empathize and gain knowledge about people with identities and cultures different from your own, embrace unique working styles without judgment, and adapt your behaviors to work well across cultures. In my studies in sociocultural anthropology, I learned the power of cultural relativism: that no one culture is superior to another; each is equally valid with its own systems, language, and beliefs. Remember not to center on your own cultural experience as the norm, but rather develop the mindset that many different cultures are the norm.

6. **Collaboration.** Give people autonomy, trust them, and empower them to fully contribute. Ensure teams are deeply diverse and inclusive, and create safe environments where every person on your team has a voice and is comfortable speaking up. Leverage the power of diversity to make better decisions, and make sure you remove any process biases that can become barriers to innovation.

In their research on management strategies that predict inclusion, Catalyst found that inclusive leaders *lead outward*—through accountability, ownership, and allyship—and *lead inward*—through curiosity, humility, and courage. These inclusive leadership skills lead to greater innovation, higher employee engagement and retention, and increased problem-solving abilities.[12] Similar themes emerge across the growing body of research on inclusive leadership.

> **Spend a moment to write down a few ways you might work to improve your leadership skills to lead with empathy and allyship.**

Choose Courage

> It's not fear that gets in the way of daring leadership; it's armor. When things get tough, do we lean in to vulnerability and get curious, or do we self-protect in ways that move us away from our values?
>
> **—BRENÉ BROWN[13]**

The work of allyship can be challenging at times. Yet we have all come across challenging new ideas and concepts many times in our lives. Like driving a car, riding a motorcycle or bicycle, or learning a new skill in our field, it takes some time to grow this new strength. It takes courageously trying new things, being vulnerable when we don't always know the answers, learning when something doesn't work or we make a mistake, listening to feedback and people's unique experiences, and holding true to our values as we continuously move forward.

Leadership requires courage, and what Brené Brown calls removing our armor: that defensiveness and inauthentic posturing we think protects us, but really holds us back. Beneath our defensiveness and posturing is sometimes shame, guilt, or discomfort. With allyship, sometimes this shame and guilt arises when we realize we have benefited from unfair privilege, we have been using language that has created harm, and perhaps we have not done enough to correct systemic barriers that exclude and oppress people. We might find ourselves resisting to protect ourselves from the uncertainty, vulnerability, or discomfort that comes from questioning what we thought we knew. Our armor might be to say we don't have time for allyship, it's too difficult, we don't know enough, or that our colleagues are "fine" without us.[14]

Do you have any unresolved feelings relating to this work? If so, I highly encourage you to work through them so they don't hold you back.

Along my own journey to lead the change, I resisted—and perhaps resented—the idea that I had unfair privilege. I have worked hard while facing many systemic barriers, I told myself. And yet when I really investigated, I realized that while this is true, I still have a great deal of privilege. I resisted Black and Indigenous women saying that their intersectional experience as women was different than my own as a White woman. Early in my life, I resisted the existence of racism, firmly believing we lived in a post-racial world. I have also resisted the notion of "White feminism," "ableism," "White supremacy," and other inequities that surface even within DEI work. Now instead of resisting I recognize it and work to make power and privilege equitable.

> For a lot of us, we don't give ourselves permission to even explore what our biases are, because we worry if I actually go there and start to reveal the darkness that I hold within my mind and my body around other people, that will affirm I am a racist. So it is easier to say "I am not racist.". . . This is a really important process of exploration that, rather than fearing what we hold, we approach it with love and empathy and compassion for ourselves.
>
> **—RITU BHASIN**[15]

Leading the change begins with our own self-awareness and internal work. If you find yourself resisting someone's experiences, doubting a new concept you learn about allyship or inclusion, denying privilege or inequity—challenge yourself. Be curious: look inside yourself and find out why you're resisting. This internal work is a big piece of allyship and will give you tools (both skills and stories) to help create change in other people too.

Above all, allies take action. We can get stuck in learning because we're afraid to take action or action makes us feel uncomfortable. Be courageous and move beyond learning alone; make sure you have a bias toward action. You may not always get it right, and that's OK. Use your courage to step out of your comfort zone, take risks, lend your power, and give your time, resources, and expertise to correcting generations of inequity and marginalization. Change happens when we catalyze a series of individual behavior changes, new cultural norms, and deliberate system and process improvements.

Rethink Your Individual Work to Be More Inclusive, Equitable, and Accessible

> You have a lot of power to make changes, and you have the power to share your power, so that other people can help make changes.
>
> **—MADELENA MAK[16]**

You have the power to lead the change in your own work, whatever your work entails. Each of us can spend some time and thought to improve our individual work to be more inclusive, equitable, and accessible—whether we work in marketing, communications, product, service, creative, customer satisfaction, procurement, administration, data, legal, engineering, research, sales, finance, strategy, innovation, HR, DEI, or something else. Model allyship in the work you do and how you go about doing it:

Share your allyship process with colleagues, with friends, and even publicly. Let people know what you're working on as an ally, whether it's ungendering your language, learning a new skill, deepening your knowledge of a culture, minding your microaggressions, or another practice you've learned. You can also ask people to give you feedback or hold you account-able to your commitment. When you do this, you model courage and growth, and normalize allyship.

Make a plan to incorporate more inclusive, equitable, and accessible processes into your daily work. Use the following exercise to think through how you might improve the daily individual work you do to embody allyship.

EXERCISE

Carve out 15 to 20 minutes in the next few days to sit in dedicated time, thinking through how you might make your work more inclusive, equitable, and accessible. Eliminate distractions and ensure you spend this time with your thoughts—and don't put this off, this can be very powerful! Consider using one or two of the following questions to help guide you:

- Are you getting input on your work from diverse people with diverse experiences? If not, how might you change that?
- Is accessibility in your DNA? If not, how can you build accessibility into the core of your work?
- How are you going about your work in an antiracist way?
- How can you correct and counter biases in what you do and how you do it?
- How might biases play a role in your decision-making, and what can you do to change this?
- When you look at a new brand concept, marketing piece, or product, is it created by diverse people, and are you viewing it through the lenses of diverse experiences? If not, what can you change?
- How are you getting to know the diverse experiences of your customers or users?
- Do you include diverse representation in presentations, communications, and other materials? Does this include broad, intersectional diversity across gender, race, ethnicity, disability, age, sexual orientation, religion, and other identities?

(continued)

- How might you use your platform to amplify voices, recognize and illuminate inequities and their impact, motivate allies, or otherwise activate change?
- Are you designing and developing ideas with a diverse team? If not, how could you work to diversify your team (or advocate for diversifying your team)? And in the meantime, is there another way to involve people from diverse identities in the development of your work?

If you have a colleague who is working to become a better ally, you might talk through your ideas together.

I will commit to: _____

_____

_____

_____

_____

_____

_____

_____

Once you have your commitment, create an actionable, time-based plan to incorporate your commitment into your work. When and how will you evaluate success?

Keep working to answer these questions as you progress in your lifelong journey as an ally.

Build Team Norms That Cultivate Allyship, Equity, and Inclusion

Inclusiveness starts with a spark to do better. That spark lives inside leaders, almost like a pilot light. It's always there, ready and waiting to create a bigger flame. . . . The hardest part about becoming an inclusive leader can be that initial work to switch the pilot light on, to become aware that you are already equipped with the ability to make a difference and to learn how much your efforts are needed.

—JENNIFER BROWN[17]

You already have what my friend and colleague Jennifer Brown calls the "spark" to become an inclusive leader, and most of the tools to make it happen are within you. There are a number of ways you can work to build new culture and team norms that facilitate change in your workplace. If you are a manager or working to become one, what you do and how you do it can make a big difference: Catalyst found that 45 percent of employees' experiences of inclusion are explained by their manager's inclusive leadership behaviors.[18]

Develop an Inclusive Team Culture

Think back to "The Role of Allyship in Diversity, Equity, and Inclusion," where we discussed the Stages of Inclusion. Work to ensure you are cultivating a culture where diverse identities and perspectives are *welcome*, where people feel *safe* to be who they are and fully contribute, *engaged* because they are contributing to the team and company's success, *committed* because leadership cares about their professional growth and well-being, and feel they *belong* because they are valued, connected, and supported.

In a study called "Project Aristotle," Google researchers conducted an in-depth analysis of what makes an effective team. They found that effective teams are interdependent and collaborative, and work together to plan, solve problems, make decisions, and review progress. In order for this interdependency and collaboration to thrive, the most important quality of a successful team is psychological safety: where team members feel safe to take risks and be vulnerable in front of each other.[19] Psychological safety is the foundation for engagement, commitment, and belonging.[20]

Create Psychological Safety on Your Team

Amy Edmondson defines *psychological safety* as "a climate in which people are comfortable expressing and being themselves."[21] Help create an environment where people on your team feel psychologically safe to do the following:

Express and be themselves. People who feel safe don't feel the need to cover, code switch, or otherwise hide a portion of their identity; they are comfortable expressing and being themselves. Eliminate out-groups so that everyone on the team feels they are an equal member of the team. Consider introducing shared values to broaden the group's feeling of belonging together. Make sure you follow through on commitments to reduce biases and microaggressions. And prioritize DEI on your team, develop shared goals around DEI, and enroll everyone in working to achieve these goals.[22]

Take risks, make mistakes, and share concerns without fear of retribution. On teams that work well, people are not intimidated, reticent, or consistently stressed. For this to happen, leaders and colleagues need to be open to new ideas, provide thoughtful feedback, and be available for support and collaboration with all team members. Approach people with a growth mindset, and view mistakes as growth opportunities. If you're a leader, take responsibility for team risk and share credit for team successes.[23]

Feel confident to speak up. When people are fearful that they will be humiliated, ignored, or blamed if they speak their minds, they shut down. Too many leaders don't tolerate disagreement or even the raising of uncomfortable issues. Become the kind of leader where people around you are confident about speaking up. Work to have equal distribution of speaking time across all team members in your meetings, where each idea is heard and respected.[24]

Know their unique skills and talents are valued and utilized. People thrive on teams where their expertise is valued rather than questioned or disrespected, their unique skills and talents are utilized, and their contributions are aligned with team goals. If you are a manager, empower and trust team members to make decisions, help team members understand how their work relates to the larger goal of the team, and always provide formal and informal recognition for accomplishments as well as feedback. Create a team norm for recognizing contributions and major milestones. Often cultures overvalue the leadership style of the CEO or the dominant culture, and undervalue other equally important styles of leadership. Instead, recognize and value different leadership styles.

Trust and respect colleagues. Teams thrive where people feel they are not judged, everyone respects the expertise of their colleagues and can rely on them to meet goals and timelines, and all team members are encouraged to take reasonable risks. Create time and space for team members to get to know each other, build empathy for one another, and develop a collective intelligence together. Consider holding team get-togethers like lunches or afternoon meet and greets, offsites, volunteer outings, or other activities that build informal connections.

Foster Engagement, Commitment, and Belonging

There are a many ways to cultivate a more inclusive team culture that fosters engagement, commitment, and belonging. Secondary to psychological safety, Google found that effective teams develop dependability ("I can rely on team members to complete quality work on time"), structure and clarity ("I understand my role, plan, goals, and processes"), meaning ("I find a sense of purpose in my work"), and impact ("My work is making a difference for the team or organization").[25] The following are a few actions you can implement:

Develop shared vision and goals. Create clarity, structure, and meaning by developing a shared vision for the team's collective work and connecting it to a larger impact. *How does your team's work contribute to a better world, or a key company priority? And what are your collective goals in achieving this vision together?*

Establish mutual accountability and process clarity. From your team's collective goals, individuals should create their own goals, timelines, and plans of action. Strive to make the goals transparent and measurable, discuss processes and review progress together, overcommunicate any changes, and take responsibility for achieving your own plan as a model for your team.

Run inclusive meetings. In many workplaces, team culture and collaboration center around meetings—whether you're working in an office together or working remotely. Here are some things to consider in developing an inclusive environment in your meetings:

▸ **Develop an agenda and ground rules.** A great way to generate meeting norms around minding microaggressions and giving equal distribution of speaking time is to build this into some basic meeting ground rules. Also create an agenda and share it before the meeting, so people can prepare to contribute. Enforce the ground rules during the meeting to ensure all voices are heard and respected.

▸ **Preplan for accessibility and accommodation.** Ask ahead of time if anyone needs accommodation. If you know someone on your team has accessibility needs, don't make them ask for it, just make it happen—whether it's providing an accessible meeting place, a sign language interpreter, a PDF version of documents for their screen reader, or something else. Meetings should take into account different time zones and parenting needs, and if you are offering food and beverages, make them inclusive (vegetarian, vegan, kosher, halal, gluten free, dairy free, etc.).

▸ **Communicate the meeting's purpose.** Help everyone in the room understand the main objectives of the meeting so the team has a collective goal and knows how best to contribute. Take a moment to let each person know why you've asked them to join the meeting.

▸ **Capture notes during the meeting.** Develop a meeting notes template and a location where all notes are stored so the notes can be referenced later. The note taker(s) should work to capture all ideas and attribute them, and document key decisions. It's crucial to rotate this responsibility for notetaking, as office tasks like these tend to disproportionately fall on people with underrepresented identities.

▶ **Make space for the quiet ones.** Introverts and people with developmental or intellectual disabilities may need extra time to think through their ideas before speaking them. While brainstorming, you might ask people to write down their ideas before you discuss them. Make it a norm to allow for pauses in the conversation where new voices can enter. Invite people who have not contributed to share their thoughts—perhaps ask them if they have any thoughts to add, if we've missed anything, or if they agree with the group's conclusions so far. If you know this is an area they are passionate about, you might say, "I know this is an area you're passionate about and wanted to be sure you had an opportunity to share thoughts if you'd like." Don't force it; allow people to contribute after the meeting if they aren't ready yet.

▶ **Conclude the meeting with clear next steps and outcomes.** Discuss and capture decisions made in the meetings, as well as next steps following the meeting. Clearly establish any responsibilities coming out of the meeting, and share the notes with all attendees.

Encourage career growth in individual team members. If you're a manager, talk to your team members about their career aspirations and create transparent pathways to growth. Outline concrete pathways for promotion, leadership development opportunities, compensation raises, and bonuses. *What are the metrics for achieving a promotion, and what milestones must be met along the way? What are the feedback loops a team member can rely on to determine if they are adequately reaching those milestones? What are their opportunities to shine and be recognized for their achievements, and how will this play a role in promotion, compensation, or bonuses?* These processes are often very opaque in organizations, and can lead to unfair and biased decision making, as well as low morale and engagement.

Support physical and mental health. To foster a healthy team, it's important to support individuals in all their dimensions, including their physical and mental health, as well as any individual needs. Hopefully, your organization offers inclusive benefits that address physical and mental well-being, such as gym, martial arts, yoga, or meditation benefits; coverage for conventional, traditional, and alternative medicine; coverage for women and LGBTQIA+ health; mental health resources; paid time for volunteering; flexible hours; ability to work from home; parental leave; sabbaticals; floating holidays so people can incorporate their own cultural holidays; and professional development and learning opportunities. Managers and people teams should help everyone understand and navigate these benefits. Develop team norms that encourage physical wellness, taking time off from work, and openly discussing mental health—especially during challenging times for individuals, groups, the company, or the world.

Enroll Your Team in Taking Action as Allies

In addition to modeling allyship in your own work, consider enrolling the team in modeling allyship together. This will engage team members around allyship and may also create an example for other teams in the organization to emulate. Here are some actions you can take:

Integrate empathy and allyship learning into your work culture. Group learning can take the form of weekly or monthly training, facilitated conversations, and events. Many companies have formal offsites dedicated to DEI and allyship. More informal learning activities could include volunteering together; informal or formal sharing of customs, holidays, and cultural milestones that people on the team experience; and having a learning portal that includes articles, books, podcasts, training, and other materials.

On some of my past teams, we rotated monthly sharing in our all-hands meetings: for 10 to 30 minutes, a person shared a bit about something that they felt passionate about related to their identity. This can go a long way to building empathy for each other. You can also share a new term or concept related to DEI each week in your team meeting. I also highly recommend having an informal place for team members to share resources—our company has a "DEI Articles to Read" Slack channel, where anyone can share an article or paper about a topic related to DEI.

In both formal and informal learning environments, make sure you are creating a psychologically safe space free from harassment, bullying, and microaggressions. Create and enforce a code of conduct or ground rules, and make sure there is someone monitoring discussions who is trained in how to take action if discussions become unsafe.

Make commitments as a team to reduce biases and microaggressions. A good way to develop team commitments is to experience a training together on allyship, biases, and/or microaggressions, and then follow up as a team to commit to taking individual and collective action. You can also read this book together. Afterward, debrief as a team and spend some time creating your own individual goals, plus collaborate to develop a few collective goals you'll work on together.

As a team, give each other permission to normalize intervening when biases and microaggressions occur. If you're leading a team, prime your team to be aware of biases and microaggressions when they are hiring, giving performance reviews, and other moments that can have a big impact on someone's career. And forgive yourselves and each other when you make mistakes, make apologies and corrections, and commit to having a growth mindset.

Empower change agents. If you're a manager, give your team time, resources, and recognition for work they do to create change in the organization. This may be participating in ERGs or affinity groups, mentoring, training, or working with the DEI team. This is important work. Often companies will allow team members to devote 10 to 20 percent of time to these efforts, or pay them overtime or bonuses for doing DEI work.

Build Accountability for Diversity, Equity, Inclusion, and Allyship

Once you make a commitment to learning and growth, hold yourself accountable to consistent learning and action. *How and when will you check in with yourself?* You might consider having an accountability partner with whom you share your goals, and hold each other accountable. This can work really well if your partner is in a lot of the same meetings, and can point out to you—publicly or privately, your choice—when biases or microaggressions show up in your words and actions. You can also ask your team to help hold you accountable to your commitments.

If you've developed goals as a team, also ensure you build in checkpoints and hold each other accountable. If you are a manager, tie individual performance to company values and team goals around DEI. And of course, don't wait until the performance review to check in on these, check-ins and incremental feedback should always happen between reviews as well. If someone is repeating microaggressions or consistently not hitting their goals, work with them, and hold them accountable for making improvements.

If your executive team has made a commitment to DEI and allyship, help hold them accountable as well. Often executives prioritize this work when they hear from their teams that it's important. We have a number of clients and partners who originally reached out to us because their employees told them it was time to take the next step. When providing feedback to leaders, be kind, use specific examples, and ask to see action.

Adopt Inclusive Ideation and Decision-Making Processes

Work with your team members to reduce bias in approach through inclusive design and development processes. Decision-making and problem-solving are more innovative and inclusive when done with a diverse group of people, so put together a diverse team to develop solutions.[26] Build inclusive team norms for projects using the methods shared earlier in this chapter, and adopt an inclusive process where solutions are created collaboratively. Here are some ideas that have proven to be effective:

First, align the group on the goal and outcome. Establish with everyone at the beginning of the work that your collective objective is to come up with a truly inclusive and equitable solution. Then share what all goals and desired outcomes are—if you can, co-create the goals and outcomes together.

Establish ground rules and prime your team to reduce biases. Ideally, create ground rules ahead of time, and ask the group if they have any to add. You can find several examples online. Ask everyone to keep inclusion in mind, go beyond their initial intuition, ask questions that help surface any biases, and remember to work together toward the bigger, inclusive goal.

Create a safe space for everyone to contribute, take risks, and know their voice is heard and respected. Allow time for open brainstorming, where everyone's voice and ideas are heard. Make space for introverts by having people write their ideas on sticky notes or some other written format, and sharing them at the same time. Check in at the end to ensure everyone feels they have been heard and included in the decision-making process.

Humanize. Whether you're looking to hire someone or to create a new product line, humanization and empathy are key. Without this, we fill in the gaps with our preconceived ideas of who a person is and what they want—opening ourselves up to biased judgments. If you're making a hiring decision, ensure you're getting to know the human not just the résumé or test—think of how the person can add to your culture, and what new experience they can bring to help you better innovate.

When building a new product or strategic direction, as Steve Blank says, "get out of the building and talk to people."[27] To build with the human in mind, create a team that looks like the people you're building for, and talk with potential customers or users. Diverse human problems require diverse human solutions.

Normalize the acknowledgment and countering of biases. Hold each other accountable for staying true to your shared goals and outcomes, and call each other in when you notice biases. (Review common biases in "Step 2: Do No Harm.") Ensure you are mitigating against groupthink and confirmation bias by encouraging alternative perspectives, allowing space for healthy disagreement, and examining risks. As you come up with your solution, list the assumptions you are making, test those assumptions through data and interactions with real people, and ask pointed questions. Who *wouldn't* this solution work for? You don't have to design for everyone, but it's important to know whom you're leaving out. Check your assumptions against data as well. If you find your solution isn't inclusive and equitable, rework and retest until it is.

Roll out the solution in an inclusive way. When you've created your solution, recognize the diverse team that worked together to achieve it. For new hiring and other team-focused decisions, show empathy for candidates, and value their time and unique experiences regardless of the outcome.

As you roll out new products, ensure you're meeting your target customers where they are through inclusive outreach strategies. For new strategies, ensure you are collaborating to implement the strategies as well. Build in feedback mechanisms with your team, candidates, and customers so you can improve your processes and solutions.

EXERCISE

Pick a project you are working on or just about to embark upon, and use the frameworks discussed in this chapter to design an inclusive ideation process. You may want to design this process with a few other colleagues (ensure it's a diverse team), so you have their support and expertise as you create this new process.

Use this inclusive design process throughout the length of the project. Be open to improving the process along the way with input from your team. When the project is complete, debrief with the team.

- *What was successful?* Remember to celebrate the wins!
- *What was challenging?* Acknowledge and give space to all perspectives.
- *How could we improve?* Make sure you create a plan for implementing some of these opportunities for improvement, get individual commitments to enact that plan, and hold yourselves accountable for following through.

Here are some things we learned and want to ideate on next time:

_____

_____

_____

_____

_____

Collaborate with Your Team to Improve DEI

Work together as a team to improve your team systems and processes to be more diverse, equitable, and inclusive. Doing this work together can build empathy and psychological safety in addition to developing long-term systemic and culture improvements. Ensure you are dedicating adequate time and resources to doing this work effectively. The following paragraphs offer some ideas:

Enroll your team in hiring diverse team members. If you're a manager, share why having a diverse team is valuable, and enroll your team in the collective vision for a more diverse and inclusive team. Then establish some team goals (for example, goals for hiring from different demographics, goals for considering diverse candidates, or goals for finding a pipeline of more diverse candidates). Support each other and hold yourselves accountable for achieving these goals. A pre-step to this may be to redesign your hiring process to be more diverse and inclusive (see "Step 7: Transform Your Organization, Industry, and Society).

Collaborate with your team to improve your team systems and processes together. Have a design meeting to develop your team's DEI plan—there are several ideas to consider in this chapter and the next. Choose a few key areas where your team believes there is high need and impact. Develop an action plan together to address these goals, and work to achieve them. Make sure you build in checkpoints along the way, elicit help from professionals if needed (this could be HR or DEI folks in your company, or consultants), and hold yourselves accountable to build, test, and deploy new solutions.

Offer to pilot a new DEI program in the organization. Often DEI folks in organizations are under-resourced in terms of staff, and/or they spend a lot of their time convincing teams to do the DEI work. They might welcome an offer to pilot a new training program, process change, or system implementation with your team. Let them know your team is open and ready to take on something new and be a resource for them.

Volunteer together. A great way to reinforce DEI values and build team cohesion is to volunteer together. Discuss as a team a few local, national, or global organizations that work to improve DEI in your field. Hone in on one or two together, and commit to volunteering as a team—it could be a two-day, three-month, or yearlong engagement depending on your availability and the organization's needs. You might mentor, teach, or use your collective skills to help an advocacy program improve their product, service, marketing, accounting, or other area where your expertise fits with their needs. Be someone they can rely on to get things done, and be open to doing whatever they need, including admin work. If an organization doesn't share opportunities to volunteer on their website, don't be afraid to connect with the organization via their contact@ email, or email the founder directly. Most advocacy organizations have needs for volunteers!

[
What actions will you take to lead the change with your team?
]

STEP 7: TRANSFORM YOUR ORGANIZATION, INDUSTRY, AND SOCIETY

Y ou're learning, unlearning, and relearning. You're taking steps to do no harm. You're taking action as an advocate and standing up to do what's right. You're helping lead the change in your work and on your team. The next step is to help create much-needed systemic change in our workplaces, in our industries, and across society. The following pages contain several different ways you can help to create a world that aligns with your values and motivation for change. Whether you work at a large organization or a small business or startup—or you're retired and wanting to give back—there is a lot you can do.

Create More Equitable and Inclusive Systems and Processes in Your Workplace

> We have got the systems that are at play: judicial, the employment systems, the education, the housing, the financial, the list goes on and on. What's at the root of those systems is power. System upon system, structure upon structure. It is an interconnected web, . . . You have to really understand all of the interconnectedness, and understand your place in it, and then take action.
>
> **—RACHEL WILLIAMS[1]**

We discussed several systemic interventions that can reduce biases and microaggressions in the workplace in "Step 5: Stand Up for What's Right." Not all inequities and forms of exclusion are micro, however; we also have macroaggressions and systemic inequities in our workplaces. The norms around systems, processes, and even culture were often created in different generations, before there was a focus on a diverse workforce. As a result, these don't work for everyone and often need to be re-envisioned. We all have a role to play in fixing these systemic inequities in our workplaces.

While it would take another book to deeply address the many methods for improving DEI, the following are some ideas for you to consider. (If you'd like to learn more, we have some training and toolkits at changecatalyst.co to deepen your understanding in several of these areas.) Your next step is to choose what change you want to implement, collaborate with the folks that can help you create the change, and ensure everyone is held accountable for creating the change.

There is an action plan template at the end of this chapter. I recommend choosing one or two projects that would be quick wins, as well as some more long-term projects that will create significant systemic change. This way you can celebrate achievements, show success, recognize members of your team for the hard work they put in, and also invest in deeper change. Use your inclusive leadership and decision-making skills to ensure the team is empowered and inclusive, courageous, collaborative, committed, culturally intelligent, cognizant of biases, and curious about diverse viewpoints. Don't get caught up in planning for too long; choose a lean, agile, or kaizen process to learn, build, test, deploy, and iterate. You may not get it all perfect the first time; make sure you're building in feedback loops and allowing the project to evolve over time. Here are specific things you can do:

Work to develop an inclusive hiring experience for candidates with under-represented backgrounds and identities. Raise the bar by committing to increase your diversity beyond the status quo of your industry, and hold yourself and your teams accountable for significantly improving year over year.

Do an audit and reboot of your hiring process to remove biases and microaggressions and make it more inclusive and accessible, so you're not missing out by excluding people. Map out your hiring experience and redesign it with and for diverse talent from outreach to job descriptions, screening, interviews, offer, and onboarding. Remember all you've learned about historical oppression, systemic inequities, cultural marginalization, biases and microaggressions, and their impact—and design a complete hiring experience that centers around welcoming, safety, and belonging for everyone, especially people with historically underrepresented and excluded identities.

Make sure you and your team are not blaming the pipeline for a lack of diversity; do the work to find the diverse pipeline that is out there through expanding your networks. And work to improve the pipeline. Since most industries have excluded people for some time (it's an intergenerational problem), you might consider developing programs that bring in new talent early in their careers—like apprentice or internship programs—and grow leaders from within your company. You can also recruit talent from adjacent industries.

Diversify the board and key leadership roles. You might consider making diversity a requirement of your board or adopting a policy of interviewing at least three to four quality candidates from diverse, underrepresented identities for each role (an updated version of the Rooney Rule).[2] Note that interviewing just one candidate from an underrepresented identity for a role can significantly decrease their chances of being hired, so do the work to find several good candidates.[3] If there are no open positions currently, create a succession plan—it may include associate board members and/or future leadership teams.

Diversity in most organizations dwindles at leadership levels, due to biases and inequities throughout people's careers. Audit your compensation and promotion processes to ensure they are equitable. It's important to do these together: one of our clients audited their compensation a few years ago, and was pleasantly surprised that it was nearly equal across gender. Then they took one more step to audit their promotions, and found severe inequities: on average, women were remaining in the same position for three years longer than men. They launched an internal investigation and found the issue centered around performance review biases, lack of quality feedback between reviews, disparities in how projects were assigned, and in-group/out-group experiences on the team (e.g., project assignments often formed in the bar where several of the men met after work to watch football games). The company immediately instituted a multifaceted approach to address the inequity.

The best way to develop diverse leaders is to develop them from within. Establish transparent and flexible professional growth and leadership development pathways. You might offer executive coaching, tuition reimbursement, mentorship opportunities, volunteer roles with leadership positions, and speaking and writing opportunities. Of course, make sure these programs have a focus on inclusive leadership.

Align your brand, messaging, and storytelling with your inclusive values. Conduct a cross-platform brand audit to see how your brand and messaging align with your DEI values. You might develop a style guide that includes diversity and accessibility, and a quality control process that includes auditing for diversity and inclusion. Make sure your images and messaging are diverse and inclusive, you're thinking about proactive messaging during times when it's important to diverse employees and customers, and of course, that you are taking action on what you say in your messages. Consider using your brand platform to counter stereotypes and other biases, and speaking out against systemic racism, sexism, ableism, heterosexism, eurocentrism, and other forms of discrimination.

Build inclusive and ethical products and services. A good portion of my work is in the tech industry, which has notoriously built products that have violated ethics, developed solutions that lacked inclusion and accessibility, and launched artificial intelligence and other products that are racist and sexist—which have caused loss of life and injustice.

Encourage your organization to design and develop products and services with a diverse team that is representative of your customers. If that's not possible right now, bring in diverse consultants and potential customers to be part of the design process. Build accessibility into your work from the beginning, as it's much easier to do it as part of the process than retroactively. And audit your products and services before they go out the door to ensure they are ethical, accessible, and inclusive, and that the images and messages you're conveying reflect diversity and inclusion.

Earlier in her career, my colleague Nancy Douyon found a gap in the product design process at Google and worked to fill it by leading research on end-to-end experience for new product launches with ethics, accessibility, and inclusion in mind. Nancy said this about the importance of her work:

> In the work I do as a UX researcher, designer, engineer—I help build technology from this corner of the world for the entire world. I'm impacting so many countries and it's all from the perspectives of first world America and Silicon Valley. It's imperative with the work that I do that we get other insights in, so that we're building audits that are more inclusive and globally minded versus just building something that only works for white male Americans.
>
> And I have seen in my work, time and time again, products that have had so many issues—whether it's a dispenser that can't pick up your skin color, or whether it is some AI that's labeling Black people as gorillas, or a chat bot that's running around finding Jewish people and insulting them. . . . We want to make sure we understand the perspective of the audience that we're trying to build better solutions for.[4]

Enact an inclusive and transparent reporting and supporting process. I've worked in the entertainment and tech industries, which are both notorious for harassment. When I worked on films and TV, sexual harassment was prevalent—while on set I experienced regular pats on the butt; arms thrown around my waist; strokes on my arm or hair; comments about my figure, my skin, or my hair color; questions about my sexuality or sexual history. . . . Daily. Hourly. On every set I worked on, harassment and sexualization was prevalent.

This experience combined with seeing women directors not given the same chances as men, and women writers not given the same credit or pay as men, contributed to my leaving the industry. Even though I was really good at it and gaining success. As so many people with underrepresented identities do—I left because I didn't want to fight every . . . single . . . day. There was no reporting structure; in fact, the people I would have reported harassment to were the same people harassing.

Later in my life, I was sexually harassed as an executive and while it was resolved, it was the straw that broke my ability to thrive at the company. That was when I stopped wanting to be there and began making plans to leave. Many people who have been harassed leave the workplace, because it can eat away at your ability to do your work well, tear up your confidence, or at the very least be very distracting. It can be incredibly demeaning when your colleague thinks of you as a sexual object rather than as a leader.

To fight harassment in your organization, create a transparent reporting process, with multiple people available to report to, where people can trust that real action will be taken and there will be no retaliation. But don't stop there. Work to create a process for supporting people as well—after someone experiences harassment, bullying, microaggressions, systemic inequities, what will you do to repair the impact? They may need a break, to be reassured that they are valued, the ability to transfer teams, a safe space to talk about their experience, therapy, executive coaching, or other methods of support. Provide those opportunities for healing, and don't assume what someone needs—ask.

Make sure your supply chain is diverse. A supplier diversity program can be incredibly impactful in the local community, supporting small women-, minority-, veteran-, disabled-, LGBTQIA+-owned businesses to grow and thrive. Vendors are often chosen based on networks, perpetuating the same network bias issues as our hiring practices. There are several companies doing this well who are publicly sharing their impact, and many templates for this are available online.

If sustainability and overall social impact is important to your company as well, combine impact measurements and ask vendors to report sustainability, social impact, and DEI efforts. Like all DEI programs, make sure you are measuring and holding teams accountable for achieving supplier diversity goals. You might share your commitment to supplier diversity—and even give some publicity to your suppliers—on your company website to share how you are doing the work.

Ensure your physical spaces and events are diverse and inclusive. Our surroundings can help facilitate welcoming, safety, engagement, commitment, and belonging—or they can do the opposite. At one company I worked with, a breastfeeding colleague had to sit on a stool in a corner of the dusty supply closet next to the mop and bucket to pump breast milk, carefully coordinating with the office manager and taping a handmade sign to the unlockable door so she wasn't disturbed. A Muslim colleague had nowhere to pray in the office, so he "made up for" his daily prayers when he got home, but always felt guilty about it. Neither colleague felt a sense of belonging in the company.

Wayne, my team, and I have been hosting diversity and inclusion events around the world for many years, and we've found little, thoughtful actions can make a big difference in how someone feels—whether in the office or at an event. Here are some of the things we've learned:[5]

- ▸ Put together a diverse design team.
- ▸ Design marketing materials and an outreach strategy that are inclusive and find people where they are.
- ▸ Have a code of conduct that protects people, and enforce it.
- ▸ Organize inclusive content and diverse speakers.
- ▸ Create informal gathering spaces as well as quiet spaces for introverts and people with developmental and intellectual disabilities.
- ▸ Choose a space that is accessible by public transit and easily accessible for wheelchair, walker, and cane users. Provide areas designated for wheelchair users at the front, middle, and rear of the event space, and make sure pathways are wheelchair accessible (ADA compliant in the United States).
- ▸ Post signage that is inclusive of people with disabilities (low enough for people in wheelchairs to see, high contrast and large font sizes for people with low vision and color blindness, available in braille for people who are Blind).
- ▸ Design decor that reflects DEI.

- Arrange live captioning, sign language interpreters, and volunteer guides for people who are Blind—without people having to ask, because inclusion is walking into a space and belonging, not having to ask to belong.
- Train volunteers and vendors to use inclusive language, prime them to filter their biases and microaggressions, and teach them how to support people with disabilities who need accommodation.
- Arrange for a mother's room, prayer room, and all-gender, accessible restrooms.
- Launch a diverse, inclusive, and accessible website and agenda (available in PDF). Make sure you ask if people have additional accessibility needs.
- Offer inclusive snacks, beverages, and meals (vegetarian, vegan, kosher, halal, gluten free, dairy free, and so on, with ingredients labeled).
- Provide a ticket option that is free (scholarships can work), and a sliding fee scale.
- Cultivate a diverse supply chain.
- For online events, most of this still applies. In addition, choose an event platform that is inclusive and accessible—most are not yet. Just like in-person events, hire live captioning (no, AI can't do this well yet)—and sign language interpreters if you can. Offer accessible PDFs of your agenda, and describe your slides for people who are Blind, Low Vision, or on the phone. Make sure to build in breaks for the captioners and interpreters.

You can apply most of the preceding principles to your office design as well as events.

Work to build systems and processes that don't currently exist or need to be redesigned with DEI in mind. Take a leadership role in developing programs to address DEI. You might put together a DEI committee or advisory board, and keep in mind that coalitions work best when they comprise a wide diversity of people across offices, regions, and departments. Use the inclusive decision-making processes to guide the group.

I recommend starting with an assessment: measuring what matters through surveys (demographic, inclusion, and engagement), listening sessions, and one-on-one interviews. Also consider working with your HR or people teams to do an equity audit across compensation and promotion. Once you know the state of DEI, you can begin to prioritize, develop goals, and create an action plan for achieving them.

Create Change in Your Industry

> If you are an ally . . . particularly to persons of color, you should be trying to promote institutions, environments, policies, that would be protective of that community. You should be a friend, generally to that community.
>
> —DR. KEVIN SIMON[6]

As we have seen throughout this book, there are so many ways that inequities appear in our systems, processes, cultures, words, and actions. Collectively we have the power to change this beyond our workplaces as well. Here are a few examples:

Convene industry leaders and work toward change together. One of the most impactful steps you can take in any sector is to convene industry leaders and collectively commit to creating change, then hold each other accountable. It can be powerful for leaders to come together formally or informally to discuss the state of the industry, share learnings, brainstorm solutions, and build best practices. You don't have to be an industry executive to convene leaders. When we first started this work at Change Catalyst in 2014, as entrepreneurs and consultants we worked to convene tech industry leaders to focus on solutions to DEI. We did it by asking people to come together, developing a shared purpose, and building relationships one at a time.

You can also facilitate smaller meetings or convene people with similar roles to your own across your industry. You might host industry-wide events, industry roundtable discussions, town hall gatherings, CEO meetings, online groups, invite-only events, or backroom conversations alongside another event. It could even start with a coffee, lunch, or happy hour meeting and turn into something bigger.

Shine a spotlight on DEI in your industry. Industry leaders are now paying attention to DEI in the tech, entertainment, and advertising industries because people in those industries spoke up and helped lead the change. *Aside from convening, how can you spotlight DEI and contribute to building DEI best practices in your industry?* You might start by telling your own story if you've experienced exclusion and propose pathways to change, elevating and amplifying voices of people with underrepresented identities in your industry, and writing articles and social media posts addressing the need for a focus on DEI. Publicizing your organization's diversity metrics and strategies can be a good catalyst for change, if you're in a position to do this or advocate for it. Also encourage your colleagues at other companies to do the same.

Partner with and support organizations working on systemic change in the industry. They often need corporate backing to do the work they do—whether they focus on events, research, education programs, policy, or other advocacy. Help fund their work if you're in a position to, or find other creative ways that you can partner together for mutual gain.

At industry events, advocate for diversity and inclusion. Often industry event organizers have not done the work they should do to make their events diverse and inclusive. If you see an event is not diverse or accessible, they don't have a code of conduct, or they have messaging that isn't inclusive—contact the organizers. Assume good intent, and work to educate them. If you're asked to speak at an event where the event or panel is not diverse, offer to help make it more diverse through your connections.

Continue Creating Change Across Society

While this book is about how to be an ally in the workplace, as we've learned, the inequities and injustices across our society affect us all. Here are a few ways to get started continuing to create change across society:

Raise children who have empathy and work for justice, inclusion, and equity. Talk with them about why you are working on being a good ally, and perhaps enroll them in working with you to create change. Buy toys and books for children that represent diverse experiences and cultures. Work with your child's school to ensure they are offering diverse and inclusive classroom and after-school programs, physical spaces, language development programs, textbooks, and readings; and they are encouraging empathy, understanding, and collaboration.

Do your civic duty. Vote, advocate, and demand change. Call your local, state, and national leaders to let them know you care and want change. Vote for candidates with underrepresented identities, who have a reputation for correcting systemic inequity and injustice, and building economic wealth and health for everyone. Help organizations that are fighting voter suppression. If you protest as an ally, do listen to the organizers and follow their lead. Help keep people safe—remember, never instigate violence or vandalism at a peaceful protest. Some allies peacefully put their bodies between police and protestors with underrepresented identities to help keep them safe.

If you're like most people with busy lives, you view a summons for jury duty as an unwanted hindrance to your work and personal schedule. Reframe your thinking and do your jury duty. Biases are prevalent in the court systems. People with underrepresented identities need allies, as they are disproportionately incarcerated and receive longer sentences.

Align your dollars with your values. Consider how and where you spend money and strive to align your dollars with your values. Financially support organizations working to create change. Make investments in companies and portfolios that support DEI and social impact. Support businesses owned by women, people with underrepresented racial and ethnic identities, veterans, people with disabilities, people who are LGBTQIA+, and immigrants.

When you see something, do something. Intervene when you see harassment, bullying, biases, and microaggressions outside your workplace as well. And record in case the recording can be useful in prosecution later. Be an upstander.[7]

You have the power to create change. Keep learning, keep advocating!

Create an Action Plan

Leading the change and transforming your workplace requires commitment and taking steady steps to pave the path for change. *What actions will you take to develop inclusive team norms and/or create more equitable and inclusive systems and processes in your workplace?*

EXERCISE

With Table 9.1 as a guide, take some time to think about what specific actions you will take as a leader.

TABLE 9.1   Goals and Action Steps for Leaders

Action Plan

	Goal 1	Goal 2	Goal 3
My goal			
Action steps to achieve this goal			
Who needs to be involved			
Any learning needed			
Resources required			
Success metrics			
Timeline			

10

ALLYSHIP IS A
JOURNEY

The path of allyship is different for each of us. It can be uncomfortable—and it's our job as allies to get comfortable with discomfort. It can make us confront our fears, question long-held beliefs, and rethink our worldview—and it's our job to choose vulnerability and courage, as we grow to become more empathetic humans. It can also open new worlds and new understanding, help us build new relationships, lead better, love better, and live in alignment with our values. Allyship is a lifelong journey of learning, showing empathy, and taking action.

Through primary and secondary research, and my work with clients to build allyship in leaders and across organizations, I've found that the allyship journey lies on a continuum of change—or Stages of Allyship. As shown in Figure 10.1, allies tend to evolve on similar paths. We might begin with *denial*. I certainly did! But once we have a breakthrough, an aha moment, we begin to *observe* and test our assumptions. We then take the step of *learning* and may go through some deep and difficult unlearning and personal investigation. The learning never stops, but at some point we start to take action as an *ally*. We might remain here, or become an *advocate*, working to change systems from within them, leading the change from our position of power. And/or we might work to change the system by breaking the rules, protesting, or changing laws as an *accomplice*. A few of us continue on to become *activists*, actively working to create major shifts in institutional inequity and injustice. These are all part of the allyship journey:

FIGURE 10.1   **How Allies Evolve**

Denier. A denier might be here because they haven't yet recognized inequity. They may be causing harm without intending to, remaining complicit in the status quo. If you were here once, even recently, know that most people start here and what you do from here can make a big difference. You picked up this book, you're moving forward, and hopefully you're beginning to take action. That's what is most important now! A small percentage of people are here because they don't believe or don't want to believe in unfairness, inequity, and injustice (our research found this to be about 3 percent of the population).[1] Most people are eventually open to change and can have that moment of awakening that moves us from denier to observer.

Observer. When someone is in the observer stage, they are testing this new understanding, checking to see if it's real. Their motivation for allyship is becoming clear, but observers are not yet participating and may feel uncomfortable or excluded from participation. They are starting to understand the importance of this work and are weighing the pros and cons of taking steps to change. Developing empathy, understanding the benefits of DEI and allyship, and seeing examples of allyship will help observers become learners.

Learner. A learner is soaking in the information, and looking outside normal avenues for learning. They may be reading, asking questions, taking courses, participating in events, and expanding their network. They may take a few small actions, but they are not active allies yet. Learners may be going through feelings of guilt and shame, and may find excuses for not taking action as they work to unlearn and relearn. Learners become allies by building empathy and understanding, tapping into additional motivations (like improved leadership skills and collective team benefits) and learning tangible, actionable steps they can take to be an ally.

It's important to move from observing and learning to *action*. Allies can't stay in the safe space of nonaction; we must take uncomfortable steps forward to become active allies.

Ally. An ally takes action. They work to reduce the unintentional harm of biases and microaggressions, and may begin to intervene and become a champion. They stand up or step back as needed for people with underrepresented identities to have opportunities, gradually increasing their actions over time. Allies grow through training and coaching, continuing to build empathy, working in a culture that values allyship action, and having access to tools and processes that help them step into advocacy roles. Help allies learn from mistakes, educate them with empathy, and support them to continue taking action.

Advocate. An advocate leads the change, pushing for systemic change across company, industry, and/or society. They are a champion, advocating for someone whether or not they are in the room, and dedicating their power and influence to create systemic change. To help continue to grow their advocacy, advocates can benefit from additional resources, programs, tools, and training. Invite them to be members or sponsors of employee resource groups; provide mentor, sponsor, and volunteer opportunities; and give them inclusive leadership and change management training. When teams work together as advocates, recognize their collective accomplishments, and tell their story as an example for other teams.

My work with companies generally centers around these first five stages. Yet it is important to recognize the additional work of allyship can go beyond these—we also need accomplices and activists in our work to create systemic change.

Accomplice. An accomplice is an advocate who breaks the rules or the law to dismantle inequitable structures. Sometimes they are called co-conspirators or abettors. Accomplices cause major disruptions through protests, strikes, walkouts, major policy changes, legal challenges, and breaking the law to shine light on an unjust law or system. Depending on your role, power, and influence, this may be something you can do in the workplace as well as outside the workplace. Generally it does take some personal or professional risk to be an accomplice.

Activist. An activist dedicates their life and career to create change. They might significantly pivot their career and take a substantial pay cut to improve diversity, equity, inclusion, allyship, and/or advocacy. Often activists are the teachers of allies and advocates, the leaders of movements, the ones who work long hours to build coalitions, redesign systems, and lead organizations through long-term DEI change management. Activists need trust and respect, support, resources, and training to learn change management and behavior change strategies.

Often activists are people with underrepresented identities who experience microaggressions and inequity along with toxicity that can come from the work itself—they need breaks to regenerate and outlets to process toxicity and trauma that can come from doing the work long-term. If this is you: someone told me once to step out when you need to—your colleagues will fill in while you regenerate—and then come back in when you're ready.

We're all a work in progress—allyship unfolds throughout our lives as we receive new information, meet new people, and put ourselves in new and often uncomfortable situations. We might move back and forth along this continuum during our careers and find ourselves at different stages depending on which group we are an ally for. For example, someone might be an activist for women, but a learner when it comes to allyship for Black, Indigenous, and disabled people.

At any given time, I can be a learner, ally, accomplice, advocate, and activist—depending on which group I'm working to be an ally for, and what work I'm doing in my work at that moment. I'm still learning and unlearning, still catching my own biases frequently, and continuing to uncover deep-seated biases I didn't realize I had.

> *Where are you on this journey? Take a moment to consider where you are on the continuum, and what you might need to accomplish to get to the next stage or next level of allyship. The following sections include questions you might ask yourself along the way.*

How Should I Feel as an Ally?

During one of our Tech Inclusion Conferences in 2020, I received a message from someone attending the event. He said he was learning a lot about the change that needs to be made and the actions he can take. But as a White man who is not marginalized or excluded in his life and work, he wanted to know how he should *feel*. He said he was feeling shame that some people experienced racism, sexism, and ableism and he did not—and wondered if he should be feeling shame or guilt or like a "bad guy." Here is what I told him:

> *You are not alone in feeling this. I can't tell you how to feel, but I can tell you how I feel in case it's helpful. I feel this too—as a White person, there is a lot of privilege that I have that is unfair. I have feelings of guilt, and also feel a responsibility to use my privilege to correct this.*
>
> *I also know I need to listen and learn how to ensure I do no additional harm, and apologize if/when I do. And learn what people really need from me as an ally. This is not easy stuff. As I continue down my own journey as an ally, I continue to learn at deeper levels where inequities are. It is hard to unsee once you see them.*

And shame is real. Many, many people feel shame as they learn more—I've been doing this work for many years and would say that most people feel shame and/or guilt at one point or another. I would recommend not ignoring the guilt and shame because that can be unhealthy. Go to the heart of it and ask yourself why you're feeling it. When you do that, you become a better ally, and it's easier to help other people (potential allies) through the process.

That you are here, present and learning is a great thing. Thank you for asking me this.

Everyone's allyship journey is unique. When you're observing and learning, allyship can feel overwhelming. You may experience guilt, shame, or fear—but choose courage to investigate your feelings, move through them, and take action. When you're in the ally stage, intervening can be challenging and uncomfortable—but get comfortable with discomfort, have a growth mindset, and know that you'll get better at it, what's difficult now will get easier.

And when you do something as an advocate, wow—it's incredible to see the impact. Your colleagues thrive in their work and careers, your team is more innovative, and you and your colleagues are happier and healthier. Celebrate your colleagues' successes, reflect on your own accomplishments, and take pride in your team's growth.

I'm a Person with an Underrepresented Identity. Why Do I Need to Be an Ally When I'm Already Overburdened?

> I don't want to be the kind of person who only knows Native American issues. I want to be the kind of person who thinks about making sure we have ASL folks and making sure we have people who are providing closed captioning. I want to be the kind of person who can share the statistics of what's happening to our undocumented community. I want to be that kind of human being that never forgets we are all here and we are all living beings. And without that respect, none of this matters, and we are just repeating the same harm.
>
> **—VANESSA ROANHORSE[2]**

My friend and colleague Vanessa Roanhorse taught me to think about allyship as "reciprocity of love and respect"—she and I are mutual allies.[3] With a relationship of mutual allyship, we show up for each other when we're needed. I can be an ally for her by using my platform to amplify her voice, work, and culture; I can share my network and check in with her when I know times are rough (like when I found out the Diné people in the Navajo Nation were severely impacted by COVID-19 and the resulting economic crisis). She can be an ally for me by sharing her networks with me and educating me in how to be a better ally for Indigenous people. Our mutual allyship deepens our relationship, and it helps us both grow.

The reality is, we all need each other—there is a lot of work to do. We have to help one another rise and then send the ladder back down and help other people rise. It's easier for us to recognize microaggressions because we experience them too, and if we're mutually intervening for each other, we'll go further together. So take a break when you need to, but then come back and let's work together.

Healing from Our Own Trauma

Sometimes the best thing we can do as people with marginalized identities is to do our own healing. I spoke of my friend Michael Thomas in "Step 1: Learn, Unlearn, Relearn." In addition to being an attorney, Michael is a certified instructor in raja yoga from the Niroga Institute in Oakland, California. As part of his certification, he worked with incarcerated men in restorative justice circles, where they discussed the harm they have caused, as well as the harm they have experienced themselves. What he learned is that if you disengage from your own past harm and don't work to heal from it, you risk causing harm to other people.[4]

This is deep, important inner work. Because as we learned, unresolved trauma can be harmful to ourselves and each other. Trauma can be passed from generation to generation through fetal cells, as well as culture and family norms. It can also affect how we treat our colleagues, friends, and neighbors. Many of us have experienced intergenerational or personal trauma. And each of us can break the cycle.

When we don't resolve our trauma, we can also internalize trauma, internalize racism, sexism, ableism, and other forms of discrimination—and begin to believe it ourselves. In her TED talk in 2019, America Ferrera talked about how as a Latina actress, she needed to change her beliefs and values about herself to affect change:

> Change will come when each of us has the courage to question our own fundamental values and beliefs. And then see to it that our actions lead to our best intentions. I am just one of millions of people who have been told that in order to fulfill my dreams, in order to contribute my talents to the world, I have to resist the truth of who I am. I for one, am ready to stop resisting and to start existing as my full and authentic self. . . . My identity is my superpower.
>
> —AMERICA FERRERA[5]

For both Michael and I, yoga and meditation have been incredibly powerful tools for healing and growth. Individual or group therapy, executive coaching, journaling, and gathering with other people who have experienced similar trauma can also help.

I suspect when you picked up this book you didn't think you'd be asked to investigate so deeply, but it's important: *do you have unresolved trauma?* If you do, I encourage you to work to heal from it—for yourself first and foremost, as well as your colleagues, your family, your neighbors, and people around the world who all need you.

> By not touching upon your emotions it becomes easier to harm someone else, it becomes easier to ignore someone. . . . We can do harm to each other if we haven't done our own work. Allies: do your own work.
>
> **—MICHAEL THOMAS**[6]

What Do I Do When I Mess Up?

You're going to mess up, we all do. The first step is to be open to the experience of making mistakes. Often, we immediately become defensive, but that doesn't help anyone. Be open to feedback as an ally. *Invite* feedback. Listen to feedback with empathy and work to understand the impact.

Then communicate your understanding and genuinely apologize. Don't expect someone to forgive you immediately, give them time. Let them know how you will correct yourself moving forward. It may be a situation where there were significant consequences for the other person—if for example, you didn't invite them to an important meeting, or said something in front of colleagues that impacted their reputation or ability to fully participate. In that case, tell the person how you might repair the situation, and ask them for feedback about what they think would work best. Come to a conclusion together.

Commit to taking action so that it doesn't happen again. You may have to work to rebuild any lost trust. The best way to do that is to follow through with treating the impact, demonstrate change (don't let it happen again), and continue to become a stronger advocate.

Be transparent and authentic about what you've learned—with yourself, the person you harmed, and publicly if you're comfortable sharing your learning process. Don't share the name or details of the other person without their permission of course, but you can share your journey of allyship so that other people learn from your mistakes, and learn how to repair them.

The more that allyship becomes a norm in your culture, the easier this will become. Work to develop a culture where people give and receive feedback, recognize and address microaggressions, and learn to become better allies together.

What Is Canceling (or Public Shaming) and Should I Do It?

Cancel culture is a public backlash, boycott, withdrawal of support, ostracization, or embarrassment after someone does or says something offensive, abusive, ignorant, racist, sexist, ableist, heterosexist, anti-Muslim, anti-Semitic, anti-trans, and so on. Canceling can significantly impact the reputations of individuals, brands, and companies and can damage careers and families. In some cases it can also encourage sympathy for the offenders.

While the term is relatively new (many say it originated in the 1991 film *New Jack City*, but didn't become popular until over a decade later via Black Twitter), it is similar to "call-out culture" and other public shaming that has been around since the Civil Rights Movement.[7] Does it work? Former US President Barack Obama answered this way: "There is this sense that 'the way of me making change is to be as judgmental as possible about other people and that's enough.' . . . That's not activism. That's not bringing about change. If all you're doing is casting stones, you're probably not going to get that far. That's easy to do."[8]

If your goal is to change someone's behavior, public shaming is not generally an effective tool. Feelings of failure, shame, or guilt can make someone step out of their commitment to allyship. They are *less* likely to be vulnerable and have the courage to take risks. So it's important not to publicly shame anyone who is moving along the stages of allyship, but instead to meet them where they are, provide constructive, empathetic feedback, and offer them the tools they need when they need them.

Almost every time we host a conference or large event at Change Catalyst, someone "shames" our team publicly (usually on Twitter) for not being inclusive enough in some way: we don't have Indigenous speakers (we had seven that year), we don't have accessibility (we host one of the most accessible tech conferences), we aren't involving the local community (we work intimately with the local community), we're White feminists (for years, we've been deeply active in broadening diversity, equity, and inclusion for people of all underrepresented groups)—each time these public tweets have been wrong, often revealing a bias of the tweet's author. What do these tweets do? They cause controversy, reduce our ticket sales, center around the person tweeting rather than the work we do to create change, and make our team exhausted and deflated—because it takes a lot of work to put on an inclusive conference, and to be shamed for doing the opposite is hard. I love that people want change to happen, but this is just not an effective approach.

At around the same time our conference is happening, usually several major tech conferences are held that are much less diverse and inclusive, and no one says a word to them. Rather than publicly shaming the people who are working to create change because we don't think they are doing it right, let's spend our time focused on making deeper, more powerful change, together.

If your goal is behavior change, lead with empathy and assume good intent until you know otherwise. Seek to educate and support someone in their growth as an ally. Consider *calling people in* first, instead of calling them out. If you don't believe there are Indigenous speakers, for example, ask someone if they have Indigenous speakers joining them. If they say no, you might tell them why it's important and suggest some possible speakers, or push them toward organizations where they might find Indigenous speakers.

> I picture "calling in" as a practice of pulling folks back in who have strayed from us. It means extending to ourselves the reality that we will and do fuck up, we stray and there will always be a chance for us to return. Calling in as a practice of loving each other enough to allow each other to make mistakes; a practice of loving ourselves enough to know that what we're trying to do here is a radical unlearning of everything we have been configured to believe is normal.
>
> **—NGỌC LOAN TRẦN[9]**

I am often called in, regularly receiving feedback from people who have been incredibly helpful. It's how I learned the difference between people-first language and identity-first language (thank you, Andrea Vu Chasko), that it's important to have live CART captioning for Deaf and Hard of Hearing people who don't use Sign Language (thank you, Svetlana Kouznetsova), that we need prayer rooms near single-stall or gendered restrooms with a sink where people can wash before prayer (thank you, Antonia Ford), and much more.

My rule of thumb is this: if a person or an organization has good intent but they've made a mistake, I seek to call them in, ask questions, and then educate (not shame) them. If I don't get a response the first time, I try again. If I still don't hear back, sometimes I'll let it alone because they aren't ready—they are not even at the learning stage of allyship. There are so many people and organizations that do *want* to change but don't know *how*, that I prefer to focus on helping them. You make the call here, though—if they are still creating harm, you may want to say something publicly to hold them accountable.

Public accountability is not the same thing as shaming. What I have learned over the years is that when companies are held publicly accountable—through press, regulation, policies, customer feedback, and peer pressure—things change more rapidly, suddenly budgets are allocated, and DEI work is prioritized from the top. This looks like asking questions, holding them to their public statements (e.g., if they've made a public statement about Black Lives Matter or #MeToo) or publicly stated diversity goals, convening stakeholders and requesting commitments, and creating policies and regulations to keep them in check and hold companies accountable.

How Do I Convince People Allyship (or DEI) Is Important?

> We live in a society that wants immediate transformation. It doesn't work that way. You have to meet the people where they're at. You have to understand where they are coming from, and what their reservations are if they have any. You have to understand what it is that drives them.
>
> **—LIONEL LEE[10]**

I get this question all the time in my trainings, keynotes, and podcast: "What do I say to convince someone who can't be convinced?" I'd like to say, "Just hand them this book and send them on their way!" But there is some work to do first to get them to the learner stage.

First, decide where you want to spend your energy. Early on in my DEI work, I realized I was expending a lot of energy on the people who are actively opposed to diversity, equity, and inclusion. It was depleting me to the point where I didn't have the energy to do my training and advocacy work. Then I realized: there are so many more people who do care, but just don't know what to do as an ally. They are ready to be activated, and just need to be equipped with information, tools, and actions. So I made a decision to focus on the people who are observers, learners, allies, and advocates—and sometimes accomplices and activists—to help them create change. *Where will you focus your energy?* It's all important.

Wherever people are on the allyship journey, if you want to help them move forward, you must meet them where they are. People in denial have not had their awareness moment yet. We often want to throw information at people to make them understand, but that isn't usually how behavior change works. Everyone has their own entry point into allyship; find out what theirs might be.

Think back to a time when you were in denial: *what made you aware?* It's often a life-changing experience, like having a child and realizing you want them to live in an equitable world, seeing a Black person murdered on camera or watching the world rise up against systemic injustice, hearing a traumatic experience a colleague or a friend went through, or experiencing trauma yourself. Or perhaps it was at a training or event, or a story you read in the news.[11]

You can't re-create this awareness moment for someone—except perhaps by sharing deeply your own experience or working with a group of people to share your experiences together. You might start with an open, safe dialogue. Listen with empathy. Find out their feelings, learn what they are resisting. Share your own feelings and experiences. Remember, change takes time; you probably won't convince anyone in one conversation, though it's possible. I encourage, you not to become too attached to the outcome for a specific person because often it takes years for people to emerge from denial.

Once people have an awareness moment, they become an observer. They are checking to see if inequity is a real thing and if being an ally is someone they want to become. They're sort of trying it on for size in the dressing room—so you can be there in the store bringing them items to try on, but they are the only ones who can decide what they will walk out the door wearing. Be a role model, and help them learn ways that allyship can benefit them. Once they're ready to learn, give them some basics—stories, data, historical context—and yes, now you can give them this book!

Not everyone will become an ally. Sometimes you just can't get them there, and you need to check in with yourself from time to time to be sure you're spending time and energy in places that matter and are good for your well-being. And do take care of yourself—having conversations with people early in their journey can be emotionally challenging.

What If My Company Isn't Focused on DEI, or My Leadership Doesn't Care—How Can I Create Change?

This can be frustrating and difficult if you're from an underrepresented group, I'm sending lots of good energy your way. If your company and leadership aren't focused on DEI, you can do a lot of work as an ally on your own: doing no harm, advocating, standing up for what's right, and even leading the change in your individual work and in your industry.

If there is no DEI work being done at your company, advocate for it. You might form a committee or coalition to discuss ways that you can create and advocate for change. Perhaps put together the business case for leadership: share statistics about the importance of DEI to business, any internal data you have around turnover and lack of diversity, and any DEI work being done in your industry by competitors. They also might need to better visualize what DEI work means—ask leadership if your committee can put together a rough idea of some things you might start to work on first. Make sure that list is short and has some quick wins where you can point to success!

If you're hitting too many roadblocks or not feeling welcome or safe, you may consider if this company is the right one for you. Only you can know that. *Do you want to spend your energy where it's not possible to create change, or do you want to work for a company where you can make a real difference?* If you're not in a healthy work environment, consider making a careful plan to find new opportunities.

What Can I Do If I'm Not in a Leadership Position?

You can lead the change no matter what position you're in! Start by learning and doing no harm, of course, and then model allyship for your colleagues and help them learn along their allyship journey. Mentor and send the ladder back down to those who are earlier in their career. Advocate for change in your company, and even help create that change if you have the time. Volunteer and find other ways to help create change in your industry. Work on your inclusive leadership skills to be ready when you are a leader. If you're leading any projects—or even meetings—you can put these skills into practice. And share your experience as an ally on social media, blogs, and internal company channels.

Why Do Some People Not Want Me to Intervene?

Wayne and I were in Puerto Rico several years ago giving a DEI training to CEOs of medium-sized businesses. In the room were 29 White Latinos, one White Latina, me, and Wayne, who is Black. They were all generally receptive to the work we were doing, except one person in the room: the woman. She denied that this was an important issue, vehemently saying that DEI wasn't important and that people should earn their spot based on merit.

This is common in my work, that the one person in the room from an underrepresented identity does not want to talk about diversity. I see this surface on social media as well. People have worked so hard to get where they are as the "only," carefully navigating spaces where they didn't fully belong, adapting and assimilating language and mannerisms, covering and masking if they needed to along the way. It's survival. They might not want to be called out as different, made part of the out-group, have people focus on them when talking about DEI, open themselves up to stereotypes and other biases, or feel stereotype threat and tokenism. They might just want to do their job and be part of the team. They also may be exhausted or done fighting.

Another way this shows up is people saying they are OK with harassment or jokes made about their identity or even telling jokes themselves. Or when you try a microintervention tactic after a microaggression, but the person experiencing the microaggression blows it off or gets angry at you for pointing it out.

The best thing you can do for them as an ally is to get more people like them in the room so they don't bear the full weight of representation and responsibility. When you're working to intervene or advocate on their behalf, respect their wishes and avoid calling attention to them. Intervene privately or in ways that are less overt—for instance, redirecting a conversation away from a microaggression or opening up a conversation to make sure they have room to speak.

Sometimes people don't want other people to intervene because they don't trust the person to intervene in a way that would help the situation. Build that trust, talk with the person about what might work best for them. And regardless, check in with them when they've experienced a microaggression—always work to treat the impact.

How Is Allyship Different in the Remote Workplace?

During the COVID-19 pandemic, I received this question a lot. And as companies continue to grow their remote workforce and workplaces become more dispersed across regions and countries, this is an important question. Almost everything in this book applies to the remote workplace as well as the physical workplace. When you're conversing via chats, video, and other internal software, there are a few more things to keep in mind:

Tone doesn't come through the chat. Sometimes I can tell something is not sitting right with one of my team members, and I ask what's wrong. They might tell me "I'm sorry I disappointed you." Disappointment was nowhere on my mind; I was just working to achieve a solution to a problem! Sometimes you have to describe context, check in with each other, and remind each other that tone doesn't come through the chat, and not to assume tone. This can be especially important when working with people from different regions of the world.

People will say things via chat that they wouldn't say in person. In many of the companies I work with, the worst microaggressions happen in backroom chats. Have a code of conduct that everyone knows about, where you can easily reference it and point to violations. If you're in a large company, there should be a person or team dedicated to ensuring safety and inclusion on internal platforms. Use microinterventions. Know where and how to report people if violations continue, and who to contact immediately if multiple people are violating the code of conduct.

If you witness a microaggression in a video or phone call, still use microinterventions. This works pretty much the same way it does in person, though you may choose to educate someone privately more often in the remote workplace.

In video, your body language and facial expressions are heightened. Consequently, because it's all you can see, it's really important to mind microaggressions and consider microaffirmations in your body language and expressions. I often keep my video window open to watch myself, so I can quickly catch if I'm unintentionally conveying the wrong message with my face. I might be curious what is in someone's video background, but they perceive that I'm confused at what they are saying. Also if you've had a difficult meeting, give yourself a moment to reset before entering a new meeting, so you're bringing the energy you want to bring.

Be inclusive and accessible in videoconferencing. Talk through agendas and visuals for anyone who is Blind, Low Vision, or on the phone. If people drop out and then return, welcome them back and catch them up briefly. Be inclusive in scheduling meetings as well. Sometimes companies with headquarters in one area of the world will use that time zone as the normal. This is a little act of exclusion for people outside that time zone. Consider mixing it up, and holding meetings that are centered on other time zones too. Also keep in mind parenting/caregiver schedules.

Overcommunicate and provide clarity. This is something our team has to consistently remind ourselves to do. Communicate what you're working on, how you're progressing on your timelines, what you've accomplished, when you'll be offline, and how you're doing. Whether you're working toward a tight deadline together or are all working on different projects, this is crucial.

Provide clarity and feedback around goals, expectations, timelines, and tasks. Take meeting notes and document tasks so everyone is on the same page. Check in on progress and give regular feedback. You should do these in any workplace, but it's especially important in the remote setting to have these touchpoints.

Schedule formal and informal check-ins. Since we can't ask each other to coffee or lunch, run into each other in the halls, or stop by each other's offices, in the remote setting you have to schedule those times. Make it part of your company culture to do it regularly. Mentorship also can fall by the wayside in the remote setting—make sure you're setting up regular meetings together.

Recognize the impact of microaggressions and exclusion in a remote setting. It is usually more difficult to know what people are going through when remote. Some things to look for are someone not showing up to or contributing in meetings, or regularly not turning on video. If that's happening, check in on them to see what's going on. Find out how you can support them.

Work harder to collaborate and to bridge isolation. Remote collaboration isn't always simple. Use collaborative documents, innovation platforms, and other ways to get people involved and thinking in new ways. Some of my team will pair up and have coworking sessions via video to hold each other accountable and ask questions of each other when needed. Re-create the watercooler effect as well—you still need those moments to build empathy and understanding between individuals and across teams. These can be structured or unstructured weekly moments to get to know each other better.

Help new team members learn the culture. In a remote workplace, it can be more difficult to navigate the culture, systems, and processes. Help people navigate through the first few weeks, and check in with them once a month after that to make sure they are feeling welcome and finding their place on the team.

What Is Performative Allyship?

Performative allyship is saying you're an ally without putting the action behind it. It's professing your alliance to the cause of a group without doing anything in service of that group. Sometimes it's wanting to be an ally or to be perceived as an ally, but when it comes down to it, you aren't present when you're needed.

Several brands showed performative allyship after George Floyd was murdered, for example. Knowing the Black Lives Matter movement was important to their customers, they released statements in solidarity. Many people called attention to the NFL for their Black Lives Matter statement and playing of the Black National Anthem, while still having low diversity numbers and not correcting the censuring of Colin Kaepernick. If you see brands performing without taking action, work to hold them accountable to their statements—make it known that as a customer, you care about the actions behind those statements.

Allyship is more than intention. It is more than words and positioning yourself as an ally. Allyship is *earned* based on learning, getting uncomfortable, going past any fears you may have, and taking action that benefits people with underrepresented identities. Allies do the work.

How Do I Lead the Change Without Taking the Spotlight?

There is a fine line between being recognized as an ally and overpowering the voices of the people you set out to be an ally for. Allies, advocates, accomplices, and activists take the responsibility of a cause or issue as their own, while at the same time following the lead of the person or group they're advocating for and with.

My friend and colleague Corey Ponder says that allies should be "trusted sidekicks," like Robin to Batman, Maria Rambeau to Captain Marvel, Okoye to Black Panther, Steve Trevor to Wonder Woman, Bucky Barnes and Falcon to Captain America.[12] Allies are not saviors swooping in and taking the spotlight as they save the day, they are correctors—collaborating side by side to solve daily systemic inequities. Lend your power, influence, and privilege—and be humble. Speak up and speak out for change and for greater allyship. But rather than speaking for a group, whenever possible amplify the voices of that group to speak for themselves.

> Listen crucially, listen carefully and recognize that your work is not to go and drown anybody out, silence anybody or stand in the front. But often your work is to resource the people who are most affected, let them set the agenda and let them dictate your role. It can be difficult, because you have to move your ego out of the way, but that is the necessary work.
>
> —BRITTANY PACKNETT CUNNINGHAM[13]

Something Not Here That You Really Want to Know?

If you still have a question, check out my podcast "Leading With Empathy & Allyship" and other resources, or find me on social media, attend one of our events or trainings, and reach out and ask. If I can, I'll address it on my podcast or message you directly. You might also reach out to a colleague who is focused on DEI; they may be happy to help you. And of course, do your own research—the answer might be out there waiting for you.

Focus on Solutions

Being an ally can stretch us in new ways. Have the courage to take risks, make mistakes, and keep growing as an ally. Hold on to your motivation when times are challenging, stay true to your values, and focus on solutions.

In DEI and allyship work, we can get caught up in the deep problems we're working to correct. The problems are what got us here, the solutions are what will take us to the next stage together. Recognize the problems, understand them—but don't get stuck there. Focus on doing the work to fix them. Learn, show empathy, and *take action*.

I believe in you, and the collective impact we can make together, to build stronger, happier workplaces—and a better world where we can all thrive equally. One person at a time, one action at a time, one word at a time.

Thank you for your work.

EXERCISE

There is much opportunity for continued learning and action as an ally. You have your Action Plan (if you haven't done it, go back to "Step 7: Transform Your Organization, Industry, and Society" and do it now!). What commitment will you make to continue learning beyond this book? What learning would help you continue your growth, and help you take action?

Consider learning from diverse viewpoints and perspectives. Start with one way you will continue to learn and grow your understanding after reading this book.

I commit to: _____

_____

_____

_____

NOTES

Acknowledgments

1. When I started thinking about this book, it was important to me to capitalize Black—like Asian, Latinx, and Indigenous. We have been capitalizing Black for years at Change Catalyst. W. E. B. Du Bois pushed for capitalizing Negro in the 1920s; *Ebony, Essence*, and other Black magazines have capitalized Black for many years. This movement is growing, as people work to recognize Black culture, and a unique experience with systemic racism. As I began writing this, however, capitalizing every racial and ethnic identity except White did not feel right. I decided to capitalize White for several reasons.

   White is more of an identity than many White people recognize (one of several indicators here is that the majority of White people only have White friends—see ch. 3 n. 77). White people are treated differently because of our skin color and because of the history we have written, the laws we have written, and the systems we have created that have oppressed everyone else while privileging White people. Capitalizing White is uncomfortable, it can feel overly powerful and wrong because White supremacists have capitalized it while wielding violence and hate. And yet not capitalizing it minimizes—and somehow removes responsibility and accountability for—systemic racial inequities. White is not the norm, White is not invisible. We must recognize and reflect on how Whiteness does hold power and privilege in this world. And then take action to correct this systemic inequity.

   Other arguments for keeping it lowercase include that White people have less shared history and culture. Considering there are over a billion Black people in the world, Asians make up about half the global population, and the peoples we call Indigenous make up thousands of cultures on almost every continent, that argument doesn't hold for me. No race or ethnicity is a monolith.

2. Someone who is *nonbinary* (or *enby*) doesn't necessarily identify as a man or woman. Similar terms are *gender nonconforming (GNC), third gender, gender fluid*, or *two-spirit*. You can find information about these and other diversity, equity, and inclusion terms in my companion glossary to this book, "Demystifying Diversity, Equity and Inclusion Terminology" at https://changecatalyst.co/glossary.

3. I've used the term *Black* to include people of African descent from all nationalities. In the United States, Black is generally accepted. Yet I want to recognize that in the United States some of my friends, colleagues, and neighbors identify as Brown,

African American, Biracial, Mixed, or by their culture/country of origin, such as Dominican or Jamaican American. In Australia, some Indigenous people identify as Black. In the United Kingdom, historically Black has included people of African, Arab, and Asian descent. In South Africa, racialization included a distinction between Black Africans and Coloureds that was rooted in racism, colorism, and White supremacy. In several African countries, Black is not generally used. Language and ideas around race are evolving globally. While race is not tracked nor openly discussed in many communities, we must recognize and address that people were racialized, then colonized and enslaved, and continue to experience systemic racism.

4. I have learned from people with disabilities around the world that this language is complex, continues to change, and varies globally. Some identify with person-first language (people with disabilities), others identify with identity-first language (disabled people or their specific disability—e.g., Autistic, Deaf, Blind). Many people believe in a social model of disability, where people are disabled by society rather than by their bodies or diagnoses, and might use disabled people or people experiencing disability. When possible, ask how someone identifies. I'll use *people with disabilities* and *disabled people* in this book. I have not capitalized *disabled* because the community doesn't generally capitalize it currently. I have capitalized *Deaf*, *Blind*, and *Autistic* because increasingly these communities do capitalize the terms.

5. *Latinx* is a gender-inclusive term that includes people who are nonbinary. After much primary and secondary research, I've decided to use the term *Latinx* throughout this book to refer to people who are Hispanic, Latino, Latina, and Latin@. The global population is somewhere between 400 and 600 million people, so any one term is imperfect. As the language continues to evolve, another better term is likely to emerge in the future.

6. I'll use the term *Indigenous* throughout this book to refer to the 370 to 500 million people around the world who are indigenous to their land, representing 5,000 cultures, across 90 countries. They include people who are Native American, First Nations, First Peoples, Aboriginal, Torres Strait Islander, Hawaiian and Pacific Islander, Indigenous Peoples of Africa and Asia, and many other Native identities.

United Nations Development Programme, "10 Things to Know About Indigenous Peoples,'" *United Nations Development Programme,* January 2019, https://stories.undp.org/10-things-we-all-should-know-about-indigenous-people.

7. The alphabet is continuing to grow as awareness grows and identities and language change. I'll use *LGBTQIA+* throughout this book. The many identities in the alphabet (with the "+") include LGBTQQIIPP2SAAAA: Lesbian, Gay, Bisexual, Transgender, Queer, Questioning, Intersex, Intergender, Pansexual, Polyamorous, 2 Spirit, Asexual, Androgynous, Agender, Ally. Also included with the "+" are kink, demisexual, graysexual, gender nonconforming (GNC), nonbinary, third gender, genderqueer, gender fluid, and more. This will no doubt continue to expand as it becomes more inclusive.

8. Change Catalyst, "What Can You Do as an Ally | Tech Inclusion SF 2015," Nancy Douyon interviewing Parker Thompson, Kaustav Mitra, Joshua Krammes, and Don Loeb, November 28, 2015, video, 40:15, https://youtu.be/4cXHKOXDC_s. We also hosted another session on allyship that year, led by Danielle DeRuiter-Williams and Elena Isaacs.

9. In the United States, many people use the term AAPI to include both Asian Americans and Pacific Islanders. Globally, sometimes these groups are combined as API, however many people distinguish Asians as separate from Pacific Islanders. In this book, I've included people who are indigenous to the Pacific Islands as Indigenous, and people whose ancestors are from South Asia, Southeast Asia, East Asia/ Far East, Central Asia, and North Asia as *Asian*. This can also include West Asia, though people in this region most often identify as Arab, MENA (Middle East and North African), or AMEMSA (Arab, Middle Eastern, Muslim, and South Asian). I recognize that Asia is the largest continent of the world and encompasses many different cultures. Whenever possible, refer to someone using the terms they use to describe their own identity. This is often the specific country or culture of their ancestors.

Introduction

1. Clare O'Connor, "Google Fires Anti-Diversity Memo Writer, Drawing Ire in Right-Wing Circles," *Forbes,* August 8, 2017, https://www.forbes.com/sites/clareoconnor /2017/08/08/google-fires-anti-diversity-memo-writer-drawing-ire-in-right-wing -circles/#4c8942785b07.

2. Daniel Goleman, *Emotional Intelligence: Why It Can Matter More Than IQ* (Bantam Books, 1995).

3. Allison Scott, Freada Kapor Klein, and Uriridiakoghene Onovakpuri, "The 2017 Tech Leavers Study," *Kapor Center & Ford Foundation* (2017) https://www .kaporcenter.org/tech-leavers/.

4. The tech industry could and should be improving faster when it comes to diversity, equity, and inclusion. To do so, however, we must shift more resources to diversity, equity, and inclusion programs; shift to multi-level, long-term learning and development programs versus one-off trainings to solve complex problems; work strategically to change processes and behaviors; and offer change management, behavioral science, and organizational development training to staff who are leading diversity, equity, and inclusion programs.

5. Melinda Briana Epler, "3 Ways to Be a Better Ally in the Workplace," *TED,* June 2018, video, 9:37, http://go.ted.com/melindaepler.

6. I am happily married with my husband so people might think I am straight. I am bisexual though, and it's important to honor my bisexuality as an intersectional aspect of my identity.

Chapter 1: What Allyship Is and Why It Matters

1. Thomas Barta, Markus Kleiner, and Tilo Neumann, "Is There a Payoff from Top-Team Diversity?," *McKinsey Quarterly* (April 2012), https://www.mckinsey.com /business-functions/organization/our-insights/is-there-a-payoff-from-top-team -diversity; Vivian Hunt, Dennis Layton, and Sara Prince, "Diversity Matters," *McKinsey and Company* (February 2015), https://www.mckinsey.com/~/media /mckinsey/business%20functions/organization/our%20insights/why%20diversity %20matters/diversity%20matters.ashx; Vivian Hunt, Sara Prince, Sundiatu Dixon-Fyle, and Lareina Yee, "Delivering Through Diversity," *McKinsey and Company* (January 2018), https://www.mckinsey.com/~/media/McKinsey/Business %20Functions/Organization/Our%20Insights/Delivering%20through%20diversity /Delivering-through-diversity_full-report.ashx; Juliet Bourke, *Which Two Heads Are Better Than One? How Diverse Teams Create Breakthrough Ideas and Make Smarter Decisions* (Australian Institute of Company Directors, 2016); Sara Fisher Ellison and Wallace P. Mullin, "Diversity, Social Goods Provision, and Performance in the Firm," *Journal of Economics & Management Strategy* 23, no. 2 (Summer 2014): 465–481, https://doi.org/10.1111/jems.12051; Alison Reynolds and David Lewis, "Teams Solve Problems Faster When They're More Cognitively Diverse," *Harvard Business Review*, March 2017, https://hbr.org/2017/03/teams-solve-problems-faster-when-theyre-more-cognitively-diverse; Deloitte and Victorian Equal Opportunity and Human Rights Commission, "Waiter, Is That Inclusion in My Soup? A New Recipe to Improve Business Performance," *Deloitte Australia* and *Victorian Equal Opportunity and Human Rights Commission,* May 2013, Mohamed Mousa, "Does Gender Diversity Affect Workplace Happiness for Academics? The Role of Diversity Management and Organizational Inclusion," *Public Organization Review 21* (July 2020): 119-135, https://doi.org/10.1007/s11115-020-00479-0.

2. *Cisgender* and many other terms are defined in the companion glossary to this book, "Demystifying Diversity, Equity and Inclusion Terminology," at https:// changecatalyst.co/glossary.

3. If the word *privilege* here is not sitting well with you, don't worry. I used to despise the word privilege, because I worked hard to get where I am, and it wasn't easy. Please keep reading, we'll address this more a bit later.

4. Jessica Chastain, "Jessica Chastain Talks Helping Octavia Spencer Receive Equal Pay | TODAY," Interview by Kota Hotb, *TODAY,* June 26, 2018, video, 5:15, https:// www.youtube.com/watch?v=MGxC4AOxOQE.

5. Octavia Spencer, "'Women Breaking Barriers' Panel—Sundance 2018," panel moderated by Elisabeth Sereda, *Sundance TV,* January 20, 2018, video, 56:33, https:// www.youtube.com/watch?v=e63gxorVT-g.

6. Jessica Chastain (@jes_chastain), Twitter, January 24, 2018, https://twitter.com/jes _chastain/status/956178688726503424.

7. Jada Pinkett-Smith (@jadapsmith), "Prime example of sister solidarity between @ jes_chastain and @octaviaspencer [camera emoji]: @MzSpectacular4u," Twitter, January 22, 2018, https://twitter.com/jadapsmith/status/955503954711859200.

8. Ben Travis, "Chadwick Boseman Boosted Sienna Miller's 21 Bridges Salary from His Own Pay," *Empire,* September 28, 2020, https://www.empireonline.com/movies /news/chadwick-boseman-boosted-sienna-miller-s-21-bridges-salary-from-his -own-pay/.

9. Erika Harwood, "Benedict Cumberbatch Says He'll Refuse Any Project Where Women Don't Get Equal Pay," *Vanity Fair,* May 13, 2018, https://www.vanityfair .com/hollywood/2018/05/benedict-cumberbatch-equal-pay-interview; Daniel Victor, "Michael B. Jordan Adopts an Inclusion Rider for His Company," *New York Times,* March 8, 2018, https://www.nytimes.com/2018/03/08/business/media /michael-b-jordan-inclusion-rider.html; Rebecca Lee, "Oprah: Gender Pay Gap Conversation Has Hit 'Critical Moment,'" *CBS News* October 14, 2015, https:// www.cbsnews.com/news/oprah-gender-pay-gap-conversation-has-hit-critical- moment/; Rhian Daly, "Mark Wahlberg Gives 'All the Money in the World' Reshoot Fee to Time's Up Campaign," *NME,* January 13, 2018, https://www.nme.com/news /film/mark-wahlberg-gives-money-world-reshoot-fee-times-campaign-2219117; Daniel Kreps, "Bradley Cooper Pledges to Help Close Hollywood Wage Gap," *Rolling Stone,* October 17, 2015, https://www.rollingstone.com/movies/movie -news/bradley-cooper-pledges-to-help-close-hollywood-wage-gap-193354/; Andrew Marantz, "Ready for Prime Time," *New Yorker,* December 27, 2015, https://www.newyorker.com/magazine/2016/01/04/ready-for-prime-time; Lacey Rose, "Ellen Pompeo, TV's $20 Million Woman, Reveals Her Behind-the-Scenes Fight for 'What I Deserve,'" *Hollywood Reporter,* January 17, 2018, https:// www.hollywoodreporter.com/features/ellen-pompeo-tvs-20-million-woman- reveals-her-behind-scenes-fight-what-i-deserve-1074978.

10. John Carlos and Dave Zirin, *The John Carlos Story: The Sports Moment That Changed the World* (Haymarket Books, 2011).

11. "Black Athletes Make Silent Protest," *BBC On This Day,* October 17, 1968, http:// news.bbc.co.uk/onthisday/hi/dates/stories/october/17/newsid_3535000/3535348.stm.

12. Amy Bass, *Not the Triumph But the Struggle: the 1968 Olympics and the Making of the Black Athelete* (University of Minnesota Press, 2002).

13. "Black Power," *The Famous Pictures Collection*, May 22, 2013, http://www .famouspictures.org/black-power/.

14. Martin Flanagan, "Olympic Protest Heroes Praise Norman's Courage," *Sydney Morning Herald,* October 10, 2006, https://www.smh.com.au/sport/olympic-protest -heroes-praise-normans-courage-20061010-gdokc5.html.

15. Charles Curtis, "Colin Kaepernick: I Won't Stand 'to Show Pride in a Flag for a Country that Oppresses Black People,'" *For the Win/USA Today Sports,* August 27, 2016, https://ftw.usatoday.com/2016/08/colin-kaepernick-49ers-national-anthem -sit-explains.

16. Chris Biderman, "Transcript: Colin Kaepernick Addresses Sitting During National Anthem," *Niners Newswire,* August 28, 2016, https://ninerswire.usatoday.com/2016/08/28/transcript-colin-kaepernick-addresses-sitting-during-national-anthem/.

17. Cindy Boren, "Megan Rapinoe Won a Woman of the Year Award. She Thanked Colin Kaepernick," *Washington Post,* November 12, 2019, https://www.washingtonpost.com/sports/2019/11/12/megan-rapinoe-won-woman-year-award-she-thanked-colin-kaepernick/.

18. John D Halloran, "Megan Rapinoe Kneels For Anthem at NWSL Match," *American Soccer Now,* September 4, 2016, http://americansoccernow.com/articles/megan-rapinoe-kneels-for-anthem-at-nwsl-match.

19. Megan Rapinoe, "You Can't Get Rid of Your Girl That Easily," *The Players' Tribune* June 23, 2019, https://www.theplayerstribune.com/articles/megan-rapinoe-united-states-world-cup-youre-not-gonna-get-rid-of-your-girl-that-easily.

20. Lindsey Horan and Megan Rapinoe, "Doing This for Women Everywhere," *The Players Tribune,* September 24, 2019, video, 3:33, https://www.theplayerstribune.com/videos/doing-this-for-women-everywhere-megan-rapione-lindsey-horan.

21. Megan Rapinoe, "Why I Am Kneeling," *The Players' Tribune,* October 6, 2016, https://www.theplayerstribune.com/articles/megan-rapinoe-why-i-am-kneeling.

22. "Megan Rapinoe Accuses Football of Failing Players Over Racism," *The Independent,* November 8, 2019, https://www.independent.co.uk/sport/football/womens_football/megan-rapinoe-football-racism-fifa-bulgarian-fa-raheem-sterling-a9194426.html; Boren, Cindy (see n. 15).

23. Megan Rapinoe, "Megan Rapinoe's Parents Taught Her That You Need to Help People, Period." Interview by Stephen Colbert, The Late Show with Stephen Colbert, June 11, 2020, video, 7:42, https://youtu.be/r22dokLryrA.

24. Mark Sandritter, "A Timeline of Colin Kaepernick's National Anthem Protest and the Athletes Who Joined Him," *SBNATION,* September 25, 2017, https://www.sbnation.com/2016/9/11/12869726/colin-kaepernick-national-anthem-protest-seahawks-brandon-marshall-nfl.

25. Kyle Wagner, "Colin Kaepernick Is Not Supposed to Be Unemployed," *FiveThirty Eight,* August 9, 2017, https://fivethirtyeight.com/features/colin-kaepernick-is-not-supposed-to-be-unemployed/.

26. Disclosure: Reddit was one of my clients as Founder and CEO of Change Catalyst, where I worked directly with Alexis and the executive team.

27. Alexis Ohanian Sr., "What Did You Do?," AlexisOhanian.com, June 5, 2020, https://alexisohanian.com/news/2020/6/5/what-did-you-do.

28. Ibid.

29. Nick Statt, "Reddit Names Y Combinator CEO Michael Seibel as Alexis Ohanian's Replacement," *The Verge,* June 10, 2010, https://www.theverge.com/2020/6/10/21285835/reddit-board-replacement-alexis-ohanian-michael-seibel-y-combinator.

30. The principal author of the document was disability rights attorney and activist Robert L. Burgdorf Jr.

31. "NCD Honors the Life and Legacy of Major Owens," *National Council on Disability Newsroom,* 2013, https://ncd.gov/newsroom/2013/102313.

32. Craig Collins, "The Capitol Crawl," *Equal Access, Equal Opportunity: 25th Anniversary of the Americans with Disabilities Act* (Faircount Media Group, 2015): 48–50–53, 55, 57; Phil Pangrazio, "A Brief History of Disability Rights & the Americans with Disabilities Act (ADA)," *LivAbility Magazine*, July 14, 2015, https://ability360.org/livability/advocacy-livability/history-disability-rights-ada/.

Chapter 2: The Role of Allyship in Workplace Diversity, Equity, and Inclusion

1. Arelis R. Hernandez, Mark Berman, and Mary Beth Gahan, "Texas Police Officer Antagonized People in Small Town Prior to Shooting, Residents Say," *Washington Post,* October 10, 2020, https://www.washingtonpost.com/nation/2020/10/10/texas-police-officer-antagonized-residents-small-town-prior-shooting-residents-say/.
2. They decided three cases: *Bostock v. Clayton County, Altitude Express Inc. v. Zarda*, and *R.G. & G.R. Harris Funeral Homes Inc. v. Equal Employment Opportunity Commission.*
3. Jamie M. Grant, Lisa A. Mottet, Justin Tanis, Jack Harrison, Jody L. Herman, and Mara Keisling, "Injustice at Every Turn: A Report of the National Transgender Discrimination Survey," *National Center for Transgender Equality* (2011).; Andy Saldaña, Jaime Woo, Emma Schwartz, Marion Daly, and Rian Finnegan, "LGBTQIA and Traveling for Work," *Tech Inclusion New York 2018* by Change Catalyst, June 27, 2018.
4. Marion Daly, "LGBTQIA and Traveling for Work," *Tech Inclusion New York 2018* by Change Catalyst, June 27, 2018.
5. United Nations Department of Economic and Social Affairs, "Factsheet on Persons with Disabilities: Disability and Employment," *United Nations,* accessed June 2021, https://www.un.org/development/desa/disabilities/resources/factsheet-on-persons-with-disabilities/disability-and-employment.html.
6. U.S. Bureau of Labor Statistics, "Persons with a Disability: Labor Force Characteristics—2020," *U.S. Department of Labor,* February 26, 2020.
7. Michelle Yin, Dahlia Shaewitz, and Mahlet Megra, "Leading the Way, or Falling Behind? What the Data Tell Us About Disability Pay Equity and Opportunity in Boston and Other Top Metropolitan Areas," *American Institutes for Research*, July 2020, https://rudermanfoundation.org/white_papers/leading-the-way-or-falling-behind-what-the-data-tell-us-about-disability-pay-equity-and-opportunity-in-boston-and-other-top-metropolitan-areas/.
8. William A. Erickson, Sarah von Schrader, Susanna M. Bruyere, and Sara A. VanLooy, "The Employment Environment: Employer Perspectives, Policies, and Practices Regarding the Employment of Persons with Disabilities," *Rehabilitation Counseling Bulletin* 57 (November 2013): 195–208, https://doi.org/10.1177/0034355213509841; Lena Strindlund, Madeleine Abrandt-Dahlgren, and Christian Ståhl, "Employers' Views on Disability, Employability, and Labor Market Inclusion: A Phenomenographic Study," *Disability and Rehabilitation* 41, no. 24 (2019): 2910–2917, https://doi.org/10.1080/09638288.2018.1481150; Simon Dixon, Ceri Smith,

and Anel Touchet, "The Disability Perception Gap: Policy Report," *Scope* (May 2018), https://www.scope.org.uk/campaigns/disability-perception-gap/.

9. Phillip Carter and Cathy Barrera, "Challenges on the Home Front: Under-employment Hits Veterans Hard," *ZipRecruiter* and *Call of Duty Endowment,* accessed December 2020, https://www.ziprecruiter.com/blog/underemployment-hits-veterans-hard/.

10. Pooja Jain-Link, Julia Taylor Kennedy, et al., "Being Black in Corporate America: An Intersectional Exploration." *Coqual (Formerly CTI)* (December 2019), https://coqual .org/reports/being-black-in-corporate-america-an-intersectional-exploration/.

11. Ibid.

12. Julie Kashen, Sarah Jane Glynn, and Amanda Novello, "How COVID-19 Sent Women's Workforce Progress Backward," *Center for American Progress*, October 30, 2020, https://www.americanprogress.org/issues/women/reports/2020/10/30/492582 /covid-19-sent-womens-workforce-progress-backward/.

13. United Nations Department of Economic and Social Affairs, "Goal 5: Achieve Gender Equality and Empower All Women and Girls," *United Nations,* 2020, https:// sdgs.un.org/goals/goal5.

14. Rachel Thomas, Marianne Cooper, Gina Cardazone, et al., "Women in the Workplace 2020," *McKinsey and Company* (2020), https://wiw-report.s3.amazonaws.com /Women_in_the_Workplace_2020.pdf.

15. Scott, Kapor Klein, and Onovakpuri (see Introduction, n. 3).

16. Christianne Corbett and Catherine Hill, "Solving the Equation: The Variables for Women's Success in Engineering and Computing," *American Association of University Women* (2015), https://ww3.aauw.org/research/solving-the-equation/.

17. Lorelle L. Espinosa, "Pipelines and Pathways: Women of Color in Undergraduate STEM Majors and the College Experiences That Contribute to Persistence," *Harvard Educational Review* 81, no. 2 (June 2011): 209–241, https://doi.org/10.17763 /haer.81.2.92315ww157656k3u.

18. Vivian Hunt, Sara Prince, Sundiatu Dixon-Fyle, and Lareina Yee. "Delivering Through Diversity." *McKinsey and Company* (January 2018), https://www.mckinsey .com/~/media/McKinsey/Business%20Functions/Organization/Our%20Insights /Delivering%20through%20diversity/Delivering-through-diversity_full-report .ashx.

19. Frank L. Schmidt and John Edward Hunter, "The Validity and Utility of Selection Methods in Personnel Psychology: Practical and Theoretical Implications of 85 Years of Research Findings," *Psychological Bulletin* 124, no. 2 (September 1998): 262–274, https://doi.org/10.1037/0033-2909.124.2.262.

20. I'm often asked for studies showing this data. The research is abundant and continues to grow—a quick search of academic articles will provide hundreds of references, as well as many of the articles throughout the endnotes in this book. See ch.1 n. 1 in particular.

21. Sundiatu Dixon-Fyle, Kevin Dolan, Vivian Hunt, and Sarah Prince, "Diversity Wins: How Inclusion Matters," *McKinsey and Company* (May 2020), https://www

.mckinsey.com/featured-insights/diversity-and-inclusion/diversity-wins-how
-inclusion-matters.

22. Melinda Briana Epler, Shivaani Lnu, Rainier Renzo Santos, Sally Moywaywa, Anto-
nia Ford, Merve Bulgurcu, and Wayne Sutton, "State of Allyship Report," *Change Catalyst* (2021), https://changecatalyst.co/allyshipreport.

23. These numbers are based on our global data and are higher than many research
projects on discrimination in the workplace. This could be due to participation
bias—people drawn to take an allyship survey may be more likely to have experienced discrimination.

24. Throughout this book, I'll abbreviate to *DEI*. You might encounter *EDI* or *EID*, or
see an additional *B* for *belonging*, *J* for *justice*, and/or *A* for *allyship*.

25. "Genders" could include gender identity, role, and/or expression.

26. Kimberlé Crenshaw, "Kimberlé Crenshaw on Intersectionality, More Than Two
Decades Later," interviewed by Columbia Law School News, *Columbia Law School*,
June 8, 2017, https://www.law.columbia.edu/news/archive/kimberle-crenshaw
-intersectionality-more-two-decades-later.

27. Kristyn A. Scott, Joanna M. Heathcote, and Jamie A. Gruman, "The Diverse Organization: Finding Gold at the End of the Rainbow," *Human Resource Management*
50, no. 6 (November 2011): 735–755, https://doi.org/10.1002/hrm.20459.

28. This definition follows our own findings as well as research from Coqual (formerly
CTI). In a study published in 2020, Coqual found four key elements of belonging at
work included seen, connected, supported, and proud. Maslow's hierarchy of needs
even includes belonging. Julia Taylor Kennedy, Pooja Jain-Link, et al., "The Power of
Belonging: What It Is and Why It Matters in Today's Workplace," *Coqual*, Belonging Series Part 1 (2020), https://coqual.org/reports/the-power-of-belonging/.

29. Epler, Lnu, Santos, Moywaywa, Ford, Bulgurcu, and Sutton (see n. 22).

30. Raw data from David McCandless, Miriam Quick, and Stephanie Tomasevic,
"Diversity in Tech: Employee Breakdown of Key Technology Companies," *Information Is Beautiful*, accessed December 2020, https://informationisbeautiful.net
/visualizations/diversity-in-tech/. Note that we have not used the "average" number
given in the database because it does not take into account the total population at
each tech company. The way this is calculated it assumes an equal weight for all tech
companies. However, some companies on this list are much larger than others: for
example, 30 percent women at Google in 2014 was 14,327 people, where 49 percent
women at Pandora was just 750 people. Our Change Catalyst team went back to the
data on the original diversity reports for each company, and calculated the total
populations of each group based on the company population in 2014.

31. "Women, Minorities, and People with Disabilities in Science and Engineering: Data
Tables," *National Center for Science and Engineering Statistics*, accessed December
2020, https://ncses.nsf.gov/pubs/nsf19304/data.

32. Melinda Briana Epler and Brenda Darden Wilkerson. "Women Championing
Women," July 7, 2020, in *Leading With Empathy & Allyship* Episode 13, by Change
Catalyst, video, 54:01. https://changecatalyst.co/brenda-darden-wilkerson/.

Chapter 3: Step 1: Learn, Unlearn, Relearn

1. Alex Altman, "Why the Killing of George Floyd Sparked an American Uprising," *Time*, June 4, 2020, https://time.com/5847967/george-floyd-protests-trump/.
2. Global Data and Insights team at Wikimedia Foundation, "Community Insights/ Community Insights 2020 Report," *Wikimedia Meta-wiki* (September 2020), https:// meta.wikimedia.org/wiki/Community_Insights/Community_Insights_2020 _Report; Edward Galvez, "What We Learned from Surveying 4,000 Members of the Wikipedia and Wikimedia Communities," *Wikimedia Foundation,* September 13, 2018, https://wikimediafoundation.org/news/2018/09/13/what-we-learned-surveying -4000-community-members/; "Wikipedia Editors Study: Results from the Editors' Survey, April 2011," *Wikimedia Foundation,* April 2011, https://upload.wikimedia.org /wikipedia/commons/7/76/Editor_Survey_Report_-_April_2011.pdf.
3. Global Data and Insights team at Wikimedia Foundation (see n. 2); AubreyWil- liams, "Wikimedia Foundation Diversity and Inclusion Information About Our Workers—2019 by the Numbers," *Wikimedia Foundation,* October 1, 2019, https:// wikimediafoundation.org/news/2019/10/01/wikimedia-foundation-diversity-and -inclusion-information-about-our-workers-2019-by-the-numbers/.
4. Joy Harjo, *Crazy Brave: A Memoir* (W. W. Norton & Company, 2013).
5. Estimates for the Taíno population of Hispaniola before colonization range from 100,000–1,000,000. New World Encyclopedia Contributors, "Indigenous Peo- ples of the Americas," *New World Encyclopedia,* March 2, 2018, https://www .newworldencyclopedia.org/p/index.php?title=Indigenous_peoples_of_the_Americas; Abdul Rob, "Taíno: Indigenous Caribbeans," *Black History Month,* December 2, 2016, https://www.blackhistorymonth.org.uk/article/section/pre-colonial-history/taino -indigenous-caribbeans/; National Library of Medicine, "AD 1493: Spanish Settlers Enslave the Taíno of Hispaniola," *Native Voices,* accessed December 2020, https:// www.nlm.nih.gov/nativevoices/timeline/170.html?tribe=Tainog.
6. Alexander Koch, Chris Brierley, Mark M. Maslin, and Simon L. Lewis, "Earth System Impacts of the European Arrival and Great Dying in the Americas After 1492," *Quaternary Science Reviews* 207, no. 1 (March 2019): 13–36, https://doi.org /10.1016/j.quascirev.2018.12.004; Alexander Koch, Chris Brierley, Mark Maslin, and Simon Lewis, "European Colonisation of the Americas Might Have Caused Global Cooling, According to New Research," *World Economic Forum,* February 1, 2019, https://www.weforum.org/agenda/2019/02/european-colonisation-of-the-americas -caused-global-cooling/.
7. Here I had hoped to name some of the cultures that disappeared as a result of colo- nization, yet sadly there are few records available.
8. "Spanish Arrival in Aramai Lands" and "Who are the original peoples of San Fran- cisco and of the San Francisco Peninsula?" *The Association of Ramaytush Ohlone,* accessed April 2021, https://www.ramaytush.org.
9. Find Indigenous Territories in your region at Native Land Digital: https://native -land.ca/. Learn more about land acknowledgments at US Department of Arts and Culture: https://usdac.us/nativeland or National Indigenous Australians Agency:

https://www.indigenous.gov.au/contact-us/welcome_acknowledgement-country. Note: some resources may be incomplete, showing Indigenous peoples who are recognized by the government; there are many peoples who are still waiting and fighting to be recognized.

10. Mike Males, "Who Are Police Killing?," *Center on Juvenile and Criminal Justice*, August 26, 2014, http://www.cjcj.org/news/8113?_ga=2.116428229.2143113355.159 9963089-686649359.1599963089.

11. Jake Flanagin, "Native Americans Are the Unseen Victims of a Broken US Justice System," *Quartz*, April 27, 2015, https://qz.com/392342/native-americans-are-the -unseen-victims-of-a-broken-us-justice-system/.

12. Nicole Busker, Deborah Rho, and Marina Mileo Gorsuch, "American Indian Women Were Disproportionately Stopped, Searched and Arrested by Police in Minneapolis in 2017," *Federal Reserve Bank of Minneapolis*, February 20, 2018, https://www.minneapolisfed.org/article/2018/american-indian-women-were -disproportionately-stopped-searched-and-arrested-by-police-in-minneapolis-in -2017.

13. Flanagin (see n. 11).

14. Jim Bell, "Indigenous Incarceration Rate 'a Travesty,' Canada's Prison Watchdog Says," *Nunatsiaq News*, January 22, 2020, https://nunatsiaq.com/stories/article /indigenous-incarceration-rate-a-travesty-canadas-prison-watchdog-says/.

15. "A Brief Aboriginal History," *Aboriginal Heritage Office,* accessed December 2020, https://www.aboriginalheritage.org/history/history/.

16. Sixthofdecember, "Cape Coast Castle Door of No Return," photograph, *Wikimedia Commons*, September 2, 2012, https://commons.wikimedia.org/wiki/File:Cape _Coast_Castle_Door_of_No_Return_02_Sept_2012.jpg.

17. W. E. B. Du Bois, *Black Reconstruction in America: an Essay Toward a History of the Part Which Black Folk Played in the Attempt to Reconstruct Democracy in America, 1860-1880* (Harcourt, Brace and Company, 1935).

18. Carl Zimmer, "Scientists Find the Skull of Humanity's Ancestor, on a Computer," *New York Times,* September 10, 2019, https://www.nytimes.com/2019/09/10/science /human-ancestor-skull-computer.html.

19. This period in history is often called "New Imperialism" or the "Scramble for Africa" (a callous term that makes my stomach and heart churn). These terms created from the colonizers' perspective need to be revised.

20. Adam Hochschild, "Leopold II: King of Belgium," *Encyclopaedia Britannica*, accessed May 2021, https://www.britannica.com/biography/Leopold-II-king-of-Belgium.

21. Mary Elliot, curator, "Four Hundred Years After Enslaved Africans Were First Brought to Virginia, Most Americans Still Don't Know the Full Story of Slavery," *New York Times Magazine*, August 19, 2019, https://www.nytimes.com/interactive /2019/08/19/magazine/history-slavery-smithsonian.html.

22. "Trans-Atlantic Slave Trade—Estimates," *Slave Voyages*, accessed December 2020, https://www.slavevoyages.org/assessment/estimates.

23. Ibid.

24. The Emancipation Proclamation abolished slavery for everyone except people who are incarcerated.

25. Gary Orfield, Erica Frankenberg, Jongyeon Ee, and Jennifer B. Ayscue, "Harming Our Common Future: America's Segregated Schools 65 Years After Brown," *UCLA Civil Rights Project*, May 10, 2019, https://www.civilrightsproject.ucla.edu/research /k-12-education/integration-and-diversity/harming-our-common-future-americas -segregated-schools-65-years-after-brown.

26. Malala Yousafzai, "Malala Yousafzai Addresses United Nations Youth Assembly," July 12, 2013, by United Nations, video, 17:42, https://youtu.be/3rNhZu3ttIU.

27. "Block the Vote: Voter Suppression in 2020," *ACLU*, February 3, 2020, https://www .aclu.org/news/civil-liberties/block-the-vote-voter-suppression-in-2020/; PBS, "Not All Women Gained the Vote in 1920," *American Experience*, July 6, 2020, https:// www.pbs.org/wgbh/americanexperience/features/vote-not-all-women-gained -right-to-vote-in-1920/; Suzanne Gamboa, "For Latinos, 1965 Voting Rights Act Impact Came a Decade Later," *NBC News*, August 6, 2015, https://www.nbcnews .com/news/latino/latinos-1965-voting-rights-act-impact-came-decade-later -n404936; Rebecca Schleifer, "Disabled and Disenfranchised," *Huffington Post*, September 5, 2012 (updated November 5, 2012), https://www.huffpost.com/entry /disabled-voting-rights_b_1853234.

28. Robert Crotti, Thierry Geiger, Vesselina Ratcheva, Saadia Zahidi, et al., "Global Gender Gap Report 2020," *World Economic Forum*, https://www.weforum.org/reports /gender-gap-2020-report-100-years-pay-equality.

29. "The Simple Truth About the Gender Pay Gap," *American Association of University Women*, December 2020, https://www.aauw.org/resources/research/simple-truth/.

30. George Takei, "Reject Hate," *Films for Action*, August 8, 2012, https://www .filmsforaction.org/news/reject-hate/.

31. Sharita Gruberg, Lindsay Mahowald, and John Halpin, "The State of the LGBTQ Community in 2020," *Center for American Progress*, October 6, 2020, https://www .americanprogress.org/issues/lgbtq-rights/reports/2020/10/06/491052/state-lgbtq -community-2020/.

32. Mark Lee, Liam Miranda, Katalina Hadfield, Jake Mazeitis, Gabrielle Winger, et al., "Dismantling a Culture of Violence: Understanding Anti-Transgender Violence and Ending the Crisis," *Human Rights Campaign Foundation* (December 2020), https://hrc-prod-requests.s3-us-west-2.amazonaws.com/files/assets/resources /Dismantling-a-Culture-of-Violence-010721.pdf.

33. Stephen W. Hawking, Foreword to "World Report on Disability," *World Health Organization* (2011).

34. Natalie Drew, Michelle Funk, Stephen Tang, Jagannath Lamichhane, et al., "Human Rights Violations of People with Mental and Psychosocial Disabilities: An Unresolved Global Crisis," *The Lancet* 378, no. 9803 (November 2011): 1664–1675, https://doi.org/10.1016/S0140-6736(11)61458-X.

35. "Factsheet on Persons with Disabilities," (see ch. 2, n. 5); Collins (see ch. 1, n. 32).

36. Ta-Nehisi Coates, *Between the World and Me* (Spiegel & Grau, 2015).

37. Many disabled people prefer not to use "phobia" in the context of hatred and discrimination because a phobia is a diagnosable mental health condition. Many people in the LGBTQIA+ and Muslim communities prefer not to use "homophobia" and "islamophobia," because anti-LGBTQIA+ and anti-Muslim sentiment is not really fear, it's deeper hatred and systemic discrimination. For these reasons, I'll use the somewhat equivalent "isms" in this book. Thanks, Najeeba Syeed, for starting me down this path of realization.

38. Kriston McIntosh, Emily Moss, Ryan Nunn, and Jay Shambaugh, "Examining the Black-White Wealth Gap," *Brookings Institution*, February 27, 2020, https://www.brookings.edu/blog/up-front/2020/02/27/examining-the-black-white-wealth-gap/.

39. Rhitu Chatterjee, "How the Pandemic Is Widening the Racial Wealth Gap," *NPR*, September 18, 2020, https://www.npr.org/sections/health-shots/2020/09/18/912731744/how-the-pandemic-is-widening-the-racial-wealth-gap; Kimberly Amadeo, "Racial Wealth Gap in the United States," *The Balance*, November 23, 2020, https://www.thebalance.com/racial-wealth-gap-in-united-states-4169678; United States Census Bureau, "Wealth, Asset Ownership, & Debt of Households Detailed Tables: 2016," September 19, 2019, https://www.census.gov/data/tables/2016/demo/wealth/wealth-asset-ownership.html; "Economic Inequality Across Gender Diversity," *Inequality.org*, accessed December 2020, https://inequality.org/facts/gender-inequality/#gender-wealth-gaps.

40. Heather Long and Andrew Van Dam, "The Black-White Economic Divide Is as Wide as It Was in 1968," *Washington Post*, June 4, 2020, https://www.washingtonpost.com/business/2020/06/04/economic-divide-black-households/.

41. Nanette Goodman, Michael Morris, and Kelvin Boston, "Financial Inequality: Disability, Race and Poverty in America," *National Disability Institute* (February 2019), https://www.nationaldisabilityinstitute.org/wp-content/uploads/2019/02/disability-race-poverty-in-america.pdf; Katie M. Jajtner, Sophie Mitra, Christine Fountain, and Austin Nichols, "Rising Income Inequality Through a Disability Lens: Trends in the United States 1981–2018," *Social Indicators Research* 151 (May 2020): 81–114, https://doi.org/10.1007/s11205-020-02379-8.

42. American Psychological Association, "Stress in America™: The Impact of Discrimination," *Stress in America™ Survey* (March 2016), https://www.apa.org/news/press/releases/stress/2015/impact-of-discrimination.pdf.

43. "Stress in America™ 2020: A National Mental Health Crisis," *American Psychological Association*, October 2020, https://www.apa.org/news/press/releases/stress/2020/report-october.

44. A. T. Geronimus, "The Weathering Hypothesis and the Health of African-American Women and Infants: Evidence and Speculations," *Ethnicity and Disease* 2, no. 3 (Summer 1992): 207–221, https://pubmed.ncbi.nlm.nih.gov/1467758/.

45. Laura SmartRichman and Charles Jonassaint, "The Effects of Race-Related Stress on Cortisol Reactivity in the Laboratory: Implications of the Duke Lacrosse Scandal," *Annals of Behavioral Medicine: A Publication of the Society of Behavioral Medicine* 35, no. 1 (February 2008): 105–110, https://doi.org/10.1007/s12160-007-9013-8;

Harvey L. Nicholson Jr. and Di Mei, "Racial Microaggressions and Self-rated Health Among Asians and Asian Americans," *Race and Social Problems* 12 (May 2020): 209–218, https://doi.org/10.1007/s12552-020-09293-1; Kevin L. Nadal, Katie E. Griffin, Yinglee Wong, Kristin C. Davidoff, and Lindsey S. Davis, "The Injurious Relationship Between Racial Microaggressions and Physical Health: Implications for Social Work," *Journal of Ethnic & Cultural Diversity in Social Work* 26, no. 1–2 (2017): 6–17, https://doi.org/10.1080/15313204.2016.1263813; Rae Ellen Bichell, "Scientists Start to Tease out the Subtler Ways Racism Hurts Health," *NPR*, November 11, 2017, https://www.npr.org/sections/health-shots/2017/11/11/562623815/scientists-start-to-tease-out-the-subtler-ways-racism-hurts-health; Zaneta M. Thayer and Christopher W. Kuzawa, "Ethnic Discrimination Predicts Poor Self-Rated Health and Cortisol in Pregnancy: Insights from New Zealand," *Social Science and Medicine* 128 (March 2015): 36–42, https://doi.org/10.1016/j.socscimed.2015.01.003; Diane S. Lauderdale, "Birth Outcomes for Arabic-named Women in California Before and After September 11," *Demography* 43, no. 1 (February 2006): 185–201, https://doi.org/10.1353/dem.2006.0008.

46. David R. Williams, Jourdyn A. Lawrence, Brigette A. Davis, and Cecilia Vu, "Understanding How Discrimination Can Affect Health," *Health Services Research* 54, no. S2 (December 2019): 1374–1388, https://doi.org/10.1111/1475-6773.13222.

47. Erika Weisz and Jamil Zaki, "Empathy-Building Interventions: A Review of Existing Work and Suggestions for Future Directions," in *The Oxford Handbook of Compassion Science*, edited by Emma M. Seppälä, et al., 205–218 (Oxford University Press, 2017) https://doi.org/10.1093/oxfordhb/9780190464684.013.16.

48. Ronald Wyatt, "Pain and Ethnicity," *Virtual Mentor* 15, no. 5 (May 2013): 449–454, https://doi.org/10.1001/virtualmentor.2013.15.5.pfor1-1305; Centers for Disease Control and Prevention, "Racial and Ethnic Disparities Continue in Pregnancy-Related Deaths: Black, American Indian/Alaska Native Women Most Affected," *CDC Newsroom*, September 5, 2019, https://www.cdc.gov/media/releases/2019/p0905-racial-ethnic-disparities-pregnancy-deaths.html.

49. James, Herman, Rankin, Keisling, et al. (see ch. 2 n. 3).

50. Williams, Lawrence, Davis, and Vu (see n. 46).

51. Alan Mozes, "COVID-19 Ravages the Navajo Nation," *WebMD*, June 9, 2020, https://www.webmd.com/lung/news/20200609/covid-19-ravages-the-navajo-nation#1; Cody Nelson, "Covid Ravages Navajo Nation as Trump Makes Election Play for Area," *The Guardian*, October 8, 2020, https://www.theguardian.com/us-news/2020/oct/08/navajo-nation-coronavirus-pandemic.

52. Dominique Derbigny, "On the Margins: Economic Security for Women of Color Through the Coronavirus Crisis and Beyond," *Closing the Women's Wealth Gap*, April 2020, https://womenswealthgap.org/wp-content/uploads/2020/11/OnTheMargins_DDerbigny.pdf.

53. Bessel Van der Kolk, *The Body Keeps the Score: Brain, Mind, and Body in the Healing of Trauma* (Penguin Books, 2014).

54. Eduardo Duran (Tiospaye Ta Woapiye Wicasa), *Healing the Soul Wound: Trauma-Informed Counseling for Indigenous Communities* (Teachers College Press, 2019).
55. Joy DeGruy, *Post Traumatic Slave Syndrome: America's Legacy of Enduring Injury and Healing*, 2nd ed. (Joy Degruy Publications Inc., 2017).
56. M. Y. Brave Heart and L. M. DeBruyn, "The American Indian Holocaust: Healing Historical Unresolved Grief." *American Indian and Alaska Native Mental Health Research* 8, no. 2 (1998): 56–78, https://pubmed.ncbi.nlm.nih.gov/9842066/.
57. Rachel Yehuda and Amy Lehrner, "Intergenerational Transmission of Trauma Effects: Putative Role of Epigenetic Mechanisms," *World Psychiatry* 17, no. 3 (October 2018): 243–257, https://doi.org/10.1002/wps.20568; Nora K. Moog, Claudia Buss, Sonja Entringer, Daniel L. Gillen, et al., "Maternal Exposure to Childhood Trauma Is Associated During Pregnancy with Placental-Fetal Stress Physiology," *Biological Psychiatry* 79, no. 10 (May 2016): 831–839, https://doi.org/10.1016/j.biopsych.2015.08 .032; Bichell (see n. 45); Richman and Jonassaint (see n. 45); Thayer and Kuzawa (see n. 45); Lauderdale (see n. 45); Elizabeth Fast and Delphine Collin-Vézina, "Historical Trauma, Race-based Trauma and Resilience of Indigenous Peoples: A Literature Review," *First Peoples Child & Family Review* 5, no. 1 (2010): 126–136, https://doi.org /10.7202/1069069ar; Karina L. Walters, Selina A. Mohammed, Teresa Evans-Campbell, Ramona E. Beltrán, David H. Chae, and Bonnie Duran, "Bodies Don't Just Tell Stories, They Tell Histories: Embodiment of Historical Trauma Among American Indians and Alaska Natives," *Du Bois Review: Social Science Research on Race* 8, no.1 (April 2011): 179–189, https://doi.org/10.1017/S1742058X1100018X; Nathaniel Vincent Mohatt, Azure B. Thompson, Nghi D. Thai, and Jacob Kraemer Tebes, "Historical Trauma as Public Narrative: A Conceptual Review of How History Impacts Present-Day Health," *Social Science & Medicine* 106 (April 2014): 128–136, https:// doi.org/10.1016/j.socscimed.2014.01.043; Amy Bombay, Kim Matheson, and Hymie Anisman. "Intergenerational Trauma: Convergence of Multiple Processes Among First Nations Peoples in Canada," *International Journal of Indigenous Health* 5, no. 3 (November 2009): 6–47, https://jps.library.utoronto.ca/index.php/ijih /article/download/28987/23916/.
58. Evans-Campbell and Walters called the combination of historical trauma and contemporary trauma from discrimination and microaggressions in Indigenous communities "Colonial Trauma Response." Teresa Evans-Campbell, "Historical Trauma in American Indian/Native Alaska Communities: A Multilevel Framework for Exploring Impacts on Individuals, Families, and Communities," *Journal of Interpersonal Violence* 23, no. 3 (March 2008): 316–338, https://doi.org/10.1177 /0886260507312290.
59. Her sister was one of 1,017 Indigenous women killed in Canada from 1980 to 2012. Steve Scherer, "Canadian Inquiry Calls Deaths of Indigenous Women 'Genocide,'" *U.S. News & World Report*, June 3, 2019, https://www.usnews.com/news /world/articles/2019-06-03/canadian-inquiry-calls-deaths-of-indigenous-women -genocide.

60. Mia Mingus, "Dreaming Accountability," *Leaving Evidence*, May 5, 2019, https://leavingevidence.wordpress.com/2019/05/05/dreaming-accountability-dreaming-a-returning-to-ourselves-and-each-other/.

61. Daryl A. Wout, Mary C. Murphy, and Claude M. Steele, "When Your Friends Matter: The Effect of White Students' Racial Friendship Networks on Meta-perceptions and Perceived Identity Contingencies," *Journal of Experimental Social Psychology* 46, no. 6 (November 2010): 1035–1041, https://doi.org/10.1016/j.jesp.2010.06.003.

62. Melinda Briana Epler and Michael Thomas, "Understanding Intergenerational Trauma & Its Impact in the Workplace," June 2, 2020, in *Leading With Empathy & Allyship* Episode 8, by Change Catalyst, video, 55:29, https://changecatalyst.co/michael-thomas/; Melinda Briana Epler and Angel Acosta, "Moving from Structural Inequality to Human Flourishing," July 14, 2020, in *Leading With Empathy & Allyship* Episode 14, by Change Catalyst, video, 57:03, https://changecatalyst.co/angel-acosta/.

63. Fast and Collin-Vézina (see n. 57); Bombay, Matheson, and Anisman (see n. 57); Williams, Lawrence, Davis, and Vu (see n. 46); Froma Walsh, *Strengthening Family Resilience*, 3rd ed. (The Guilford Press, 2016). Michael A. Grodin, Linda Piwowarczyk, Derek Fulker, Alexander R. Bazazi, and Robert B. Saper, "Treating Survivors of Torture and Refugee Trauma: A Preliminary Case Series Using Qigong and T'ai Chi," *Journal of Alternative and Complementary Medicine* 14, no. 7 (September 2008): 801–806, https://doi.org/10.1089/acm.2007.0736; Jennifer Taylor, Loyola McLean, Anthony Korner, Elizabeth Stratton, and Nicholas Glozier, "Mindfulness and Yoga for Psychological Trauma: Systematic Review and Meta-analysis," *Journal of Trauma & Dissociation* 21, no.5 (2020): 536–573, https://doi.org/10.1080/15299732.2020.1760167; Latifa Jackson, Zainab Jackson, and Fatima Jackson, "Intergenerational Resilience in Response to the Stress and Trauma of Enslavement and Chronic Exposure to Institutionalized Racism," *Journal of Clinical Epigenetics* 4, no. 15 (August 2018): 1–7, https://doi.org/10.21767/2472-1158.1000100; Devin G. Atallah, "A Community-based Qualitative Study of Intergenerational Resilience with Palestinian Refugee Families Facing Structural Violence and Historical Trauma," *Transcultural Psychiatry* 54, no. 3 (May 2017): 357–383, https://doi.org/10.1177/1363461517706287; Evans-Campbell (see n. 58); Ashley Quinn, "Reflections on Intergenerational Trauma: Healing as a Critical Intervention," *First Peoples Child & Family Review* 3, no. 4 (2007): 72-82, https://doi.org/10.7202/1069377ar; Mark Lusk, Sam Terrazas, Janette Caro, Perla Chaparro, and Delia Puga Antúnez, "Resilience, Faith, and Social Supports Among Migrants and Refugees from Central America and Mexico," *Journal of Spirituality in Mental Health* 23, no. 1 (2021): 1–22, https://doi.org/10.1080/19349637.2019.1620668.

64. Lena Rawley, "Petra Collins Captures Her Family in This New Exhibition," *The Cut*, March 31, 2017, https://www.thecut.com/2017/03/petra-collins-captures-her-familys-past-in-pacifier.html.

65. Stacy L. Smith, Marc Choueiti, Kevin Yao, Hannah Clark, and Katherine Pieper, "Inclusion in the Director's Chair: Analysis of Director Gender & Race/Ethnicity Across 1,300 Top Films from 2007 to 2019," *Annenberg Foundation and USC Annenberg*

Inclusion Initiative, January 2020, https://www.courthousenews.com/wp-content /uploads/2020/09/film-diversity.pdf.

66. Stacy L. Smith, Marc Choueiti, Katherine Pieper, et al., "Inequality in 1,300 Popular Films: Examining Portrayals of Gender, Race/Ethnicity, LGBTQ & Disability from 2007 to 2019," *Annenberg Foundation* and *USC Annenberg Inclusion Initiative*, September 2020, https://assets.uscannenberg.org/docs/aii-inequality_1300_popular _films_09-08-2020.pdf.

67. Bechdeltest.com, accessed 2021.

68. Manohla Dargis, "Sundance Fights Tide with Films Like 'The Birth of a Nation,'" *New York Times*, January 29, 2016, https://www.nytimes.com/2016/01/30/movies /sundance-fights-tide-with-films-like-the-birth-of-a-nation.html?smprod=nytcore -ipad&smid=nytcore-ipad-share&_r=0.

69. Johanna Weststar, Eva Kwan, and Shruti Kumar, "Developer Satisfaction Survey 2019: Summary Report," *International Game Developers Association*, November 2019, https://s3-us-east-2.amazonaws.com/igda-website/wp-content/uploads/2020 /01/29093706/IGDA-DSS-2019_Summary-Report_Nov-20-2019.pdf.

70. Corinne Duyvis, "#OwnVoices," *CorinneDuyvis.net*, *n.d.* accessed April 2021, https://www.corinneduyvis.net/ownvoices/.

71. Laura M. Jiménez and Betsy Beckert, "Where Is the Diversity in Publishing? The 2019 Diversity Baseline Survey Results," *The Open Book Blog* by Lee and Low Books, January 28, 2020, https://blog.leeandlow.com/2020/01/28/2019diversitybaselinesurvey/.

72. Cooperative Children's Book Center, "The Numbers Are In: 2019 CCBC Diversity Statistics," *University of Wisconsin-Madison School of Education,* June 16, 2020, https://ccbc.education.wisc.edu/the-numbers-are-in-2019-ccbc-diversity-statistics/.

73. Kazi Md. Mukitul Islam and M. Niaz Asadullah, "Gender Stereotypes and Education: A Comparative Content Analysis of Malaysian, Indonesian, Pakistani and Bangladeshi School Textbooks," *PLoS ONE* 13, no. 1. (January 2018), https://doi.org /10.1371/journal.pone.0190807; Barbara C. Cruz, "Stereotypes of Latin Americans Perpetuated in Secondary School History Textbooks," *Latino Studies Journal* 1, no. 1 (January 1994): 51–67, https://eric.ed.gov/?id=ED389648; Dionysios Gouvias and Christos Alexopoulos, "Sexist Stereotypes in the Language Textbooks of the Greek Primary School: A Multidimensional Approach," *Gender and Education* 30, no. 5 (2018): 642–662, https://doi.org/10.1080/09540253.2016.1237620; Lütfi İncikabı and Fadime Ulusoy, "Gender Bias and Stereotypes in Australian, Singaporean and Turkish Mathematics Textbooks," *Turkish Journal of Education* 8, no. 4 (October 2019): 298–317, https://doi.org/10.19128/turje.581802; Rae Lesser Blumberg, "The Invisible Obstacle to Educational Equality: Gender Bias in Textbooks," *Prospects* 38 (September 2008): 345–361, https://doi.org/10.1007/s11125-009-9086-1; Agostino Portera, "Stereotypes, Prejudices and Intercultural Education in Italy: Research on Textbooks in Primary Schools," *Intercultural Education* 15, no. 3 (2004): 283–294, https://doi.org/10.1080/1467598042000262572; Wei Wang, "Gender Role Stereotypes in Chinese Primary School Textbooks," *Asian Journal of Women's Studies* 4, no. 4 (1998): 39–59, https://doi.org/10.1080/12259276.1998.11665833.

74. Travis L. Dixon, "A Dangerous Distortion of Our Families: Representations of Families, by Race, in News and Opinion Media," *Color of Change*, January 2018, https://colorofchange.org/dangerousdistortion/.

75. Travis L. Dixon and Charlotte L. Williams, "The Changing Misrepresentation of Race and Crime on Network and Cable News," *Journal of Communication* 65, no. 1 (February2015): 24–39, https://doi.org/10.1111/jcom.12133; QinZhang, "Asian Americans Beyond the Model Minority Stereotype: The Nerdy and the Left Out," *Journal of International and Intercultural Communication* 3, no. 1 (2010): 20–37, https://doi.org/10.1080/17513050903428109.

76. Melinda Briana Epler and Muna Hussaini, "Pandemic & Parenting: How to Juggle the Impossible," October 27, 2020, in *Leading With Empathy & Allyship* Episode 24, by Change Catalyst, video, 1:00:09, https://changecatalyst.co/muna-hussaini/.

77. Christopher Ingraham, "Three Quarters of Whites Don't Have Any Non-White Friends," *Washington Post*, August 25, 2014, https://www.washingtonpost.com/news/wonk/wp/2014/08/25/three-quarters-of-whites-dont-have-any-non-white-friends/.

Chapter 4: Step 2: Do No Harm—Understand and Correct Our Biases

1. Francesca Rice, "Maya Angelou: An Extraordinarily Wise Woman," Marie Claire, April 4, 2014, https://www.marieclaire.co.uk/entertainment/people/maya-angelou-an-extraordinarily-wise-woman-84132. Similarly, Carl W. Buehner has been quoted as saying: "They may forget what you said—but they will never forget how you made them feel."

2. Alison Wood Brooks, Laura Huang, Sarah Wood Kearney, and Fiona E. Murray, "Investors Prefer Entrepreneurial Ventures Pitched by Attractive Men," *PNAS* 111, no. 12 (March 2014): 4427–4431, https://doi.org/10.1073/pnas.1321202111; Daniel S. Hamermesh, *Beauty Pays: Why Attractive People Are More Successful* (Princeton University Press, 2011); Corinne A. Moss-Racusin, John F. Dovidio, Victoria L. Brescoll, Mark J. Graham, and Jo Handelsman, "Science Faculty's Subtle Gender Biases Favor Male Students," *PNAS* 109, no. 41 (October 2012): 16,474–16,479, https://doi.org/10.1073/pnas.1211286109; Anne M. Koenig, Abigail A. Mitchell, Alice H. Eagly, and Tiina Ristikari, "Are Leader Stereotypes Masculine? A Meta-Analysis of Three Research Paradigms," *Psychological Bulletin* 137, no. 4 (2011): 616–642, https://doi.org/10.1037/a0023557; Amanda K. Sesko and Monica Biernat, "Prototypes of Race and Gender: The Invisibility of Black Women," *Journal of Experimental Social Psychology* 46, no. 2 (March 2010): 356–360, https://doi.org/10.1016/j.jesp.2009.10.016.

3. Brené Brown defines the bandwagon effect as "Feeling like you have to hop on board with the consensus, even if you might disagree, vehemently or mildly. This often happens when you're the only objector or you're the last to share and the group is already excited about an idea." Brené Brown, "The Dare to Lead Glossary: Key

Language, Skills, Tools, and Practices," BreneBrown.com (2018), https://daretolead
.brenebrown.com/wp-content/uploads/2018/10/Glossary-of-Key-Language-Skills
-and-Tools-from-DTL.pdf.

4. Paul 't Hart, "Irving L. Janis' Victims of Groupthink," *Political Psychology* 12, no. 2
(June 1991): 247–278, https://doi.org/10.2307/3791464.

5. Keith E. Edwards, "Aspiring Social Justice Ally Identity Development: A Conceptual Model," *NASPA Journal* 43, no. 4 (2006): 39–60, https://doi.org/10.2202/1949
-6605.1722.

6. Janine Willis and Alexander Todorov, "First Impressions Making Up Your Mind
After a 100-Ms Exposure to a Face," *Psychological Science* 17, no. 7 (July 2006): 592–
598, https://doi.org/10.1111/j.1467-9280.2006.01750.x.

7. Bernadette Dillon and Juliet Bourke, "The Six Signature Traits of Inclusive Leadership: Thriving in a Diverse New World," *Deloitte University Press* (2016), https://
www2.deloitte.com/us/en/insights/topics/talent/six-signature-traits-of-inclusive
-leadership.html.

8. Patrick S. Forscher, Calvin K. Lai, Jordan R. Axt, et al., "A Meta-Analysis of Procedures to Change Implicit Measures," *Journal of Personality and Social Psychology*
117, no. 3 (April 2019): 522–559, https://doi.org/10.1037/pspa0000160.

9. Catherine Hanrahan, "Job Recruitment Algorithms Can Amplify Unconscious
Bias Favouring Men, New Research Finds," *ABC News Australia*, December 1,
2020, https://www.abc.net.au/news/2020-12-02/job-recruitment-algorithms-can
-have-bias-against-women/12938870; Marc Cheong, Reeva Lederman, Aidan
McLoughney, Sheilla Njoto, Leah Ruppanner, and Anthony Wirth, "Ethical
Implications of AI Bias as a Result of Workforce Gender Imbalance," CIS & The
Policy Lab, The University of Melbourne for UniBank (December 2020), https://
www.unibank.com.au/-/media/unibank/about-us/member-news/report-ai-bias-as
-a-result-of-workforce-gender-imbalance.ashx.

10. Melinda Briana Epler and Najeeba Syeed, "Exploring Empathy, Islamophobia &
Muslim Identity," June 1, 2020, in *Leading With Empathy & Allyship* Episode 6, by
Change Catalyst, video 52:57, https://changecatalyst.co/najeeba-syeed/.

11. Paul Ekman, *Moving Toward Global Compassion* (Paul Ekman Group, 2014); Daniel
Goleman, "The Focused Leader," *Harvard Business Review*, December 2013, https://
hbr.org/2013/12/the-focused-leader.

12. Theresa Wiseman, "A Concept Analysis of Empathy," *Journal of Advanced Nursing*
23, no. 6 (1996): 1162–1167, https://doi.org/10.1046/j.1365-2648.1996.12213.x.

13. Weisz and Zaki (see ch. 3 n. 47).

14. Theresa Wiseman, "Toward a Holistic Conceptualization of Empathy for Nursing
Practice," *Advances in Nursing Science* 30, no. 3 (July 2007): E61–E72, https://doi
.org/10.1097/01.ANS.0000286630.00011.e3; Weisz and Zaki (see ch. 3, n. 45).

15. Ekman (see n. 11).

16. Elena Ruíz, "Cultural Gaslighting," *Hypatia* 35, no. 4 (October 2020): 687–713,
https://doi.org/10.1017/hyp.2020.33.

Chapter 5: Step 3: Recognize and Overcome Microaggressions

1. Derald Wing Sue, *Microaggressions in Everyday Life: Race, Gender, and Sexual Orientation* (Wiley, 2010).
2. Anthony D. Ong and Anthony L. Burrow, "Microaggressions and Daily Experience: Depicting Life as It Is Lived," *Perspectives on Psychological Science* 12, no. 1 (January 2017): 173–175, https://doi.org/10.1177/1745691616664505; Chester M. Pierce, Jean V. Carew, Diane Pierce-Gonzalez, and Deborah Wills, "An Experiment in Racism: TV Commercials," *Education and Urban Society* 10, no. 1 (November 1977): 61–87, https://doi.org/10.1177/001312457701000105.
3. Sue (see n. 1).
4. Ibid.
5. Roberto E. Montenegro, "My Name Is Not 'Interpreter,'" *Journal of American Medical Association (JAMA)* 315, no. 19 (May 2016): 2071–2072, https://10.1001/jama.2016.1249.
6. Christina Friedlaender, "On Microaggressions: Cumulative Harm and Individual Responsibility," *Hypatia* 33, no. 1 (Winter 2018): 5–21, https://doi.org/10.1111/hypa.12390.
7. Kieran Snyder, "How to Get Ahead as a Woman in Tech: Interrupt Men," *Slate,* July 23, 2014, https://slate.com/human-interest/2014/07/study-men-interrupt-women-more-in-tech-workplaces-but-high-ranking-women-learn-to-interrupt.html.
8. Eddie Wren, "The Great Gender Debate: Men Will Dominate 75% of the Conversation During Conference Meetings, Study Suggests," *Daily Mail,* September 19, 2012, https://www.dailymail.co.uk/sciencetech/article-2205502/The-great-gender-debate-Men-dominate-75-conversation-conference-meetings-study-suggests.html.
9. Michelle Obama, *Becoming* (Penguin, 2018).
10. Stella Young, "I'm Not Your Inspiration, Thank You Very Much," TED, April 2014, video, 8:43, https://www.ted.com/talks/stella_young_i_m_not_your_inspiration_thank_you_very_much.
11. Lydia X. Z. Brown, "Ableism/Language," *Autistic Hoya,* page created in or before July 2012, last updated February 27, 2021, https://www.autistichoya.com/p/ableist-words-and-terms-to-avoid.html.
12. Melinda Briana Epler and Tiffany Yu, "Advocating for People with Disabilities." May 18, 2020, in *Leading With Empathy & Allyship* Episode 5, by Change Catalyst, video 54:39, https://changecatalyst.co/tiffany-yu/.
13. Daniel Goleman, *Emotional Intelligence* (see Introduction n. 2)..
14. Paul Ekman, "Facial Action Coding System," *Paul Ekman Group,* accessed 2021, https://www.paulekman.com/facial-action-coding-system/.
15. Barbara Pease and Allan Pease, *Definitive Book of Body Language: The Hidden Meaning Behind People's Gestures and Expressions* (Bantam Dell, 2004).
16. Ibid.
17. Melinda Briana Epler and Victor Calise, "How to Make Disability Accommodation & Inclusion the New Working Norm," November 17, 2020, in *Leading With Empathy & Allyship* Episode 27, by Change Catalyst, video 57:51, https://changecatalyst.co/victor-calise/.

18. Jeromey B. Temple, Margaret Kelaher, and Ruth Williams, "Discrimination and Avoidance Due to Disability in Australia: Evidence from a National Cross Sectional Survey," *BMC Public Health* 18, no. 1347 (December 2018): 1-13, https://doi.org/10.1186/s12889-018-6234-7.

19. Judy Foreman, "A CONVERSATION WITH: PAUL EKMAN; The 43 Facial Muscles That Reveal Even the Most Fleeting Emotions," *New York Times*, August 5, 2003, https://www.nytimes.com/2003/08/05/health/conversation-with-paul-ekman-43-facial-muscles-that-reveal-even-most-fleeting.html.

20. Sue (see n. 1).

21. The term comes from "ayas̄kimew" in Innu-aimun (an Algonquin language) meaning "a person who laces a snowshoe." It is now often considered offensive or racist because it was a name assigned by people who are not Native—instead, use the names of specific Native people: Inuit, Yupik, and/or Aleut.

22. "Brief History of The Programs," *National Longhouse,* accessed December 2020, https://www.nationallonghouse.org/about-programs/basic-info/brief-history/.

23. "Adventure Guides History," *YMCA of Northwest North Carolina*, accessed April 2021, https://ymcawnc.org/programs/adventure-guides/adventure-guides-history/.

24. "A dad and daughter tradition since 1926. . . . ," *Sequoia Nation Indian Guides and Princesses*, accessed April 2021, http://sequoianation.org/; Huya Big Sky Expeditions, "Program Structure," *Huya Big Sky Expedition*, accessed April 2021, https://www.huyabigsky.org/about/program-structure.

25. Cultural appropriation is similar to cultural imperialism or cultural colonization.

26. Chauncey Alcorn, "Aunt Jemima and Uncle Ben Are Going Away. Are These Mascots Next?" *CNN*, June 19, 2020, https://www.cnn.com/2020/06/19/business/racist-brands-aunt-jemima-chiquita/index.html; Jemima McEvoy, "Eskimo Pie Becomes Edy's Pie: Here Are All the Brands That Are Changing Racist Names and Packaging," *Forbes*, June 26, 2020, https://www.forbes.com/sites/jemimamcevoy/2020/10/06/eskimo-pie-becomes-edys-pie-here-are-all-the-brands-that-are-changing-racist-names-and-packaging/?sh=5bc3c61e56a7.

27. The Jim Crow Museum of Racist Memorabilia at Ferris State University in Big Rapids, Michigan.

Chapter 6: Step 4: Advocate for People

1. Sheryl Nance-Nash, "Why Imposter Syndrome Hits Women and Women of Colour Harder," *BBC*, July 27, 2020, https://www.bbc.com/worklife/article/20200724-why-imposter-syndrome-hits-women-and-women-of-colour-harder.

2. Melinda Briana Epler and Daisy Auger-Domínguez, "Amplifying the Latinx Experience in the Workplace," May 5, 2020, in *Leading With Empathy & Allyship* Episode 4, video, 54:50, https://changecatalyst.co/daisy-auger-dominguez/.

3. Claude M. Steele and Joshua Aronson, "Stereotype Threat and the Intellectual Test Performance of African Americans," *Journal of Personality and Social Psychology* 69, no. 5 (December 1995): 797–811, https://doi.org/10.1037/0022-3514.69.5.797.

4. Jason W. Osborne, "Linking Stereotype Threat and Anxiety," *Educational Psychology* 27, no. 1 (May 2007): 135–154, https://doi.org/10.1080/01443410601069929; Ruth A. Lamont, Hannah J. Swift, and Dominic Abrams, "A Review and Meta-Analysis of Age-Based Stereotype Threat: Negative Stereotypes, Not Facts, Do the Damage," *Psychology and Aging* 30, no. 1 (March 2015): 180–193, https://doi.org/10.1037/a0038586; Arielle M. Silverman and Geoffrey L. Cohen, "Stereotypes as Stumbling-Blocks: How Coping with Stereotype Threat Affects Life Outcomes for People with Physical Disabilities," *Personality and Social Psychology Bulletin* 40, no. 10 (2014): 1330–1340, https://doi.org/10.1177/0146167214542800; Markus Appel, Silvana Weber, and Nicole Kronberger, "The Influence of Stereotype Threat on Immigrants: Review and Meta-Analysis," *Frontiers in Psychology* 6, no. 900 (July 2015), https://doi.org/10.3389/fpsyg.2015.00900.

5. Tom Porter, "How FDR Kept His Partial Paralysis a Secret from the American Public—Even While He Was on the Campaign Trail," *Business Insider*, May 10, 2019, https://www.businessinsider.com/how-fdr-hid-his-paralysis-from-american-public-even-while-campaigning-2019-4.

6. Dr. Christie Smith and Kenji Yoshino, "Uncovering Talent: A New Model of Inclusion," *Deloitte* (2013).

7. Ida Harris, "Code-Switching Is Not Trying to Fit in to White Culture, It's Surviving It," *Yes Magazine*, December 17, 2019, https://www.yesmagazine.org/opinion/2019/12/17/culture-code-switching/.

8. This was formerly called Black English Vernacular and is also called Ebonics. Many people incorrectly call African American English Vernacular (AAEV) "slang" when it is actually a dialect of English with its own distinct grammatical rules and pronunciations. Similarly, Black American Sign Language (BASL) is a dialect of American Sign Language (ASL).

9. Neil A. Lewis, "On a Supreme Court Prospect's Résumé: 'Baseball Savior,'" New York Times, May 14, 2009, https://www.nytimes.com/2009/05/15/us/15sotomayor.html.

10. Pauline Rose Clance and Suzanne Ament Imes, "The Imposter Phenomenon in High Achieving Women: Dynamics and Therapeutic Intervention," *Psychotherapy: Theory, Research & Practice* 15, no. 3 (1978): 241–247, https://doi.org/10.1037/h0086006.

11. Gail Matthews and Pauline Rose Clance, "Treatment of the Imposter Phenomenon in Psychotherapy Clients," *Psychotherapy in Private Practice* 3, no. 1, (1985): 71–81, https://doi.org/10.1300/J294v03n01_09.

12. Melinda Briana Epler and Adia Gooden, "Overcoming Impostor Syndrome," September 29, 2020, in *Leading With Empathy & Allyship* Episode 21, by Change Catalyst, video, 55:40, https://changecatalyst.co/adia-gooden/.

13. Tara Sophia Mohr, "Why Women Don't Apply for Jobs Unless They're 100% Qualified," *Harvard Business Review,* August 25, 2014, https://hbr.org/2014/08/why-women-dont-apply-for-jobs-unless-theyre-100-qualified.

14. Thema Bryant Davis (@drthema), November 15, 2020, https://twitter.com/drthema/status/1328182690902773761.

15. Dnika J. Travis, Jennifer Thorpe-Moscon, and Courtney McCluney "Emotional Tax: How Black Women and Men Pay More at Work and How Leaders Can Take Action," *Catalyst* (October 2016), https://www.catalyst.org/wp-content/uploads /2019/01/emotional_tax_how_black_women_and_men_pay_more.pdf.

16. Evan Carr, Gus Cooney, Cheryl Gray, et al., "The Value of Belonging at Work: New Frontiers for Inclusion," *BetterUp* (June 2018).

17. Derald Wing Sue and Lisa Beth Spanierman, *Microaggressions in Everyday Life,* 2nd ed. (Wiley, 2020).

18. Farah Kuster, Ulrich Orth, and Laurenz L. Meier, "High Self-Esteem Prospectively Predicts Better Work Conditions and Outcomes," *Social Psychological and Personality Science* 4, no. 6 (2013): 668–675, https://doi.org/10.1177/1948550613479806; Fred C. Lunenburg, "Self-Efficacy in the Workplace: Implications for Motivation and Performance," *International Journal of Management, Business, and Administration* 14, no. 1 (2011): 1–6; Jason Thompson and Rapson Gomez, "The Role of Self-Esteem and Self-Efficacy in Moderating the Effect of Workplace Stress on Depression, Anxiety and Stress," *Australasian Journal of Organisational Psychology* 7, no. 2 (January 2014): 1–14, https://doi.org/10.1017/orp.2014.2.

19. Melinda Briana Epler and Irma Olguin Jr. "Leading the Change," September 8, 2020, in *Leading With Empathy & Allyship* Episode 18, video, 52:49, https://changecatalyst .co/irma-olguin-jr/.

20. Epler, Lnu, Santos, Moywaywa, Ford, Bulgurcu, and Sutton (see ch. 2 n. 22).

21. Dora C. Lau, Long W. Lam, and Shan S. Wen, "Examining the Effects of Feeling Trusted by Supervisors in the Workplace: A Self-Evaluative Perspective," *Journal of Organizational Behavior* 35, no. 1 (January 2014): 112–127, https://doi.org/10.1002 /job.1861; Kuster, Orth, and Meier (see n. 18).

22. Sylvia Ann Hewlett and Kennedy Ihezie, "Sponsoring a Protégé—Remotely," *Harvard Business Review*, July 2, 2020, https://hbr.org/2020/07/sponsoring-a-protege -remotely; Sylvia Ann Hewlett, *Forget a Mentor, Find a Sponsor: The New Way to Fast-Track Your Career* (Harvard Business Review Press, 2013).

23. Nancy M. Carter and Christine Silva, "Mentoring: Necessary but Insufficient for Advancement," *Catalyst* (2010), https://www.catalyst.org/wp-content/uploads/2019 /01/Mentoring_Necessary_But_Insufficient_for_Advancement_Final_120610.pdf.

24. Sylvia Ann Hewlett, Kerrie Periano, Laura Sherbin, and Karen Sumberg, "The Sponsor Effect: Breaking Through the Last Glass Ceiling," *Harvard Business Review* (December 2010), https://30percentclub.org/wp-content/uploads/2014/08/The -Sponsor-Effect.pdf.

Chapter 7: Step 5: Stand Up for What's Right

1. Amarra Mohamed, "Color of Pride: Alice Nkom is One of the Only Lawyers in Cameroon Fighting for Queer Rights," *LGBTQ Nation*, June 11, 2019, https://www .lgbtqnation.com/2019/06/color-pride-alice-nkom-one-lawyers-cameroon-fighting -queer-rights/.

2. Melinda Briana Epler and KR Liu, "Opening Doors for the Disabled Community," October 20, 2020, in *Leading With Empathy & Allyship* Episode 23, video, 54:24, https://changecatalyst.co/kr-liu/.

3. Mary Rowe, "Micro-affirmations & Micro-inequities," *Journal of the International Ombudsman Association* 1, no. 1 (January 2008): 45–48.

4. Melinda Briana Epler and Jeannie Gainsburg, "Becoming a Skilled LGBTQ+ Advocate," October 6, 2020, in *Leading With Empathy & Allyship* Episode 22, by Change Catalyst, video, 57:24, https://changecatalyst.co/jeannie-gainsburg/.

5. Lily Jampol and Vivian Zayas, "Gendered White Lies: Women Are Given Inflated Performance Feedback Compared with Men," *Personality and Social Psychology Bulletin* 47, no. 1 (May 2020): 57-69, https://doi.org/10.1177/0146167220916622; Sarah Coury, Jess Huang, Ankur Kumar, Sara Prince, Alexis Krivkovich, and Lareina Yee, "Women in the Workplace: 2020," *McKinsey and Company* (September 2020), https://www.mckinsey.com/featured-insights/diversity-and-inclusion/women-in-the-workplace; Zuhairah Washington and Laura Morgan Roberts, "Women of Color Get Less Support at Work. Here's How Managers Can Change That," *Harvard Business Review*, March 4, 2019, https://hbr.org/2019/03/women-of-color-get-less-support-at-work-heres-how-managers-can-change-that.

6. Shelley J. Correll and Caroline Simard, "Research: Vague Feedback Is Holding Women Back," *Harvard Business Review*, April 29, 2016, https://hbr.org/2016/04/research-vague-feedback-is-holding-women-back.

7. Joan C. Williams, Su Li, Roberta Rincon, and Peter Finn, "Climate Control: Gender and Racial Bias in Engineering?," *Center for WorkLife Law and Society of Women Engineers* (2016), https://research.swe.org/wp-content/uploads/2016/11/16-SWE-020-Work-Study-11-01-LM.pdf.

8. Melinda Briana Epler and Danny Allen, "Using Data to Drive Change," September 22, 2020, in Leading With Empathy & Allyship Episode 20, by Change Catalyst, video, 56:16, https://changecatalyst.co/danny-allen/.

9. Laura Park, "400 Hours. $500," *New York Times: The Diary Project*, June 26, 2020, https://www.nytimes.com/2020/06/26/arts/latasha-harlins-laura-park.html.

10. Tiffany Jana and Michael Baran, *Subtle Acts of Exclusion: How to Understand, Identify, and Stop Microaggressions* (Berrett-Koehler Publishers, 2020).

11. Sue and Spanierman (see ch. 6 n. 17).

12. Ibid.

13. Juliet Eilperin, "White House Women Want to Be in the Room Where It Happens," *Washington Post*, September 13, 2016, https://www.washingtonpost.com/news/powerpost/wp/2016/09/13/white-house-women-are-now-in-the-room-where-it-happens/.

Chapter 8: Step 6: Lead the Change

1. Rahul Eragula, "The Exigency of Empathy in Leadership," *International Journal of Current Research* 8, no. 7 (July 2016), https://www.journalcra.com/sites/default/files/issue-pdf/16385.pdf.

2. Melinda Briana Epler and Kate Johnson, "How to Use Empathy to Create Change in the Workplace," December 15, 2020, in *Leading With Empathy & Allyship* Episode 31, by Change Catalyst, video 56:25, https://changecatalyst.co/kate-johnson/.

3. Svetlana Holt, Joan Marques, Jianli Hu, and Adam Wood, "Cultivating Empathy: New Perspectives on Educating Business Leaders," *Journal of Values-Based Leadership* 10, no. 1 (Winter/Spring 2017), https://doi.org/10.22543/0733.101.1173; "2020 State of Workplace Empathy," *Businessolver* (2020).

4. "2019 State of Workplace Empathy," *Businessolver* (2019).

5. "The Industry Spectrum: How Employees in Different Lines of Work View Workplace Empathy," *Businessolver* (2019).

6. Holt, Marques, Hu, and Wood (see n. 3); Weisz and Zaki (see ch. 3 n. 47).

7. Karina Schumann, Jamil Zaki, and Carol S. Dweck, "Addressing the Empathy Deficit: Beliefs About the Malleability of Empathy Predict Effortful Responses When Empathy Is Challenging," *Journal of Personality and Social Psychology* 107, no. 3 (2014): 475–493, https://doi.org/10.1037/a0036738.

8. Michael Beldoch, "Sensitivity to Expression of Emotional Meaning in Three Modes of Communication," in *The Communication of Emotional Meaning*, ed. Joel Davitz (McGraw-Hill, 1964).

9. Travis Bradberry and Jean Greaves, *Emotional Intelligence 2.0* (TalentSmart, 2009).

10. Carol S. Dweck, *Mindset: The New Psychology of Success* (Ballantine Books, 2007).

11. Dillon and Bourke (see ch.4, n. 7).

12. Dnika J. Travis, Emily Shafer, and Jennifer Thorpe-Moscon, "Getting Real About Inclusive Leadership: Why Change Starts with You," *Catalyst* (2020), https://www.catalyst.org/wp-content/uploads/2020/03/Getting-Real-About-Inclusive-Leadership-Report-2020update.pdf.

13. Brené Brown, "The Courage to Not Know," BrenéBrown.com, February 13, 2020, https://brenebrown.com/blog/2020/02/13/the-courage-to-not-know/.

14. Epler, Lnu, Santos, Moywaywa, Ford, Bulgurcu, and Sutton (see ch. 2 n. 22).

15. Melinda Briana Epler and Ritu Bhasin, "Living & Leading Through Fear, Bias, & Othering," June 16, 2020, in *Leading With Empathy & Allyship* Episode 10, by Change Catalyst, video, 55:25, https://changecatalyst.co/ritu-bhasin/.

16. Melinda Briana Epler, Madelena Mak, Sloan Leo, and Max Masure, "Being a Great Ally for Trans and Gender Nonconforming Colleagues." June 9, 2020, in *Leading With Empathy & Allyship* Episode 9, by Change Catalyst, podcast, 42:23. https://changecatalyst.co/trans-and-gender-nonconforming/.

17. Brené Brown, *How to Be an Inclusive Leader: Your Role in Creating Cultures of Belonging Where Everyone Can Thrive* (Berrett-Koehler, 2019).

18. Travis, Shafer, and Thorpe-Moscon (see n. 12).

19. Google, "Guide: Understand Team Effectiveness," re:Work, accessed April 2021, https://rework.withgoogle.com/guides/understanding-team-effectiveness/; Charles Duhigg, "What Google Learned from Its Quest to Build the Perfect Team," *New York Times Magazine*, February 25, 2016, https://www.nytimes.com/2016/02/28/magazine/what-google-learned-from-its-quest-to-build-the-perfect-team.html.

20. M. Lance Frazier, Stav Fainshmidt, Ryan L. Klinger, and Veselina Vracheva, "Psychological Safety: A Meta-Analytic Review and Extension," *Personnel Psychology* 70, no. 1 (2017): 113–165, https://doi.org/10.1111/peps.12183.

21. Amy C. Edmondson, *The Fearless Organization: Creating Psychological Safety in the Workplace for Learning, Innovation, and Growth* (Wiley, 2018).

22. Weisz and Zaki (see ch. 3 n. 47).

23. Basharat Javed, Sayyed Muhammad Mehdi Raza Naqvi, Abdul Karim Khan, Surendra Arjoon, and Hafiz Habib Tayyeb, "Impact of Inclusive Leadership on Innovative Work Behavior: The Role of Psychological Safety," *Journal of Management & Organization* 25, no. 1 (January 2019): 117-136, https://doi.org/10.1017/jmo.2017.3.

24. Anita Williams Woolley, Christopher F. Chabris, Alex Pentland, Nada Hashmi, and Thomas W. Malone, "Evidence for a Collective Intelligence Factor in the Performance of Human Groups," *Science* 330, no. 6004 (2010): 686–688, https://doi.org/10.1126/science.1193147.

25. Google (see n. 19).

26. Vivian Hunt, Sara Prince, Sundiatu Dixon-Fyle, and Lareina Yee, "Delivering Through Diversity," *McKinsey and Company* (January 2018), https://www.mckinsey.com/business-functions/organization/our-insights/delivering-through-diversity.

27. Steve Blank, "Tools and Blogs for Entrepreneurs," Steveblank.com, accessed January 2021, https://steveblank.com/tools-and-blogs-for-entrepreneurs/.

Chapter 9: Step 7: Transform Your Organization, Industry, and Society

1. Melinda Briana Epler and Rachel Williams, "Creating Structural Change in the Workplace," July 21, 2020, in *Leading With Empathy & Allyship*, Episode 15, by Change Catalyst, video, 57:38, https://changecatalyst.co/rachel-williams/.

2. The Rooney Rule was first used in the National Football League (NFL) by Pittsburgh Steelers owner Dan Rooney. It requires teams to interview at least one minority candidate for executives and senior leadership positions. For nearly 10 years, the rule had a significant impact on the number of Black coaches hired in the NFL. Unfortunately, its success has waned since 2012, with some discussion that it doesn't go far enough to enforce hiring and training of candidates.

3. Stefanie K. Johnson, David R. Hekman, and Elsa T. Chan, "If There's Only One Woman in Your Candidate Pool, There's Statistically No Chance She'll Be Hired," *Harvard Business Review*, April 26, 2016, https://hbr.org/2016/04/if-theres-only-one-woman-in-your-candidate-pool-theres-statistically-no-chance-shell-be-hired.

4. Nancy Douyon and Janine Yancey. "#AlwaysLearning with Nancy Douyon: How to Be a Better Ally," *Emtrain*, June 2020, video, 42:14, https://www.linkedin.com/video/live/urn:li:ugcPost:6676225946313469952/.

5. Melinda Briana Epler, Wayne Sutton, Salem Kimble, and Change Catalyst Team, "Toolkit for Startups: Creating Inclusive Events," (*Change Catalyst* and *LaunchVic*, 2018), https://changecatalyst.co/change-catalyst-tool-kits/.

6. Melinda Briana Epler and Dr. Kevin Simon, "Understanding The Effects Of Racism On Black Boys & Men," November 3, 2020, in *Leading With Empathy & Allyship*, Episode 25, by Change Catalyst, video, 56:53, https://changecatalyst.co/kevin-simon/.

7. You could also attend upstander training to learn how to do this safely and effectively. Center for Anti-Violence Education and Hollaback! both offer regular training.

Chapter 10: Allyship Is a Journey

1. Epler, Lnu, Santos, Moywaywa, Ford, Bulgurcu, and Sutton (see ch. 2, n. 22).

2. Melinda Briana Epler and Vanessa Roanhorse, "Supporting Indigenous Power, Leadership, and Community," April 28, 2020, in *Leading With Empathy & Allyship* Episode 3, by Change Catalyst, video, 43:26, https://changecatalyst.co/vanessa-roanhorse/.

3. Ibid.

4. Melinda Briana Epler and Michael Thomas, "Understanding Intergenerational Trauma & Its Impact in The Workplace," June 2, 2020, in *Leading With Empathy & Allyship* Episode 8, video, 55:29, https://changecatalyst.co/michael-thomas/.

5. America Ferrera, "My Identity Is a Superpower—Not an Obstacle," *TED*, April 2019, video, 13:54, https://www.ted.com/talks/america_ferrera_my_identity_is_a_superpower_not_an_obstacle.

6. Epler and Thomas (see n. 4).

7. Aja Romano, "Why We Can't Stop Fighting About Cancel Culture," *Vox*, August 25, 2020, https://www.vox.com/culture/2019/12/30/20879720/what-is-cancel-culture-explained-history-debate.

8. Barack Obama, "President Obama in Conversation with Yara Sahidi and Obama Foundation Program Participants," *Obama Foundation*, October 30, 2019, video, 1:20:45, https://www.obama.org/video/president-obama-conversation-yara-shahidi-obama-foundation-program-participants/.

9. Ngọc Loan Trần, "Calliing In: A Less Disposable Way of Holding Each Other Accountable," in, *The Solidarity Struggle: How People of Color Succeed and Fail at Showing Up for Each Other in the Fight for Freedom*, ed. Mia McKenzie (BGD Press, Inc., 2016).

10. Melinda Briana Epler and Lionel Lee, "Engaging Leadership," September 1, 2020, in *Leading With Empathy & Allyship* Episode 17, by Change Catalyst, video, 53:15, https://changecatalyst.co/lionel-lee/.

11. Epler, Lnu, Santos, Moywaywa, Ford, Bulgurcu, and Sutton (see ch. 2 n. 22).

12. Melinda Briana Epler and Corey Ponder, "Cultivating Empathy as a Skill," September 15, 2020, in *Leading With Empathy & Allyship* Episode 19, by Change Catalyst, video, 55:44, https://changecatalyst.co/corey-ponder/.

13. Brittany Packnett Cunningham, "Ally, Accomplice, Co-conspirator," Interviewed by Shirley Washington, *Womens Voices*, June 8, 2019, video, 5:57, https://youtu.be/QZVILjJPreM.

INDEX

ABOUT THE AUTHOR

Melinda Briana Epler has more than 25 years of experience elevating brands and developing business innovation strategies for entrepreneurs, Fortune 500 companies, and global nongovernmental organizations.

As CEO of Change Catalyst, Melinda is a strategic diversity, equity, and inclusion advisor for executives, startups, investors, and activists around the world. As part of her changemaking work, she is an inclusive leadership coach, trains executive and management teams, and builds learning and development solutions for clients. She also hosts a weekly live show and podcast series, "Leading With Empathy & Allyship."

Melinda is a TED speaker, award-winning documentary filmmaker, and former marketing and culture executive. She speaks and writes about diversity and inclusion in tech, allyship, and empathy. Melinda has spoken on hundreds of stages around the world, including SXSW, Grace Hopper, Wisdom 2.0, the World Bank, White House, Clinton Foundation, Black Enterprise, Google, Indeed, Capital One, UC Berkeley, and McKinsey.

For further information and to connect with Melinda and Change Catalyst, go to:

Website: changecatalyst.co
LinkedIn: linkedin.com/in/melindaepler
Twitter: @mbrianaepler
Instagram: @changecatalysts
Podcast: ally.cc